Survey

A Short History of Canadian Literature

by

Elizabeth Waterston Ph.D.
Professor of English
University of Guelph
Guelph, Ontario

Methuen Canadian Literature Series
Methuen
Toronto London Sydney Wellington

P9-BJA-237

Library of Congress Catalogue Card Number 72-97553
ISBN   pb   0   458   90930   0
ISBN   hc   0   458   90950   5

Designed by Carl Brett.
Printed and bound in Canada.

77 76   2 3 4 5 6

Photo credits:
Paul Newberry, 4, 78; Public Archives of Canada, 18, 48;
Toronto Star Syndicate, 34, 114; Mrs. Howard Kennedy, 64;
Miller Services, 92; Ontario Ministry of Agriculture and
Food, 100; Ken Barton Photography, Guelph, Ontario, 130,
144; Prof. Richard Vosburgh, 176.

Survey: A Short History of Canadian Literature

Contents

Acknowledgements

I acknowledge gratefully the help of colleagues, librarians, and students at the universities where I have taught Canadian Literature since 1946: Sir George Williams University, the University of Western Ontario, and the University of Guelph. The Survey Chart at the end of my book was first devised by Leslie Monkman; Allan Austin and Gerald Manning helped me update it. Glenys Stow suggested readings in Indian material, and Ray Hathorn furnished the list of French-Canadian chansonniers. Professor Gordon Roper directed my first serious work in Canadian Studies. Carl Klinck's courtesy to fellow-scholars is legendary, and I have been the happy recipient of his kindness for many years. I would also like to acknowledge the kindness of the poets and publishers who permitted me to quote from their work.

At Methuen, Sarah Swartz turned editorial conferences into stimulating and helpful experiences.

This book owes something also to my family. My father, mother, and aunt started me in Canadian Literature with Ralph Connor and L.M. Montgomery. My son Dan opened a new chapter with his Leonard Cohen records. All the girls helped put the book together—Rosemary, Charlotte, Christy, and especially Jane, who produced the index and a good deal of the bibliographies. Above all I am grateful to my husband Douglas.

Elizabeth Waterston
University of Guelph
January, 1973

Prologue:
Who Has Seen the Wind

When we begin a study of Canadian Literature we face two problems
in those two key words "Canada" and "Literature"—and a third
problem in the relation between them.

What is Canada? Surely more than just a place on the map,
a vast landmass that is the northern half of the North American
continent! Whether Canada is a dream, or a fact, or a fossilized
bit of history, a look at her literature will help throw light on
what the country is and has been. Whether we view Canada as a
political confederation, a business complex, or a multi-cultural
social phenomenon, Canadian writers should help us understand
the nature of this mysterious country.

Literature gives voice to the country. But the spirit of
Canada has sounded in folk songs and legends as well as in polished lyric poems. Political pronouncements, radio plays, letters
and diaries, as well as novels and formal dramas have been the
means of expression of Canada. A modern survey of Canadian
Literature should draw into its net many such works, for in them
we see emerging a style, a rhythm, a diction, and a form which
is Canadian.

But can we line up creative art and "survey" it? Will we find
we have amassed an incredible number of separate artworks, but
that the phrase "Canadian Literature" is meaningless? The question of nationality in literature is a touchy one. It is dangerous to
assume that just as a country produces a certain kind of wheat
and a certain kind of whiskey, it will grow a recognizable crop of
poetry. Most artists, certainly, would insist on their own individuality, their freedom from any sense of national pressure or any
necessity of "writing Canadian". Many would agree with the
contemporary poet George Johnston, who insists:

I love the slightly flattened sphere,
Its restless, wrinkled crust 's my here,
Its slightly wobbling spin's my now
But not my why and not my how:
My why and how are me.[1]

    This book proposes to explore some of the "hows" and the
"whys" of Canadian art. *Why* certain topics caught the consciousness of writers in this country at particular periods; *how* particular
writers or groups of writers shaped those topics into artworks:
this is our subject. Art and society can probably be seen as a
symbiotic relationship. The society in part shapes its artforms,
and in turn the artworks shape society. We are what we are
because of what our artists have said, as well as because of
politics and geography—and chance.

    For further probes into these questions of Canadian history
and literature, a selection of material for reading, listening, and
viewing is suggested after each chapter. Again, the listings are
a selection only. One could go into a much more extensive study
of any of the Canadian topics that make up the chapter titles.
But perhaps the better follow-up to this survey would be to begin
deeper readings of a few major works by Canadian artists. Perhaps
the books whose names appear as sub-titles of the following
chapters could furnish a list for such an adventure in Canadian
reading. The list would include work in a mixture of genres:
essays, plays, songs, and stories. The titles themselves are
intriguing. Each catches something of the sense of riddle and
paradox that is certainly one major theme of writing in Canada.

    If we were to give a title to this brief Prologue, it would be
"Who Has Seen the Wind" an enigmatic question used as the
name of a novel by W.O. Mitchell. Mitchell's book would make a
fine start into a course of Canadian readings. It begins with the
barest elements: sky, land, and a child's consciousness. The
little boy in the book grows in awareness of his family, his school,
and the eccentric, funny, mysterious people in his town and its
prairie fringes. He becomes aware of process, change, and death

[1] George Johnston, "O
Earth, Turn!" in *Canadian
Anthology*, eds. C.F. Klinck
and R.E. Watters
(Toronto,1966), p. 401.

in his environment, and in himself. Within the controlling limits of his prairie setting and his heredity, he grows in ways that are unpredictable.

Readings in Canadian Literature can give some comparable growth in awareness, and a comparable answer to the question of national art. We can see some of the winds of Canadian thought and feeling as we watch the shifts in Canadian Literature. And we are left in the end with some insight into the more mysterious winds of free human creativity.

Terrain:
The Double Hook

1

1600

Literature is a part of life caught in words. The writer is a person who fishes with a double hook. One barb he casts outward into the given forms of landscape and society: hills, snow, city streets, facial expressions, bodily movements, gestures, talk. The other barb reaches into the inner world of temperament, dream, memory, hooking up shapes of fear and desire.

Some artists use a longer and stronger barb when they fling perception toward the outer world. Others probe more subtly and deeply inward. Our earliest Canadian writers were conditioned to rely on the outer senses. Recent writers seem more introverted. Writing of the French-Canadian use of the motif of Northern journeys, Professor Jack Warwick summarizes the current theory about the inter-dependence of inner and outer geography: "The presence of a North in man is even more critical than the presence of men in the North."[1]

Canada's earliest writers were not so subtle. They were practical men. They observed some indisputable facts about this new world: Canada is a northern place. It is sea-bound on three sides and deeply indented by waterways on the fourth. It is a series of regional pockets, savagely separated by natural barriers. The climate is extreme—too hot in summer, too cold in winter; and the winter breathes heavily in the background all through the fall and spring.

For our earliest writers, Canadian experience began as an arduous voyage over the sea. Our oldest songs are sea-songs, Newfoundland jig songs about boats and fish and harbours. Our first prose is in travel journals, and most of them have a sea-sick first chapter.

By water the new Canadians moved into a northern world.

[1] Jack Warwick, *The Long Journey* (Toronto, 1968), p. 47.

The early invader of Canada, moving from the ship on the sea, to
the bateau on the river, to the canoe in the rapids, stripped himself down, closer to the elements. Alexander Mackenzie, moving
North and West to the two distant oceans, compass in hand for
physical bearings, pencil poised to record the inner weather—this
is the image of the first English-Canadian writer. The compass
swings north and west, and the air, the winey, tonic, bracing,
windy air, is usually swirling with early snow, or late snow, or
mid-winter snow.

Turn up your collar, pull your toque down over your ears, and
make a canoe trip north by west, from Montreal to French River
to Georgian Bay, Manitoulin Island, Lake of the Woods,
"Winepec", the Red River of the North, the Athabaska, through the
Tête Jaune passes maybe, down the Fraser to the coast, and
over to Nanaimo. These are the ways the explorers went, and the
explorers made up the corps of our earliest writers. There was
Henry Kelsey keeping a Diary at his Hudson Bay port around
1700, and Joseph Robson, penning *An Account of Six Years Resi-
dence on the Hudson's Bay* in 1752, and Alexander Henry keeping
a *Journal of Travels in Canada and the Indian Territories between
the Years 1760 and 1776.* There are many other travel reports
written between 1700 and 1801, when Alexander Mackenzie
added his *Voyages from Montreal, on the River St. Lawrence, through
the continent of North America, to the Frozen and Pacific Oceans.*

Travellers' View

The travellers wrote reports on navigation, reports on Indians
and wild life. As they moved inland along the waterways, they
realized how varied the regions of this northern country were.
There were gentle pastoral scenes in Prince Edward Island,
"Garden of the Gulf". There was rugged land in New Brunswick,
Newfoundland, and Nova Scotia; land sociably quilted in a
patchwork of farms along the St. Lawrence, where French Canadians huddled away from the raw Laurentian North. In Ontario,
forests and glades were set beneath escarpments that swept in

concentric cricles north from Lake Ontario toward James Bay
and Hudson Bay. Beyond Lake Superior, prairies rolled and
stretched toward the foothills. And then the Rockies, and beyond
them the picturesque coastal region.

The urge to pull this geographic variety into an artistic focus—
to fix the flux of trans-Canadian travel in an artwork—has
stirred travellers from 1600 to our own time. Travel books are
our earliest artforms. George Head, writing in 1829, is typical of
the host of travellers, many of them military, who moved inland
into the colonies and wrote of their experiences:

It was in the latter end of November, when I disembarked, after a
rough passage from Falmouth, at Halifax, the capital of Nova Scotia,
and the passage of the river St. Lawrence being already closed for
the winter, it became my duty to undertake a journey over land to
the Canadas; I therefore made my arrangements to set out as soon
as snow should fall in sufficient quantity to put the roads in good
order for travelling in a sleigh.[2]

The sea, the winter, and the passage from one region to another—
these are the staples of most travel books.

Inland waters continued to define the sense of Canada as a
place. The St. Lawrence Sea-Way, the Great Lakes, Hudson
Bay, the Red River, the Columbia and its sources all have been
determinants of our political and economic history. All have
pressed on artistic consciousness. The first poem about Canada
to catch the print-oriented world was Tom Moore's "Canadian
Boat-Song" in 1804:

Faintly as tolls the evening chime
Our voices keep tune and our oars keep time.
Soon as the woods on shore look dim
We'll sing at St. Ann's our parting hymn.
Row, brothers, row, the stream runs fast,
The Rapids are near and the daylight's past.[3]

Moore, writing about his popular poem says, "The above stanzas
are supposed to be sung by those *voyageurs* who go to the Grand

[2] George Head, *Travel
Scenes and Incidents in the
Wilds of North America*,
1829, facsimile edition
(Toronto, 1970), p. 1.
[3] Thomas Moore,
"Canadian Boat-Song", in
Songs for Canadian Boys
(Toronto, 1940), p. 24.

Portage by the Utawas River. For an account of this wonderful
undertaking, see Sir Alexander Mackenzie's *General History of
the Fur Trade.*" Readers in Moore's Regency England who took
this advice would find Mackenzie's comment: "At the Rapid
of St. Ann they are obliged to take out part, if not the whole, of
their lading. It is from this spot the Canadians consider they take
their departure, as it possesses the last church on the island."[4]

Above all, travellers wrote reports on the climate. It was
cold! There was a winter unlike anything known in Western
Europe. Earlier, Frenchmen had gone through the same country, the same climate, and the French explorers' books and the
Jesuit *Relations* record their responses. They had discovered
that winter here, instead of inducing hibernation in humans,
made it possible to travel and hunt more efficiently. For the
coureur de bois, the North and the cold called a man away from
commercialism and domestic comfort. The cold strong call of
le pays d'en haut was a welcome call. The hard freeze-up of the
waterways made a path for human sociability and commerce.

This was not in accord with the notions about winter popu-
larized in European literature of the eighteenth century. People
back in England, Scotland, Ireland, and also in New England had
regarded winter as a time of dreariness. The stylish James
Thompson, writing in 1730, added in *The Seasons* a notion of
winter as terrifying, wild, stormy, and threatening—an archetype
of death. Animal life in the small familiar animals offered a
pattern of hibernation. But the wanderers in the Canadian wilderness and the dwellers in the little towns dotting the country—
the military establishment, and trading posts and mill-towns of
the eighteenth century—all report a very different Canadian
response to the cold.

In all the small outposts of civility in Canada, local presses
reported the business of society, the busyness of keeping warm by
a constant succession of levees and balls and inspections of the
garrison. The presses proliferated early: one in Halifax in 1752,
Quebec 1764, Saint John 1783, Montreal 1785, Charlottetown 1787,

[4] Alexander Mackenzie,
*The Journals and Letters of
Sir Alexander Mackenzie*,
ed. Kaye Lamb (Toronto,
1970), p. 85.

Niagara 1793. Mostly these gazettes reflect an official world of appointments, arrivals, ceremonies, protocol, and promotion—a complex world, related to a more complicated Empire. Indeed, the presses were reporting the emergence of a Canadian "world" in a second sense—not as a place geographically, but as a social complex, in which one's "place" was social. Thus Canada became what the modern poet Margaret Avison calls an "unchill, habitable" place, because of the sociable erection of cultural defenses against the cold.[5] "*Mon pays, c'est l'hiver*"—but *l'hiver* can evoke charm and energy.

Even in lonelier places, early Canadian journals record the pleasures of winter; even in lowlier economic circumstances there is recognition of the winter employment and ease of travel in Canadian winter scenes. Yes, Canada was a cold place; but it became a place of civil warmth.

Mrs. Brooke, writing of Quebec City during the Conquest period in *The History of Emily Montague,* 1769, comments, "The cold is so amazingly intense as almost totally to stop respiration," but adds, "I have business, the business of pleasure, at Quebec." Men and women set themselves *against* nature, in civilized pleasures. Mrs. Brooke reports the pleasures of wine, brandy, of fur-lined cloaks and hoods ("vastly becoming") and of parties and flirtations, outings through the snow to see the magical beauty of Montgomery Falls frozen into an icy fantasy, and coquetry and politics indoors.[6]

There was another typical Canadian response to the fact of the cold. This is the peculiar brand of Canadian humour—wry, sly, rueful. Thomas Haliburton, Maritime humourist, in the "The Snow Wreath", 1836, catches the folk quality of comic exaggeration: if we're going to die of the cold, we might as well die laughing.[7] It's the same spirit as the response to Yukon cold sixty years later in Robert Service. "The cremation of Sam McGee" takes the unthinkable coldness of Canada and pushes it to absurdity.[8]

Canadian Literature, then, began with the given forms of land and sea, mountain, river, city, village. It began with sea

[5] Margaret Avison, "New Year's Poem" in *Canadian Anthology*, eds. C.F. Klinck and R.E. Watters (Toronto, 1966), p. 440.
[6] Frances Brooke, from *The History of Emily Montague,* in *Canadian Anthology*, pp. 4-6.
[7] T.C. Haliburton, "The Snow Wreath", in *Canadian Anthology*, p. 40.
[8] Robert Service, "The Cremation of Sam McGee", in *Canadian Anthology*, p. 305.

songs; journals of comings and goings through wintry northlands;
gazette reports of social civilities formed to ward off melancholy
thoughts of the raw land and the estranging sea; funny stories
counteracting those terrors. The process had begun of giving form
to the Canadians' responses to life in this land: escapes, dreams,
classifications, enumerations, prettifications, abusings.
Canadian life had begun to make Canadian art—and vice versa.

Later Look of the Landscape

Canada's brief history coincides with the European age of
industrialization, mechanization, and urbanization. Within one
hundred years of the first travels through Canada by English
writers, many of the elements reported by those first travellers
had disappeared. The Marquis of Lorne, a governor-general who
wrote one of the finest of travel books, caught the moment of
transition in 1884:

Often as the canoes proceed the voyager threads passages so
narrow that the boughs almost meet overhead, and the bushes, mosses
and lichens on the ripple-worn rocks, sprinkled with bright flowers,
are so close that each may be distinctly recognized. A night-camp among
such scenes, when the tawny birch-bark flotilla just floats with the
painted prows resting on clean sands, and the fire's glow falls on the
nearer pines and firs, and a clear moon shows the more distant slopes
backed by some huge crag, remains in the memory as a joy for ever.
    These canoe voyages are only memories, for nowadays at Port
Arthur we enter the railway cars, and after passing for 400 miles
through a wooded and rocky region we suddenly emerge upon the
endless meadows of Manitoba. For miles and miles we now see the
long grasses wave, and out of the treeless land rise the spires of the
churches of the new city of Winnipeg.[9]

Later poets would continue to record and protest against changes
in the look of the land. The overlay of one kind of world by another
was not regarded as a sign of progress.
    The old geographical world remained, but its features would
become muffled and blurred. The writers were changing also as the
century progressed. Canadian landforms were now being described

[9] Marquis of Lorne, *Canadian Pictures* (London, 1886), pp. 135-6.

by people whose lives had never been pitted against nature for a live-lihood as the lives of traders and fishers had been. By Confederation a new breed of writer had appeared. They were men of a more sheltered life, who could go to nature when the poetic mood was ripe and stay indoors at other times.

Yet the dominant physical features remain strong in Canadian poetry: the sea and waterways, the northern cold, and the sharp regional differences in terrain. For instance, even in days when major exploration was inland, prairie-oriented, mountain-conquering, our major poets were still sea-poets: Bliss Carman, Charles G.D. Roberts, and later E.J. Pratt. Our proudest slogan for defining nationhood was "From Ocean to Ocean—from Sea to Sea—the Dominion of Canada". But poets sensed the sea as *not* to be dominated; rather, as menacing, insistent, sad, repetitive, reductive. "The shambling sea is a sexton old", says Bliss Carman.[10]

Roberts adds the sense of the sea as a persistent, dark misgiving, a curb on new-world optimism:

Inland I hear the calling of the sea . . .
Bleak, bleak the tide, and evening coming on.[11]

It is indeed a grey sea, a Northern sea, that bounds Canada. Round these shores, as Pratt remembered, icebergs "lurch and shamble".[12]

We can still feel the tidal movements, submerged, in Canadian poetry. Earle Birney feels every day as encircled by the sea of sleep: "the ebb begins from dream".[13] A young Maritime poet, Bill Howell, feels sea-tides pulling at our sense of "reality":

Once a night, as in the day,
the sea feeds on this land.[14]

Probably you can still go three-quarters of the way around Canada, or around Canadian poetry, by sea.

Later poets would also continue using the physical facts of winter. Archibald Lampman writes a series of fine winter sonnets; Patrick Anderson describes witty imagist encounters with Montreal's zero; Ralph Gustafson records a lonely life on a Quebec

[10] Bliss Carman, "The Gravedigger", in *Poets of the Confederation*, ed. M.M. Ross, (Toronto, 1960), p. 37.
[11] C.G.D. Roberts, "Beside the Winter Sea", in *Poems of the Confederation*, p.13.
[12] E.J. Pratt, "The Titanic", in *Collected Poems*, 2nd ed., ed. Northrop Frye (Toronto, 1958). p. 214.
[13] Earle Birney, "The Ebb Begins from Dream", in *Canadian Anthology*, p. 305.
[14] Bill Howell, "From this Headland", in *Soundings*, ed. Jack Ludwig (Toronto, 1970), p. 120.

farm.[15] Earle Birney turns the whole beautiful destructive
business of winter into a social metaphor in "Man is a Snow", and
follows the winter to its own capital in "Ice Cod Bell or Stone".[16]
Canadian novelists have used snow scenes for their best effects:
the Christmas sequence and the last chapter of Ernest Buckler's
The Mountain and the Valley, Hugh MacLennan's manipulation of
snow in *The Watch that Ends the Night,* and Morley Callaghan's
symbolic white-black settings in *The Loved and the Lost.*

Finally, Canada *is* sharply varied in land forms, insistent,
angular, tied together East-West by human designs (technological,
political, and ideological) rather than by natural path-ways.
This fact becomes even clearer to modern poets who can ride
through or over the Canadian sequence of scenes at unimaginable
speeds. A modern poet's mind can be airborne, "Pulled from our
ruts by the made-to-order gale".[17] Or the poet can move by highway
through the land:

through rock cuts between valleys, across valleys
filled with mist and swollen rivers . . .[18]

Either way, the artists help us hold a varied Canadian voyage in the
mind's unifying eye.

Many modern novelists build the still-surprising differences
between geographical regions into their stories. Margaret Laurence,
for example, in *Stone Angel,* 1964, sets her heroine's present
life in the rainy forest region of the British Columbia seacoast.
In memory, however, the heroine travels back to the dusty prairie
of her childhood experience. Each region is important both to the
events and the moods of the story. The two perceptions, of fact
and of memory, are tied together in the mind of the heroine.

The Second Hook

The Canadian terrain today is very different from the clean,
cold, rock-bound shore first seen by English voyagers around 1600.
Modern eyes see a polluted nature. Rivers and seas are contaminated,

[15] Archibald Lampman,
"Winter Evening", in
Canadian Anthology, p. 131;
Patrick Anderson, "Song of
Intense Cold", in *Canadian
Anthology*, p. 417; Ralph
Gustafson, "Quebec
Winterscene", in *Canadian
Anthology*, p. 352.
[16] Earle Birney, "Man is a
Snow", in *Canadian
Anthology*, p. 306; "Elles-
mereland" in *Canadian
Anthology*, p. 308.
[17] Frank Scott, "Trans
Canada" in *Canadian
Anthology*, p. 269.
[18] Dale Zieroth, "Across
Canada, West from
Toronto", in *Storm Warnings*,
ed. Al Purdy (Toronto,
1971), p. 151.

prairies single-cropped too long, harvests blighted by the world's hunger, snow scored by snowmobiles. All these views simmer in modern writing on man and his environment. Farley Mowat may be fiercest in protest and most widely read; he is backed in every medium by other Canadian writers.

One major theme of modern Canadian literature is the need to relate in a fresh and creative way to natural forms. Margaret Avison urges:

Nobody stuffs the world in at your eyes.
The optic heart must venture: a jail-break.[19]

The strong physical challenges of Canada have elicited intense responses. Reading Canadian Literature we see Canada, not only as God created it, but as artists have been recreating it for two hundred years. We see the Canadian terrain as the writers have caught it for us. A sequence of their works helps us know Canada as a place in time as well as in space.

Visitors and settlers alike have thrown out a double hook to this strange northern land. They have created an emotional relation to it, as well as establishing a physical stake in it. The artists, too, have moved from bare perception into subtler responses. They have reached outward to the land, inward to the world of myth.

The image of a "double hook" is taken from the title of a novel by Sheila Watson.[20] Her perception hooks into the life of a group of families, living at subsistence level "in a fold of the hills", and also into a moment of sterility and drought in inner life. Her story is set, she says, "somewhere in the Cariboo district, or in the dry-belt of the heart". This is Kamloops country, a long way from the Eastern seacoast where Canadian Literature began. But the pressure of environment is still very strong and very menacing. This is not a winter novel, but a novel of arid heat, when life proceeds "under the eye of Coyote", a force of denial, suspicion, trickery. The little community has become so dried out, so subdued by the physical environment that its social life is almost

[19] Margaret Avison, "Snow", in *Fifteen Canadian Poets*, eds. Gary Geddes and Phyllis Bruce (Toronto, 1970), p. 129.
[20] Sheila Watson, *The Double Hook* (Toronto, 1959).

gone. But the hero learns lessons of responsibility. He rides out
of his own community to the nearby town, and then rides back—
to accept his position as father of a newborn child and as a man in
the community. It is an ironic book, very modern in method, but
very basic in its topic: human life in account with time and change,
and with the physical environment.

For Further Study

The study guides at the end of each chapter include items in the most accessible and reasonably priced edition, rather than the first or most scholarly edition. These lists are selective. More complete bibliographies in an easy-to-use form appear in the following:

Teaching Canada, a Bibliography, ed. A.R. Stewart and W.J. McAndrew. Orono: NEAPQ Centre at the University of Maine, 1971.

English-Canadian Literature: A Student Guide and Annotated Bibliography, eds. R.G. Moyles and Catherine Siemens. Edmonton: Athabascan, 1972.

Canadian Basic Books. Toronto: Southam, 1971.

Bibliography of Canadian Literature for Teaching, compiled by Jim French, Bill Cockburn, Lorne Dickie, mimeographed by Canadian Literature Interest Group, London Board of Education. London, Ontario, 1972.

Travellers' View

In Print:

Butler, William Francis. *The Great Lone Land, 1872.* Reprint edition. Edmonton: Hurtig Press, 1968.

Hakluyt, Richard. *Principal Voyages, Travels and Discoveries, 1589-1600.* London: Dent, 1927.

Haliburton, Thomas. "The Snow Wreath". In *Canadian Anthology,* eds. C.F. Klinck and R.E. Watters. Toronto: Gage, 1966.

Hall, E. *Early Canada.* Ottawa: Information Canada, 1967.

Head, George Esq. *Forest Scenes in the Wilds of North America,* 1829. Reprint edition. Toronto: Coles Canadiana Collection, 1970.

Henry, Alexander. *Travels and Adventures.* 1809. Reprint edition. Edmonton: Hurtig, 1969.

Klinck, C.F. et al. *Literary History of Canada.* Toronto: University of Toronto Press, 1965.

Mackenzie, Alexander. *The Journal and Letters of Sir Alexander Mackenzie.* Ed. W. Kaye Lamb. Toronto: Macmillan, 1970.

Service, Robert. *The Best of Robert Service.* Toronto: Ryerson, 1963.

Warwick, Jack. *The Long Journey.* Toronto: University of Toronto Press, 1968.

Pictures:

Beny, Roloff. *To Everything There is a Season.* Toronto: Longmans, 1967.

Kerr, D.G.G. and R.I.K. Davidson. *Canada: A Visual History.* Toronto: Nelson, 1966.

National Film Board of Canada. *Canada: A Year of the Land.* Toronto: Copp Clark, 1967.

On Film:

Alexander Mackenzie. National Film Board, 1964. Colour. 28 minutes.

Music:

Creighton, Helen, ed., *Songs and Ballads From
Nova Scotia.* Toronto: General Publishing, 1967.

Drama:

Sinclair, Lister. *The Blood is Strong.* Toronto:
Book Society of Canada, 1956.

Later Look of the Landscape

In Print:

Anderson, Patrick. "Song of Intense Cold",
In *Canadian Anthology,* eds. C.F. Klinck and
R.E. Watters. Toronto: Gage, 1966.
Atwood, Margaret. "Fragments: Beach". In
Listen! Songs and Poems of Canada, ed. Homer
Hogan. Toronto: Methuen, 1972.
Birney, Earle. "The Ebb Begins From Dream".
In *Canadian Anthology,* eds. C.F. Klinck
and R.E. Watters. Toronto: Gage, 1966.
Buckler, Ernest. *The Mountain and the Valley.*
Toronto: McClelland and Stewart, 1952.
Callaghan, Morley. *The Loved and the Lost.*
Toronto: Macmillan, 1970.
Carman, Bliss. "The Sexton". In *Poets of the
Confederation,* ed. Malcolm M. Ross. Toronto:
McClelland and Stewart, 1960.
Cockburn, Bruce. "Let Us Go Laughing".
In *Listen! Songs and Poems of Canada,* ed. Homer
Hogan. Toronto: Methuen. 1972.
Fetherling, Douglas, ed. *Thumbprints.*
Toronto: Peter Martin, 1968.
Gustafson, Ralph. "Quebec Winter Scene".
In *Canadian Anthology,* eds. C.F. Klinck and
R.E. Watters. Toronto: Gage, 1966.
Howell, Bill. "From This Headland".
In *Soundings,* eds. Jack Ludwig and Andy
Wainwright. Toronto: Anansi, 1970.
Hutchison, Bruce. *The Unknown Country.*
Toronto: Longmans, 1948.
Lampman, Archibald. "In November",
"Winter Evening". In *Poets of the Confederation*,
ed. Malcolm M. Ross. Toronto: McClelland
and Stewart, 1960.
Laurence, Margaret. *Stone Angel.* Toronto:
McClelland and Stewart, 1964.

Lorne, Marquis of. *Canadian Pictures.* London:
Religious Text Society, 1884.
MacLennan, Hugh. *Seven Rivers of Canada.*
Toronto: Macmillan, 1961.
MacLennan, Hugh. *The Watch That Ends the
Night.* Toronto: New American Library of
Canada, 1957.
Pratt, E.J. "The Titanic". In *Poets Between the
Wars,* ed. Milton Wilson. Toronto: McClelland
and Stewart, 1967.
Roberts, C.G.D. "The Salt Flats", "The
Winter Fields", "Beside the Winter Sea". In
Poets of the Confederation, ed. Malcolm M. Ross.
Toronto: McClelland and Stewart, 1960.

Pictures:

Spears, Borden, ed. *Wilderness Canada.*
Toronto: Clarke, Irwin, 1971.

On Film:

Seasons. Christopher Chapman Films. 1954.
Colour. 18 minutes.
Trans Canada Journey. National Film Board.
1962. Colour. 29 minutes.

On Record:

Glenn Gould. *The Idea of North.* Toronto:
Canadian Broadcasting Corporation. 1970.

The Second Hook

In Print:

Atwood, Margaret. *Survival.* Toronto:
Anansis, 1972.
Bell, I.F. and S.W. Port. *Canadian Literature,
1959-1963.* Vancouver: University of British
Columbia Press, 1966.
Eggleston, W. *The Frontier and Canadian
Letters.* Toronto: Ryerson, 1957.
Klinck, C.F. and R.E. Watters, eds. *Canadian
Anthology.* Toronto: Gage, 1966.
Klinck, C.F. et al. *Literary History of Canada.*
Toronto: University of Toronto Press, 1965.

Mickleburgh, Brita, ed. *Canadian Literature.*
Toronto: McClelland and Stewart, 1972.
Milne, W.S. *Canadian Full Length Plays in English.*
Ottawa: Dominion Drama Festival, 1964.
Pacey, Desmond. *Creative Writing in Canada.*
Toronto: Ryerson, 1967.
Smith, A.J.M. *The Book of Canadian Poetry.*
Toronto: Gage, 1948.
Smith, A.J.M. *The Book of Canadian Prose.*
Vol. 1. Toronto: Gage, 1965.
Story, Norah. *The Oxford Companion to
Canadian History and Literature.* Toronto:
Oxford, 1967.
Sylvestre, Guy, Brandon Conron and C.F.
Klinck, eds. *Canadian Writers: A Biographical
Dictionary.* Toronto: Ryerson, 1966.
Thomas, Clara. *Our Nature, Our Words.*
Toronto: New Press, 1972.

Toye, William. *A Book of Canada.* Toronto:
Collins, 1962.
Watson, Sheila. *The Double Hook.* Toronto:
McClelland and Stewart, 1959.
Watters, R.E. and I.F. Bell. *On Canadian
Literature, 1806-1860: A Checklist of Articles,
Books and Theses on English Canadian Literature,
its Authors and Language.* Toronto: University
of Toronto Press, 1966.
Weaver, Robert, ed. *Canadian Short Stories:
First Series.* Toronto: Oxford, 1960.
Weaver, Robert, ed. *Canadian Short Stories:
Second Series.* Toronto: Oxford, 1968.

Native Peoples :
Beautiful Losers

2

1713

Alexander Henry wrote in 1809 of the Michilimackinac massacre, as he had witnessed it:

The dead were scalped and mangled; the dying were writhing and shrieking under the unsatiated knife and tomahawk; and, from the bodies of some ripped open, their butchers were drinking the blood, scooped up in the hollows of joined hands, and quaffed amid shouts of rage and victory. I was shaken, not only with horror, but with fear.[1]

John Richardson wrote in 1832 in a romantic novel about the same Pontiac rising of 1763:

A tall and noble looking warrior, wearing a deerskin hunting frock closely girded round his loins, appeared to command the deference of his colleagues. . . . With a bold and confiding carriage, the fierce Pontiac moved at the head of his little party.[2]

Canadian Indians, envisioned by English-Canadian writers: two opposing versions. Noble Savage or implacable foe; tragic victim or grotesque menace—the Indian was a puzzling presence on the early Canadian scene.

In early days, settlers reported the ways of the native peoples with a mixture of dread and scorn. Later, as the Indians slipped into "harmless" ways, the dread disappeared. In its place emerged a sentimental romantic picture of the "Noble Savage"—a primitive being better, stronger, more dignified than his civilized counterpart. The smaller the menace presented by the native peoples, the greater the tendency to idealize their ancient ways. Canadian Literature ultimately presents the image of the Indian as losing the land to more sophisticated peoples, but as keeping his own cultural dignity and grace. The image of the Eskimo is

[1] Alexander Henry, "The Massacre at Fort Michilimackinac", in *The Book of Canadian Prose*, ed. A.J.M. Smith (Toronto, 1965), p. 73.
[2] John Richardson, *Wacousta*, New Canadian Library edition (Toronto, 1967), p. 108.

tinged with humour rather than dignity; but again English-
Canadian Literature presents the legend of a good-natured people
victimized by changing times and by technology. These myths of
the native peoples perhaps masked the actual facts: degradation,
exploitation, expropriation in the nineteenth century; prejudice
and rejection in the twentieth century.

From the beginning, literary treatment of the Indian in Canada differed from that in the colonies which were to emerge as
the United States. It differed, partly because the beginnings of
literature in Canada came so much later than in the more southern colonies. Virginia was opened to settlement in 1607, in an age
of wonder at the brave new beings in a brave new world. The
Mayflower Pilgrims landed at Plymouth in 1620, bringing with
them Reformation ideas concerning the unregenerate state of
the souls of the heathen in their dealings with the Indians. In
contrast, English settlement was not firmly established in Newfoundland until 1713, nor in Halifax until 1749, nor in Niagara and
Quebec until 1759. By this time eighteenth century attitudes to
the Indians had supplanted earlier attitudes. Pope cried, in 1733:

Lo, the poor Indian! whose untutored mind
Sees God in clouds, or hears him in the wind,
His soul, proud science never taught.[3]

The mid-eighteenth century rationalist assumed that the Indian
would be the better for learning Western ways.

The Indian in these more northerly regions had already
been partially assimilated into French life in Quebec and the
Maritimes, thanks to the proselytizing Jesuits and the frater-
nizing *coureurs de bois*. Alexander Henry, recording his life among
the Indians between 1760 and 1776, was one of many to feel their
kindness as well as their savagery. Alexander Mackenzie, in 1789,
was more scornful of the "dirty, lazy savages", less interested in
their ceremonies, more repelled by their "unattractive, sickly"
appearance.[4] But Mackenzie, and Henry, and their fellow-
traders all accepted the eighteenth century assumption that the

[3] Alexander Pope, "An
Essay on Man", epistle I,
1.99 in *Norton Anthology
of English Literature*, ed.
M.H. Abrams (New York,
1968), Vol. I, p. 1722.
[4] Alexander Mackenzie,
"Among the Indians of the
Pacific Coast", in *The Book
of Canadian Prose*,
pp. 92-100.

Indians were capable of being "civilized", and would be the better for it.

Farther north, European notions of dress, family customs, transportation, and home-building seemed less viable. Eskimos, coping so well with their Arctic climate, were less subject to the pressure to "improve themselves". But few travellers followed Mackenzie into the Arctic circle. The figure of the Eskimo did not become as familiar to readers as did the Indian. Until the North became more accessible through air travel, attitudes to the native peoples of Canada were generally concerned with the stereotype of the Indian.

Indian as Romantic Stereotype

By the beginning of the nineteenth century, Rousseauistic respect for the "Noble Savage" had begun to supplant the tone of patronizing scorn. Major John Richardson's novel *Wacousta*, 1832, was the first Canadian work to make creative use of the romantic attitudes towards the Indian. As a novelist, Richardson was very much under the influence of Sir Walter Scott. His intricate plots, his sensational romantic scenes, his use of picturesque scenery, strangeness, and terror of incident, all show a debt to the great Scottish novelist.

For the addition of Indian characters to this romantic mix, Richardson could follow the lead of a contemporary American writer, James Fenimore Cooper. Cooper's *The Pioneers* had appeared in 1823, *Last of the Mohicans* in 1826, and *The Prairie* in 1827. But the first of these novels had shown the Indian as a rather degraded being, lingering on the edges of the white man's villages. Not until 1840 would Cooper follow Chingachkook back to his primitive strength in the wilderness, in *The Pathfinder* and *The Deerslayer*. Richardson's novel pre-dated Cooper's in glamourizing the Indian. *Wacousta* began the popular Canadian series of romantic novels in which warriors, red-coats, Indian maidens and swooning English gentlewomen tangle in a complex of intrigues, ambushes, oratory, and peril by land and lake. Richardson outdoes Fenimore Cooper in shock and surprise. The two authors offer an interesting comparative study, not only for the facts they present about Indians, but for the insight into attitudes toward the Indians held by Canadians and Americans.

Wacousta exploits the still-fresh memories of the Pontiac conspiracy of the 1760's. The siege of Detroit, successfully withstood because of a warning by friendly Indians, contrasts with the horrible massacre at Michilimackinac. Indian brutality is revealed; but the most savage character in the plot, Wacousta himself, is no Indian, but an English nobleman "gone native", and fostering dark plots of revenge. Pontiac, the real Indian chief, appears in dignity and power, more sympathetic a character than the English commander De Haldimar.

In his detailed description of the Council at Detroit, Richardson includes an impassioned speech by Pontiac, presenting the Indians' case:

"Why did the Saganaw come into the country of the Red-skins?" haughtily demanded the chief. "Why did they take our hunting ground from us? Why have they strong places encircling the country of the Indians like a belt of wampum round the waist of a warrior?"[5]

A major figure in *Wacousta* is the mysterious Indian maiden, Oucanasta, who loves young De Haldimar, saves him from a series of perils, but finally relinquishes him to his white ladylove. "The Saganaw is safe within his fort," she says, "and the girl of the palefaces will lay her head upon his bosom. . . . Oucanasta will go to her solitary wigwam among the redskins."

The conquering white man perhaps pacifies his conscience in this romantic motif. The beautiful loser is seen as a willing victim.:

A heavy sigh escaped her laboring bosom; and as the officer

[5] *Wacousta*, p. 118.

now rose and quitted her hand she turned slowly and with dignity
from him, and crossing the drawbridge was in a few minutes lost in
the surrounding gloom. [6]

Indians as Observed by Travellers

It was hard to maintain a pose of romantic idealization in the
face of evidence piling up from the experience of travellers and
the observations of anthropologists and folklorists. Travellers in
Canada in the 1840's and 1850's, in particular, piled-up a case for
the non-romantic side of Indian life. Missionaries commented on
the subsistence level of living. Anna Jameson in her *Winter Studies
and Summer Rambles* wrote sympathetically about the Indians
at the forks of the Credit River, and made a perilous journey up
Lake Huron to observe Indian Treaty days at Manitoulin Island.[7]
An increasing number of travellers noted the sad effects of civilization. Yet Mrs. Moodie found in her Indian neighbours a kind
of sympathy lacking in the borrowing "Yankees" who bedevilled
her early days in the bush.[8] All these travellers' experiences
were limited to the tribes of the East coast and Eastern wood-
lands: Algonquins—Abenakis, Micmacs, Malecites, Ojibways—
Hurons, and Iroquois—Mohawks, Oneidas, Onondagas, Cayugas,
Senecas, and Tuscororas.

Travel books of the 1850's contain some accounts of the Eskimos, but most of these Northern accounts are connected with
the flurry of interest in the North-West passage stirred up by the
disappearance of the Franklin expedition—and the focus of
Northern travel was mostly on this mystery, rather than on the
ways of the native people.

An upsurge of interest in the native peoples, not as observed
by white men, but as members of a self-contained culture with
indigenous folkways, arts and crafts, mythology, rituals and mores
spread to Canada from the States in the mid-nineteenth century.
H.R. Schoolcraft, an American whose work fired the imagination
of Longfellow, began publishing in 1839. Schoolcraft was visited

[6] *Wacousta*, p. 297.
[7] Anna Jameson, *Winter Studies and Summer Rambles*, New Canadian Library edition (Toronto, 1965).
[8] Susanna Moodie, *Roughing It in the Bush*, New Canadian Library edition (Toronto, 1962), ch. 18.

by many travellers to the Detroit and Windsor regions; his attitudes infused the work of British observers and, eventually,
of Canadian writers.

This anthropological approach coincided with the opening of
the Canadian West where there were tribes of Indians as yet
unaffected by the white man's conventions. Songs and legends
were recorded by travellers among the Blackfoot, the Crees, the
Blood, and other Indians of the plains, preserving part of the
native culture. Paul Kane's *Wanderings of an Artist among the
Indians of North America*, 1855, gives vivid word pictures to
accompany his paintings of Indians.[9] Sir George Simpson, the
Earl of Southesk, Milton and Cheadle added colourful anecdotes
to the literature of the prairie Indians.[10]

Paul Kane pushed all the way to the Pacific coast. There he
observed other tribes: Nez Percés, Walla Walla, Klikilat, Nootka,
Babine, Chinmesyan, Chinook, Skinpah, and Cowichan.

Soon these tribes would witness the influx of gold seekers. But
on the West coast, when the colony of British Columbia emerged
in the 1850's, there was special interest in preserving the Indian
legends. Governor Douglas' wife, herself part Indian, passed
along the old legends to her family. Her daughter, Martha Douglas
Harris, became one of many folklorists to collect stories of the
western tribes.[11]

At the time of Confederation the Canadian Indians were
regarded with a mixture of paternalism, interest, and respect;
but their ancient culture was being eroded in all areas of the new
nation. Charles Mair's *Tecumseh*, a verse-drama written in 1868,
shows both the romantic idealization of the Indian and his mis-
treatment. Mair presents a vision of fierce Pontiac and noble
Tecumseh in heroic blank verse. The full drama, published in
1886, presents the admirable Indian chiefs in ironic contrast with
ignoble whites. Interestingly, the coarse white townfolk are
Yankees, ugly specimens of debased "civilization," named Gerkin,
Slagh, Twang and Bloat. One of them summarizes the contemp-
tuous attitude to the red man: "Whisky's better'n gunpowder,
and costs less than fightin' em in the long run."[12]

[9] J.R. Harper, *Paul Kane's
Frontier* (Toronto, 1971).
[10] George Simpson, *Narra-
tive of a Journey* (London,
1847); W.B. Cheadle,
North-west Passage by Land
(London, 1865); Earl of
Southesk, *Saskatchewan and
the Rocky Mountains*
(Edinburgh, 1875).
[11] M.B. Smith, "The Lady
Nobody Knows", in *British
Columbia: a Centennial
Anthology*, ed. R.E.
Watters (Toronto, 1958),
p. 472 ff.
[12] Charles Mair, *Tecumseh*
(Toronto, 1926), p. 107.

Mair's drama is interesting not only for its use of the Noble Savage theme, but also for its supplement of notes, in which the author shows how carefully he has been reading scientific bulletins on Indian customs. These notes on initiation rites, calumets, war chants, wampum, and so on, show the scientific realism that was already replacing romantic stereotyping.

Newspaper accounts of the Riel rebellion brought the grievances of Indians and half-breeds (métis) to the reading public of the 1880's. The railroad to the West, rushed into construction by the need of coping with Riel, remained as a means of access to the prairies and to prairie tribes. The men who carried the railway line further westward added their reports on Indian life. W.F. Butler, Sandford Fleming, and George Grant helped fix the image of the Indian in their widely-read accounts.[13]

Almost all the travellers assumed that Indian ways would be wiped out by the new age of technology. Nineteenth century folklorists recorded Indian songs and legends with a sad feeling of recording a disappearing culture.

Indian Myths, Songs, and Legends

Folklorists have found in Indian tales a unique response to the concepts of time, of personality, and of personal possessions, and, above all, to the phenomena of nature. Early important collections of Indian myths and legends were compiled by such anthropologists as Franz Boas, S. T. Rand, and J. D. Edgar. Cyrus MacMillan retold many of the legends in a form attractive to children in the 1930's. Among modern collections of Indian legends, the most interesting are those produced by Indian people, for instance *The Tales of Nokonis*[14] and the book *Forbidden Voice*.[15]

The legends of the Canadian Indians focus on two central figures: a cultural hero, called Glooskap in Eastern versions, and an evil trickster, called Malsunis or Raven. Among some peoples, the two figures become one in Nanabush, the hero-trickster, sometimes called Wiskedjak or Coyote.[16]

[13] Sandford Fleming, *England and Canada*, (London, 1884); G.M. Grant, *Ocean to Ocean* (Toronto, 1873); W.F. Butler, *The Great Lone Land* (London, 1872).
[14] Patronella Johnston, *Tales of Nokonis* (Toronto, 1970).
[15] Alma Greene, *Forbidden Voice* (London, 1970).
[16] Norah Story, "Indian Legends and Tales", in *Oxford Companion to Canadian History and Literature* (Toronto, 1967), pp. 376-380.

Some legends explain, often in a comic vein, the phenomena of nature—why the trillium is white, why the birch bark has fine brown scars, why the skunk smells as he does, or how a star floated down to become a water lily. Other legends touch on the mysteries: the souls of the dead, the powers of dancers, fire, and the birth of evil.

Indian songs also form part of Canadian oral literature. They include lullabies, love chants, war songs, and ritual songs connected with the seasons, the crops, and the hunt.[17] Some of the Indian songs were included in the first major collection of Canadian poetry, W. D. Lighthall's *Songs of the Great Dominion,* 1889. Some are included in the modern record collection by folk singer Alan Mills, *Canada's Story in Song.*

By the end of the nineteenth century Indian customs were dimming. But Indian legends had become a part of all Canadians' heritage.

Poets' Use of the Legends

Three interesting nineteenth century poets show the problems of using Indian materials: Pauline Johnson, daughter of a Mohawk Chief and an English gentlewoman, and a consummate showman and extrovert; Duncan Campbell Scott, by profession Civil Servant in the Department of Indian Affairs, by temperament mystic, aesthetic; and Isabella Valancy Crawford, freelance writer with no particular expertise on Indian affairs but with deep poetic sensitivity to the legends, the myths, and the rhythms of the Indian people. The three raise the general question of the necessity of "writing from personal experience". Johnson, who grew up in the Indian tradition was most inclined to sentimentalize. Scott, firmly shaping the actual changes in Indian life through the agency of his Department, wrote a poetry which is haunting and evocative, but indefinite. Crawford, the writer with the *least* personal experience of Indian ways seems to have written best and most sensitively.

Pauline Johnson's poetry is the easiest to read. Some is didactic—indignant at exploitation:

[17] "Song to the Wanderer", "Dead Man's Song", "Wabanaki Song", "Hard Times", in *Listen! Songs and Poems of Canada*, ed. Homer Hogan (Toronto, 1972), pp. 31, 33, 36, 63.

By right, by birth ,we Indians own these lands,
Though starved, crushed, plundered, lies our nation low . . .[18]

Some is pretty, using soft similes of wings, bubbles, ferns, opal
tints, and lullabies. From 1885 on, Pauline Johnson was one of
Canada's celebrities. Her reading tours electrified audiences with
the drama of her change from a first appearance, slim and straight,
in beaded white doe-skin, to the second-act sophistication of
her beauty in full formal court dress. Her poetry sentimentalized
her own inheritance. It gave Canadians a pleasant, perhaps
facile familiarity with the idyllic life of canoe, wampum, flint,
and feather. Miss Johnson was respected and loved. Her harsher
notes of social protest were accepted—and forgotten.

Duncan Campbell Scott emphasized the strong violent aspects
of Indian traditions. Perhaps as escape from the routine of his
Ottawa life as civil servant, Scott created poetry which has the
hypnotic beat and the powerful story line of Indian legends. Scott
tends to focus on sombre aspects of Indian life—the plight of
the half-breed for instance. "On the Way to the Mission", "The
Mission of the Trees" and, "Night Burial" are poems about
murder, cannibalism, and starvation. "The Forsaken" presents
a code of valiant endurance.

In the most haunting of his poems, Scott returns to the
portrayal of a young Indian girl as victim and sacrifice, interestingly reminiscent of Richardson's Oucanasta. He adds a level of
ritual mystery to the poem by linking the story with natural
seasonal cycles. "At Gull Lake" presents an Indian girl, caught
between the two worlds of red man and white trader. Hers is a
story of sacrifice, set in an autumn world. Keejigo is cast out from
her society, isolated, blinded; then the seasons circle on toward
winter and moonrise: "after the beauty of terror, the beauty of
peace. [19]

Isabella Valancy Crawford, at her best, makes Indian poetry,
rather than making English poetry of Indian life. Crawford does
more than recreate moments of experience from Indian life. She
tries to recreate the Indian sense of the universe. She uses Indian

[18] Pauline Johnson, "A Cry
from an Indian Wife", in
Flint and Feather (Toronto,
1912), p. 19.
[19] D.C. Scott, "At Gull
Lake", in *Poets of the
Confederation*, ed. M.M.
Ross (Toronto, 1960), p. 119.

myths and metaphors as a form of realizing the world of nature
in an Indian way. She mythologizes the changes of the seasons;
she captures the sense of time as measurable in experience rather
than in achievement. Professor Northrop Frye claims for her "the
most remarkable mythopoeic imagination in Canadian poetry. She
puts her myth in an Indian form, which reminds us of the re-
semblance between white and Indian legendary heroes in the
New World, between Paul Bunyan and Davy Crockett on the one
hand and Glooscap on the other."[20] These myths, Frye suggests,
best show the way the imagination responds to the impact of the
Canadian landscape.

Like the poets, the novelists of the late nineteenth century
had been stirred to use the traditional tales and legends of the
Indians as recorded by the post-romantic observers. Best among
the results were: William Francis Butler's *Red Cloud,* 1882; G.M.
Adam, *An Algonquin Maiden,* 1887; Egerton Ryerson Young's
Oowikapum, 1895; W.A. Fraser's *The Blood Lilies,* 1903, and W.D.
Lighthall's *Hiawatha the Hochelagan,* 1906. All of these novels
show an effort to study the Indian in his own right, not as
a shadow at the edge of white settlements.

Mazo de la Roche in the 1920's chose to write instead about
integration between white and Indian cultures. In 1923, before she
wrote her best-seller *Jalna,* de la Roche published *Possession.* This is
the story of a young architect who moves into an old house on
Lake Ontario, and finds himself involved in the lives of the Indian
fruit-pickers who hire out as seasonal workers. The young hero is
bewtiched by Fawnie, a beautiful and wayward Indian girl. Fawnie,
buoyant, vital, malicious, half-civilized, is funny and tragic. She
lies and she connives. She has no taste—at least in the white
community's eyes. Her relationship with the young hero brings
frustration to both.

Fawnie's father is an old Indian chief, who mourns with
dignity the loss of his ancestral lands. "I will tell you," he says,
"tales of the old days—not so long ago either—when my people
owned all this." The new owners agree. "What he says is
true. . . . We have taken their land, and civilization demoralizes

[20] Northrop Frye, "The
Narrative Tradition in
English CanadianPoetry",
in *The Bush Garden*
(Toronto, 1971), p. 148.

them." Then the opposite point is made: "Yes, but we have
made a better land of it, and I think they are better employed
picking berries than scalping each other.[21] The old chief dies,
and his funeral is a grotesque travesty. Fawnie lives on, conniving
and subdued, a burden and a reproach to her white husband.

One of the excellent things about Fawnie is her sense of
humour. She is a refreshing change from earlier Indian characters,
so often seen in sombre tones. Anthropologists emphasize the
importance in Indian thought of the notion of a trickster-god,
whose pranks dominate the universe.[22] Fawnie is a first recognition
of the Indians' tone of humour and gaiety.

There is no such lightness in the major Canadian poem about
the encounter between red man and white. E.J. Pratt's *Brébeuf and
His Brethren,* 1940, presents Jesuit missionaries and Iroquois in
heroic terms. The taunting, cruel Indians are forced to admire
the endurance and defiance of the Frenchman, although they
cannot accept or tolerate him in their world. In the theatre,
two modern plays by George Ryga reflect the persistence of
smouldering animosity: *Indian* and *The Ecstasy of Rita Joe.*

The comic sense is picked up again in Mordecai Richler's
The Incomparable Atuk, 1963. Here it is an Eskimo who serves as
absurd anti-hero, a mocking commentator on civilized Canada. It
is interesting to find the Eskimo at last emerging as a factor in
Canadian art. Richler in *Atuk* makes fun of the contemporary
fad for primitive Eskimo art and shows how a smart Eskimo
exploits that fad.

New Indian Voices

Young poeple have developed new sympathy for the native peoples of America. Indian fashions have become associated with the
desired return to natural ways, natural foods, and simple dress.
In the Canadian version of *Hair* the "tribe" of young rebels
slipped naturally into an Indian life style. Awareness of Canadian
discrimination against Indians has been urged as a warning against
an over-critical attitude toward American racial prejudice. Talk

[21] Mazo de la Roche,
Possession (Toronto, 1923),
p. 80.
[22] Paul Radin, *The Trickster*
(New York, 1956).

about "red power" has spilled over from the "black power" movement. All these elements have increased the interest, respect,
and sympathy, as well as the sense of guilt, of young white
Canadians toward the Indians. West Coast poets in particular
use Indian materials in this new mood. George Bowering's "Indian
Summer" and Victor Coleman's "Fish: Stone: Song" illustrate
such new uses. [23]

Indians in Canada have appeared strongly among our new
poets and painters. The singer-poets, Buffy Sainte-Marie and Willy
Dunn, and poets such as Sarain Stump join older writers like
Chief Dan George. [24] But the Canadian Indian appears in the eyes
of his own artists neither as a fierce warrior nor as a Noble
Savage. Indian singers show us poverty, denial of right,
drunkenness, loneliness, with only occasional affirmations of a
counter-culture with natural harmony, ease, and security. The
anthology *The Only Good Indian,* 1971, reminds us of the ironic
streak in Indian outlook.

Duke Redbird, who played the lead role in the first production
of *The Ecstasy of Rita Joe,* is also a painter and a poet. Redbird's
poetry is featured in *Red on White,* a most exciting experiment in
mosaic composition edited by Marty Dunn. Duke Redbird
protests against technocracy:

> I lie
> murdered on this concrete prairie . . .[25]

But he is hopeful that the white Canadian may learn from the
Indians an alternative attitude to nature and time, childhood,
and possessions, and death.

In all these modern Indian writers there are echoes of some of
the strains heard earlier in Canadian history. The works of Chief
Dan George and Alma Greene's *Forbidden Voice* are reminiscent
of the dignified oratory of Tecumseh. Duke Redbird's life-story
of fantastic adventures in circuses, on the road, in Rochdale,
Yorkville, and Ottawa shows some of the trickster quality of
the Coyote stories, the sense of magic transformations and jaunty
opportunism and humour that is also part of the Canadian Indian.

[23] George Bowering,
"Indian Summer", in *Fif-
teen Canadian Poets*, eds.
Gary Geddes and Phyllis
Bruce (Toronto, 1970),
p. 227; Victor Coleman,
"Fish: Stone: Song",
in *Fifteen Canadian Poets*,
p. 240.
[24] See *I Am an Indian*, ed.
Waubageshig (Toronto,
1971).
[25] Duke Redbird, *Red on
White*, ed. Marty Dunn
(Toronto, 1971), p. 54.

The Beauty of Losers

Perhaps as a mark of a guilty conscience, English-Canadian writers have played most insistently on the theme of the sacrificial victim, the beautiful loser, whether Oucanasta, Keejigo, or Fawnie. In this way, perhaps, white Canadians absorb the Indian presence into a deep level of imaginative experience. Leslie Fiedler, the controversial American critic, speaks of the importance in all American literature of the figure of the "dark other"— the black man, as measure and symbol of the essential nature of man. In Canadian Literature, the Indian may serve as "dark other" in this deep sense.

Certainly, in *Beautiful Losers*, 1966, the strange and strained novel by Leonard Cohen, the Indian girl has a powerful and puzzling function. Catherine Tekakwitha appears in *Beautiful Losers* as an obsessing memory of legendary purity. "Lily out of the soil watered by the Gardener with the blood of martyrs", she trails "the fragrance of the forests" into our world. Cohen mocks the Indian girl; her sainthood, her miracles, her self-martyrdom are treated sardonically. Yet a cry to her threads through this curious, distraught book, this fantasy of modern Montreal, this compound of slogans and machines, of *Québec Libre*, drug addiction, homosexuality, cinema techniques, slot machines, and mass meetings. Through this perverted world runs the thought of the martyred maiden of the Iroquois like the thought of a sparkling miracle of spring and faith:

They called the new village Kahnawake. . . . Close by was a small clear spring where she came each day for water. She kneeled on the moss. The water sang in her ears. The fountain rose from the heart of the forest, crystal and green were the tiny orchards of the moss. . . .[26]

To reach this reverent borderland of a dream of innocence, we must also accept the offensive, excremental perversity of Cohen's vision of modern society. But in the heart of this sinister forest, Cohen finds the clear spring of the Indian martyr, saint of the beautiful losers.

[26] Leonard Cohen, *Beautiful Losers* (New York, 1966), p. 101.

For Further Study

Indian as Romantic Stereotype

In Print:

Grey Owl [pseud.]. *Tales of an Empty Cabin.*
Toronto: Macmillan, 1936.
Grey Owl. *A Book of Grey Owl.* Toronto:
Macmillan, 1964.
Mair, Charles. *Tecumseh, a Drama.* Toronto:
Radisson Society, 1926.
Richardson, John. *Wacousta.* Toronto:
McClelland and Stewart, 1967.

On Film:

Caribou Hunters. MP 378. 17 minutes.
Joseph Brant and the Six Nations Indians.
MP 313. 10 minutes.

Other Media:

Jackdaw Kit. *Indians of Canada.* Toronto:
Clarke, Irwin. Documents, newspaper clippings,
recordings, tickets, photographs, posters.
Jackdaw Kit. *Louis Riel.* Toronto: Clarke,
Irwin.

Indians as Observed by Travellers

In Print:

Butler, W.F. *The Great Lone Land.* London:
S. Low, Marston, Low and Searle, 1873.
Cheadle and Milton. *The Northwest Passage by
Land.* Toronto: Coles Canadiana Collection, 1970.
Harper, Russell. ed. *Paul Kane's Frontier.*
Toronto: University of Toronto Press, 1971.
Harrington, Richard. *The Face of the Arctic.*
New York: Henry Schuman, 1952.
Jameson, Anna. *Winter Studies and Summer
Rambles.* Toronto: McClelland and Stewart, 1965.
Long, John. *Voyages and Travels of an Indian
Interpreter.* Facsimile edition. Toronto: Coles
Canadiana Collection, 1971.

Mackenzie, Alexander. *The Journals and Letters
of Sir Alexander Mackenzie.* Ed. W. Kaye Lamb.
Toronto: Macmillan, 1970.
Moodie, Susanna. *Roughing It in the Bush.*
Toronto: McClelland and Stewart, 1962.
Mowat, Farley. *People of the Deer.* Toronto:
Little, Brown, 1951.
Smith, A.J.M. *The Book of Canadian Prose.*
Toronto: Gage, 1965.
Southesk, James Carnegie, Earl of.
Saskatchewan and the Rocky Mountains. Toronto:
J. Campbell, 1875.
White, James, ed. *Handbook of the Indians of
Canada.* Toronto: Coles, 1971.

On Film:

Longhouse People. National Film Board. 1950,
Colour. 24 minutes.

Indian Myths, Songs and Legends

In Print:

Fowke, Edith. *Canada's Story in Song to 1959.*
Toronto: Gage, 1961.
Jenness, Diamond. *Indian Tribes of Canada.*
Toronto: McGraw-Hill, 1933.
Johnston, Patronella. *Tales of Nokonis.*
Toronto: Musson, 1970.
Macmillan, Cyrus. *Glooskap's Country.*
Toronto: Oxford, 1956.
Radin, Paul. *The Trickster: A Study in American
Mythology.* Comments by Jung and Kerenyi.
New York: Greenwood, 1956.
Symington, Fraser. *The Canadian Indian.*
Toronto: McClelland and Stewart, 1969.
Thornton, M.V. *Indian Lives and Legends.*
Vancouver: Mitchell, 1966.
Toye, William. *How Summer Came to Canada.*
Toronto: Oxford, 1969.
Toye, William. *The Mountain Goats of
Temlaham.* Toronto: Oxford, 1969.

On Film:

Legend. National Film Board. 1970. Colour.
15 minutes.
Legend of the Raven. Crawley Films. 1957.
Colour. 14 minutes.

Other Media:

Chief Henry Speck, *Kwakiutl Art.* British
Columbia Indian Designs Ltd., 367 Water St.,
Vancouver 3, B.C.
National Gallery of Canada. *The Art of the
Canadian Indians and Eskimos.* Ottawa:
Information Canada, 1969.

On Record:

"Huron Lullaby". In *Canada's Story in Song.*
Sung by Allan Mills. Toronto: Gage, 1960.

Poets' Use of the Legends

In Print:

Crawford, Isabella Valancy. *Collected Poems.*
Toronto: W. Briggs, 1905.
Johnson, Pauline. *White Wampum.* London:
Lane Press, 1895.
Scott, Duncan Campbell. *New World Lyrics
and Ballads.* Toronto: Morang, 1905.
(Selections from all three, Crawford, Johnson
and Scott, are in the *Oxford Book of Canadian
Verse,* ed. A.J.M. Smith. Toronto: Oxford,
1960, or the same author's anthology, *The Book
of Canadian Poetry.* Third edition. Toronto:
Gage, 1957).
Van Steen, Marcus. *Pauline Johnson.* Toronto:
Musson, 1965.

Native Peoples in Twentieth Century Literature

In Print:

Markoosie. *Harpoon of the North.* Montreal:
McGill-Queen's University Press, 1970.
Parker, Sir Gilbert. *Pierre and his People.*
Toronto: Copp Clark, 1897.
Pratt, E.J. *Brébeuf and his Brethren.* Toronto:
Macmillan, 1940.

Richler, Mordecai. *The Incomparable Atuk,*
London: A. Deutsch, 1963.
Roberts, Theodore. *The Red Feathers.* Boston:
Page, 1907.
de la Roche, Mazo. *Possession.* Toronto:
Macmillan, 1923.
Ryga, George. *The Ecstacy of Rita Joe and Other
Plays.* Toronto: New Press, 1970.

On Record:

Pratt, E.J. *Brébeuf and his Brethren.* TBC
Recording Ltd. 1262 Don Mills Rd., Don Mills
Ontario. A recording of the poem by E.J. Pratt,
set to music by Healy Willan, and performed
by the choir of St. Mary Magdalen Church.

New Indian Voices

In Print:

Cardinal, Harold. *Unjust Society.* Edmonton:
Hurtig, 1969.
Dunn, Marty. *Red on White: The Biography
of Duke Redbird.* Toronto: New Press, 1971.
Fidler, Dick. *Red Power in Canada.* Toronto:
Vanguard, 1970.
George, Chief Dan. "Lament for Confederation".
In *Listen! Songs and Poems of Canada,*
ed. Homer Hogan. Toronto: Methuen, 1972.
Gooderham, George K., ed. *I Am an Indian.*
Toronto: Dent, 1969.
Greene, Alma. *Forbidden Voice.* London:
Hanlyn, 1970.
Peterson, Len. *The Great Hunger.* Toronto:
Book Society of Canada, 1971.
Stump, Sarain. *There is my People Sleeping.*
Sidney, B.C.: Grays, 1970.
Waubageshig, ed. *The Only Good Indian.*
Toronto: New Press, 1971.

On Film:

Duke Redbird. *Charley Squash Goes to Town.*
National Film Board. 1969. Colour. 4 minutes.

The Beauty of Losers

In Print:

Cohen, Leonard. *Beautiful Losers.* Toronto:
McClelland and Stewart, 1966.

Canada

French and English Canada:
Two Solitudes

3

1763

"Two old races and religions meet here and live their separate legends, side by side." Hugh MacLennan, in *Two Solitudes,* writes of the bicultural, bilingual phenomenon that is Canada. His title, "Two Solitudes", has become proverbial. A dramatic fact about Canada, and a critical problem, is the nervous coexistence of the two founding cultures: French and English. English-Canadian literature has faced the French fact for two hundred years; but the tone of the encounter from the very beginning has been hesitant, distant, and stiff.

The first Canadian novel was Frances Brooke's *The History of Emily Montague,* 1769, which she wrote while living in Quebec City. Mrs. Brooke was wife of the chaplain of Wolfe's forces, and one would expect close involvement with the theme of Conquest and with the nature and needs of the conquered from a Christian gentlewoman in her position. Yet as her novel threads its elegant and sentimental way through the flirtations and courtships of Quebec society, there is hardly a touch of interest in the economic, theological, or political questions posed by the coexistence of two ethnic groups, traditional enemies, in one small colony.

The History of Emily Montague is an epistolary novel—a good form for catching the minutiae of response to life in an unfamiliar country, and a logical and realistic form in its times, considering how much of business, courtship, and politics had to be conducted by letter from colony to homeland. But of the 228 letters in *Emily*, only five focus on the French Canadians. True, there are a few passing references to the lazy peasants, the vain seigneurs, the parochial curés, the vivacious but shallow ladies, the dirty monks. And there are three longish analyses of *habitant* farming.[1]

[1] Frances Brooke, *The History of Emily Montague*, New Canadian Library edition (Toronto, 1961), pp. 59-61, 166-168, 175-178.

But essentially the characters in Mrs. Brooke's story are blithely
unaware of any real issues, any real differences in values or
in mores, or any probability of real clashes arising from those
differences. The novel presents two heroines, Arabella Fermor, an
English coquette and Emily Montague, an English rose-maiden.
Then Mrs. Brooke, in good romantic style, adds a third female: a
dangerously seductive French-Canadian widow, Mme des Roches
of Kamaraskas.

   Emily Montague is a charming period piece, fun to read if your
taste runs to Jane Austen and Anthony Trollope. As the earliest
novel set in North America it has great historic interest. As the first
piece of imaginative literature preserved in English Canada, it is
also noteworthy for its clear manifestation of the "two solitudes"
phenomenon.

The French Presence

   Even in Mrs. Brooke's day, the French-Canadian life drew much
attention from travellers. Social patterns had evolved in French
Canada different from French-in-France patterns. Seigneurial
life—warm, zealous, and conservative—developed in the villages
sparked by those adventurous outriders, the *coureurs de bois*.

   In the cities of Quebec and Montreal, a second kind of
society emerged. Convents, universities, law courts, and cathedrals
fostered in the cities a tradition of Jansenist intensity and martyr-
dom. Stubborn land-centered peasant life built villages and farms
that were family-oriented and rich in folklore. Aristocratic
families maintained tenuous ties with Paris and Versailles; *habitants*
settled more permanently into the new habitat. A dichotomy of
life within French-Canadian society was evolving, very different
both from the more levelled bourgeois life of New England and
from the slave-based gentility of the South. The Quebec Act of
1774 guaranteed the survival of the social pattern as well as
of the language. The French Revolution, raging from 1789, broke
many of the ties with French intellectual developments and

intensified local loyalties.

All travellers in the early days were intrigued by these
people: "conquered, but not oppressed", "inoffensive, unchangeable",
above all "picturesque". Issac Weld, George Heriot, John
Lambert, Jospeh Sansom, Francis Hall—the important travel-
writers of the early 1800's—share the same focus. Not the
grandeur of the approach up the St. Lawrence, nor the sublimity
of Niagara; not the hillocks in the roads nor those unimaginably
menacing "muskeetoes"; not the Indians worshipping their Great
Turtle nor the English-speaking farmers pioneering in the
Maritimes—none of these dominate the early reports on Canada
in the nineteenth century. No, it is the French presence. The
presence of the French in politics; the appearance of the
habitant in his village or farmhouse; the whispering progress of
French nuns through hospital wards—these are the features that
catch the eye of the early tourists. There was both affection and
condescension in the travellers' reports on the *habitants*. There
was, also, a growing sense of "romantic" value and interest in
those aspects of French-Canadian life which fitted very well into
contemporary tastes. For a generation becoming addicted to
Wordsworth's poetry, to Byron, to Gothic novels, here were
humble people, quaint in their bright sashes, charming in their
folk-wisdom, their ballads and legends. Here were also the
mysterious convent shadows, the flickering votive candles, the
silently-gliding nuns of Perpetual Adoration. Here were Byronic
young Frenchmen of famous old families such as the De Salaberrys
and Casgrains, bereft of old inheritance.

Of all the travellers between 1800 and 1820, Lieutenant
Francis Hall best reflected these interests. His anecdotes are finely
handled. A curé at Les Eboulements offers wine and strawberries
and urbane discourse. At La petite Rivière, in a country home,
the skin of a sea-wolf is hung against white-washed walls. A
dame and her daughter turn from their carding to offer a friendly
meal: omelet fried with bacon and served with maple syrup; later,
by the light of an iron lamp, they add a mess of milk porridge. [2]

[2] Francis Hall, *Travels in
Canada and the United States
in 1816 and 1817* (London,
1818). This book, like
many travellers' accounts,
is available in microfilm.
Rare early editions are held
in libraries, as listed in
R.E. Watters' *Check List of
Canadian Literature*
(Toronto, 1972).

Why did no creative writer appear to turn these materials into
poetry, sketch, or short story? Down in New York, Washington
Irving was converting just such materials into "The Legend of
Sleepy Hollow" and "Rip Van Winkle". Why no Canadian Irving?

By the 1830's and 1840's, English Canadians had begun to
use English-Canadian history, French Canadians to use French-
Canadian traditions in romantic novels; but there was no
interchange. John Richardson's *The Canadian Brothers,* 1840, for
instance, paralleled Doutre's *Les Fiancés de 1812,* 1844, but they
deal with two separate legends, two increasingly separated life-styles.

Then in the late 1860's, Rosanna Mullins began to use
French-Canadian materials in some of her sketches, poems, and
novels. As Madame Leprohon, she had entry into French-speaking
circles in Montreal; she caught in her art several of the aspects
of Quebec life just beginning to be explored by Francophone
artists. Again, we see a dichotomy in Mrs. Leprohon's work:
The Manor-House of Villerai, 1860, presents rural manners of the
1760's. *Antoinette de Mirecourt,* 1864, dips into the much more
sophisticated and sentimental circle of post-Conquest Montrealers,
and particularly into the temptations and tremors of a lovely
young girl secretly married to a dashing but dastardly English
soldier. *Armand Durand,* 1868, explores both country life and
city manners. In all three, this English-Canadian writer presents
a French world locked away from English Canada, and locked into
a life which is polarized between elegant wealth in the city and
stoic, inarticulate isolation in the remote villages or seigneuries.

Yet in the same period a fine French-Canadian writer was
presenting his vision of both French-Canadian worlds, happily
interrelating. Philippe Aubert de Gaspé in *Les Anciens Canadiens*
explored both the folk culture and the intellectual aspirations
of Quebec. Significantly, his book was retrospective to an age
long gone. Written in 1863, but dealing with 1783, Aubert
de Gaspé wrote in response to François-Xavier Garneau's plea

(in *Histoire du Canada,* 1845-8) for preservation of Quebec legends
and traditions. De Gaspé's work in turn became the source and
the inspiration of many historical novels romanticizing the old
regime. Jospeh Marmette produced *l'Intendant Bigot* in 1872, and
Le Chevalier de Mornac in 1873; J.-T. Lespérance published *Les
Bastonnais* in 1877. They followed Aubert de Gaspé's lead back
to the Conquest days and beyond.

Francis Parkman, the American historian, provided good
source materials for romancers; so did the English-speaking
Quebec scholar James Macpherson Le Moyne. An English-
Canadian novelist picked up the materials. William Kirby, in
The Golden Dog, 1877, turned to Intendant Bigot's regime for
a tale of love, intrigue, murder, treachery. This melodramatic
romance became very popular in English Canada, and remained
a staple of school reading lists up to our own time. Kirby claimed
eleven years of research had gone into *The Golden Dog,* but it
was not research on the French-Canadian life of his own times.
Nor was it research on the realities of colonial or national politics
of any time. *The Golden Dog* remains vivid, exciting, and hollow.
Ironically, without any intimation of the reality of the menace
implied, it fixed into English-Canadian memories the menacing
couplet: "The time will come which is not yet/When I'll bite them
by whom I'm bit".

Other English Canadians picked up Kirby's lead into a dreamy
world of chivalry, intrigue, and simpering romance: W.D. Lighthall's
The Younger Seigneur, 1888, and J.G. Marquis' *Marguerite de Roberval,*
1899, are among twenty or so titles of books in which Anglophones
perpetuated the myth of archaic charming aristocracy in Quebec.

By the end of the century, the other half of the English-
Canadian myth of French Canada surfaced: the image of the quaint,
lovable habitant, superstitious, good natured, old-fashioned,
inoffensive. There is a glimmer of this picture of the *habitant* in
Gilbert Parker's historical novel *The Seats of the Mighty,* 1896. Here
in a comic peasant-soldier named Gabord, Parker develops the
dialect humour he had first recorded in *Pierre and His People,* 1892.
In 1897 the comic dialect found its master in William Henry

Drummond. Affectionate, sympathetic ,but essentially patronizing,
W.H. Drummond produced for English Canadians a long series
of lovable, amusing portraits of Little Bateese, Johnny Courteau,
and company. French Canadians were not amused when Drummond
and his admirers recited their verses:

Venez ici, mon cher ami, an' sit down by me—so
An' I will tell you story of old tam long ago—
W'en eve'ryt'ing is happy—w'en all de bird is sing
An' me! I'm young an' strong lak moose an' not fraid no t'ing.[3]

Duncan Campbell Scott also exploited the comic value of the
superstitious villagers in *In The Village of Viger,* 1896, and other
stories.

Altogether, the emphasis in nineteenth-century English
poetry and fiction was on French-Canadian people, whether in
the charming past or the amusing present, very different from
the English-Canadian "us". Ralph Connor, in his best-selling
novel, *The Man from Glengarry,* 1901, presents a stereotype picture
of a brawling, lusty French Canadian, LeNoir. He is a minor
character, subservient to the English-Canadian hero, and comically
confused. "Das mos' surprise!" cries LeNoir. "Ne comprenne pas.
I never see lak dat, me!"

The patronizing attitude of Parker, Connor, Drummond,
and their contemporaries added fuel to the resentment growing
in French Canada as the twentieth century moved toward the
First World War. A new school of writing was emerging in
Quebec. Among its themes was resentment of the Anglophones'
economic exploitation, the political deference to British imperial
interests, and the cultural condescension of English Canadians.

[3] W. H. Drummond, "Le
Vieux Temps", in *The Book
of Canadian Poetry*, ed.
A.J.M. Smith (Toronto,
1957), p. 160.

The French Angle

Violent feelings had erupted in French Canada; violence

caught and flung to French audiences by French writers, but
rarely translated into English. Perhaps the retrospective *Maria
Chapdelaine,* 1914, product of a French writer from France, spurred
native *Canadiens* to a re-assessment of current realities, in village
and city. New realities, not the established sentimental myths,
infused the books of French-Canadian writers between the wars.
With modern writers, we move from reality to nightmare or
fantasy, but never to the old dream of life. Thériault, Aquin,
Langevin, Godbout, Blais: their novels are strained, nervous,
angular. To read them is to enter a strange intense world,
different from that of English Canada—and vastly different from
the legend preserved in English Canada about French-Canadian
values and interests.

Have modern English-Canadian writers had any success in
catching the pulse of French-Canadian life? Interestingly, among
major successes in this line we must recognize the poems of
A.M. Klein. From his vantage point as a Jewish member of the
English-speaking community in Montreal, Klein observed and
caught many of the new tones in Quebec life: the gentle dignity
of nuns in "Sisters of the Hôtel Dieu", the jaunty corruption
of a small-time operator like "M. Gaston", the more dangerous
demagoguery of the orator in "Political Meeting: for Camillien
Houde".[4]

Recent French-Canadian literature has been obsessed by
growth and change within the culture. In literary terms, separatism,
neo-federalism, and quiet revolutionism have all spurred
experiments with theme and language in prose and poetry, much
more exciting than anything that is going on in English Canada.
Most modern French-Canadian writers are writers of crisis, and
in most the crisis is defined in cultural, political, and social
terms. Yet there is always a metaphysical strain. Many follow
Hector de Saint-Denys-Garneau into this view: "The whole task,
I think, the whole problem consists in freeing the human spirit—
not in freeing French-Canadians."[5]

[4] A.M. Klein, "Sisters of
Gaston", "Political Meet-
ings", in *The Book of Canadian Poetry*, pp. 359, 360,
362.
[5] H. de St. D. Garneau,
"Notes on Nationalism",
in *Canadian Writing Today*,
ed. Mordechai Richler
(London, 1970), p. 90.

Twin Solitudes

    A perceptive bilingual critic, Ronald Sutherland, in *The
Second Image* points out the significant parallels between the themes
emerging in modern Canadian Literature in both languages. Inter-
influence is improbable, he says, yet there is an evolution, parallel
though separate, a growth of "twin solitudes". Sutherland notes
a parallel Puritan tension—Jansenist in Quebec—different
from that in the States, and affecting in both literatures the
presentation of the priest or churchman and the treatment of
women and sexuality. There is a related tension in treatment of
female beauty, and in studies of impotence and guilt. The "twin"
effect also appears in French and English obsession with the
land, a parallel vision of the simple cycle of nature as deeply
meaningful and vital. In both literatures, there is new focus
on strange, amoral characters who "begin at zero" in a search for
faith and meaning. There is a parallel fear of being dominated
by an alien culture *(les Anglais*/the Americans). Treatment of child's
life in both literatures is marked by a peculiar insistence on the
anxieties of childhood, its non-innocence, its lack of joy.

    Are these parallels the results of a shared geography? We
go back to the sense of place. Perhaps Anne Wilkinson is right
in "South, North":

On native stone of sin
Cold men whet their pleasure.[6]

Professor Ronald Sutherland may overstress the parallels between
the "twin" cultures—perhaps we could find similar ties with
Australian or Scandinavian literature—but he is right in believing
that reading one literature sharpens our sense of the drift in
the other. Certainly we should ponder his categorical statements:
"The main distinguishing feature of Canadian life is the coexistence
of two major ethnic groups. To be in the emerging mainstream
of Canadian Literature, therefore, a writer must have some

[6] Ann Wilkinson, 'South,
North", in *Canadian
Anthology*, eds. C.F.
Klinck and R.E. Watters
(Toronto, 1966), p. 384.

awareness of fundamental aspects and attitudes of both language groups in Canada."[7]

The growth within the two cultures has not been matched by an interchange between them. How few of our English writers do any more with the French fact today than Mrs. Brooke did with the same fact in her time! "Nous Vivons Ensemble!" Gordon Lightfoot cries[8], but few writers either French or English have wrestled with the difficulty of explaining or using bi-culturalism.

The French-Canadian writer best known to English writers is Anne Hébert. Her work, translated by Frank Scott and others, shows intricate, introverted, often neurotic intensity.[9] D.G. Jones, in "Portrait of Anne Hébert", speaks of her deft probing of some "obscure disease", the morbid tissue of a sense of guilt and repression.[10] Jones' image of "a tatter of lace" relates interestingly to the image of an old lace-making lady in Anne Hébert's story "The House on the Esplanade."[11] Other French-Canadian poets are being presented to English readers through the editorial work of John Glassco and Fred Cogswell.[12] An anthology called *Canadian Writing Today* edited by Mordecai Richler includes an intriguing sample of current French-Canadian work in poetry, fiction, and essay in translation.

There are very few French-Canadian characters in current English-Canadian novels: Richler's Yvette in *Duddy Kravitz;* Morley Callaghan's Claude Gagnon ("the dapper French-Canadian cartoonist with the fancy striped shirt") in *The Loved and the Lost;* Réné de Sevigny in Gwethalyn Graham's *Earth and High Heaven;* "Frenchy" Camille Turgeon, isolated among English-speaking shipmates in a corvette on convoy duty in Hugh Garner's *The Storm Below.* None of them do much more than Mrs. Brooke's "Madame des Roches" to suggest the ferment and anguish of life in Quebec today.

Hugh MacLennan's *Return of the Sphinx,* prophetic story of terrorism published on the eve of the F.L.Q. outbreaks of violence, presents a fuller and more frightening range. In French, Gratien Gélinas' *Yesterday the Children Were Dancing* does a parallel job

[7] Ronald Sutherland, *The Second Image* (Toronto, 1971), p. 124.
[8] Gordon Lightfoot, "Nous Vivons Ensemble", in *Listen! Songs and Poems of Canada*, ed. Homer Hogan (Toronto, 1972), p. 15.
[9] Anne Hébert, "Manor Life", tr. Frank Scott, in *Canadian Anthology*, p. 272.
[10] D.G. Jones, "Portrait of Anne Hébert", in *Fifteen Canadian Poets*, eds. Gary Geddes and Phyllis Bruce (Toronto, 1970), p. 97.
[11] Anne Hébert, "The House on the Esplanade", in *Canadian Short Stories*, ed. Robert Weaver (Toronto, 1960), p. 319.
[12] John Glassco, ed. *The Poetry of French Canada in Translation* (Toronto, 1970); *A Second Hundred French-Canadian Poems*, tr. Fred Cogswell (Fredericton, 1971).

of striking us with terror and pity.

More subtly, Hugh Hood relates the marriage of an English
and a French Canadian to a deeper duality. The hero of Hood's
White Figure, White Ground, 1970, paints two pictures entitled
"Light Source #1" and "Light Source #2", in the course of
a summer that is tense with his relationship to his French Montreal
wife and to his English Nova Scotia cousin. Repeating the motif
of the "double hook", the artist reaches out to the white light
of a summer sea and inward to the darkness of family memories—
and relates this duality to the polarities of English- and French-
speaking societies. This is a puzzling and subtle book, moving
bicultural tension to psychological and aesthetic planes of meaning.

Less complicated, but with its own deeper level of puzzles,
is Hugh MacLennan's *Two Solitudes,* 1945. MacLennan draws the
phrase "two solitudes" from a poem about lovers. The term has
become part of Canadian folklore, as applying to our bicultural
situation. In the novel, MacLennan, himself a Maritimer who
had few close connections with French Canadians when he wrote
the novel, deals with English-French relations over two
generations and between two war periods in Montreal.

Ironically, the closer understanding in *Two Solitudes* is
between the French Canadian Athanase Tallard and the Nova
Scotian Yardley. But the novel presents a series of divided worlds:
(1) the two solitudes within a Quebec village: the curé and the
seigneur, one oriented to his faith and the parish, the other to
intellectual life, to Paris, to Montreal and Ottawa; (2) two generations as "solitudes": father and son (Athanase the Member of
Parliament and Marius Tallard the draft-evader), father and
daughter (Yardley and Janet); (3) male and female as solitudes
in love (young Paul and Heather).[13]

Technically also the book seems divided. The first half
watches conscription tension in World War One; the second
half follows young Paul through Depression days to the eve of
World War Two.

[13] Hugh MacLennan, *Two Solitudes* (Toronto, 1945).

Do all these discords fuse into artistic unity? Is *Two Solitudes* one book in the end, one heart with a double beat, a self-moved reciprocation? Or is the book two separate stories bound into an incomplete unity? The same debatable question can be asked about the crucial two solitudes of Canada.

For Further Study

The French Presence

In Print:

Brooke, Frances. *The History of Emily Montague.* Ed. C.F. Klinck. Toronto: McClelland and Stewart, 1961.
de Gaspé, Ph. Aubert. *Canadians of Old.* Trans. Charles G.D. Roberts. New York: Appleton, 1890.
Hall, Lieut. F. *Travels in Canada and the U.S. 1815-1816.* London: Longmans, 1818.
Hémon, Louis. *Maria Chapdelaine.* Trans. W.H. Blake. Toronto: Macmillan, 1921.
Klein, A.M. *The Rocking Chair and Other Poems.* Toronto: Ryerson, 1948.
Le Moine, J.M. *Maple Leaves.* Quebec: Demers, First Series, 1863; Sixth Series, 1906.
Rivard, Adjutor. *Chez Nous.* Trans. W.H. Blake. Toronto: Ryerson, 1924.

On Film:

Aquin, Hubert. *Day after Day.* National Film Board. 1962. Black and white. 28 minutes.
The Voyageurs, National Film Board. 1964. Colour. 20 minutes.

On Record:

"A la Claire Fontaine". In *Canada's Story in Song.* Sung by Allan Mills. Toronto: Gage. 1960.

The Literary Myths

In Print:

Cather, Willa. *Shadows on the Rock.* New York: Knopf, 1931.
Drummond, W.H. *Habitant Poems.* Toronto: McClelland and Stewart, 1959.
Kirby, William. *The Golden Dog.* Toronto: McClelland and Stewart, 1969.
Parker, Gilbert. *The Seats of the Mighty.* Toronto: McClelland and Stewart, 1971.

On Record:

Pratt, E.J. *Brébeuf and His Brethren.* TBC Recording Ltd. 1262 Don Mills Rd., Don Mills, Ontario.

The French Angle

In Print:

Blais, Marie-Claire. *Mad Shadows.* Toronto: McClelland and Stewart, 1960.
Carrier, Roch. *La Guerre Trilogy.* Trans. Sheila Fischman. Toronto: Anansi, 1972.
Garneau, Hector de Saint Denys. "Journal". Trans. F.R. Scott. In *Canadian Writing Today,* ed. Mordecai Richler. London: Penguin Books, 1970.
Gélinas, Gratien. *Yesterday the Children Were Dancing.* Trans. Mavor Moore. Toronto: Clarke, Irwin, 1967.
Harvey, J.-C. *Les Demi-Civilisées.* Montreal: Totem, 1934.
Kattan, Haim. "A Literature of Interrogation". In *Canadian Writing Today*, ed. Mordecai Richler. London: Penguin, 1970.
Lemelin, Roger. *The Town Below.* Trans. Samuel Putnam. Toronto: McClelland and Stewart, 1948.
LeMoyne, Jean. *Convergences.* Montreal: Edition H.M.H., 1969.
Ringuet. [pseud.]. *Trente Arpents.* Toronto: McClelland and Stewart, 1960.
Roy, Gabrielle. *The Tin Flute.* Trans. Hannah Josephson. Toronto: McClelland and Stewart, 1947.
Vallières, Pierre. *The White Niggers of America.* Toronto: McClelland and Stewart, 1971.

On Record:

Charlebois, Robert. *Robert Charlebois.* Select
Records. SSp 24.147.
Dor, Georges. *Georges Dor à la Comédie-
canadienne.* Gamma. GS117.
Ferland, Jean-Pierre. *Jean-Pierre Ferland.*
Select. SP 12.132.
Julien, Pauline. *Suite québecoise.* Gamma.
GS112.
Leclerc, Felix. *Felix Leclerc.* Philips.
B77.898L.
Leyrac, Monique. *Monique Leyrac en concert.*
Columbia. FL 332.
The Singer Composers of Quebec. Gamma. GM 502.
Vigneault, Gilles. *Gilles Vigneault à la
Comédie-canadienne.* Columbia. FL332.

Twin Solitudes

In Print:

Carman, Bliss and Lorne Pierce. *Our
Canadian Literature, English and French.*
Toronto: Ryerson, 1963.

Cogswell, Fred. *A Second Hundred Poems of
Modern Quebec.* Fredericton: Fiddlehead, 1971.
Cook, Ramsay. *Canada and the French-
Canadian Question.* Toronto: Macmillan, 1966.
Glassco, John, ed. *The Poetry of French Canada
in Translation.* Toronto: Oxford, 1970.
Hood, Hugh. *White Figure, White Ground.*
Toronto: Ryerson, 1970.
Lightfoot, Gordon. "Nous Vivons Ensemble".
In *Listen! Songs and Poems of Canada,* ed.
Homer Hogan. Toronto: Methuen, 1972.
MacLennan, Hugh. *Two Solitudes.* Toronto:
Macmillan, 1957.
MacLennan, Hugh. *Return of the Sphinx.*
Toronto: Macmillan, 1967.
Morchain, Janet and Mason Wade. *Search
For a Nation.* Toronto: Dent, 1967.
Stanley, G.F.G. *Louis Riel.* Toronto: Ryerson,
1963.
Sutherland, Ronald. *Second Image. Comparative
Studies in Quebec Literature.* Toronto:
New Press, 1971.
Wade, Mason. *French-Canadian Outlook.*
Toronto: McClelland and Stewart, 1964.
Warwick, Jack. *The Long Journey.* Toronto:
University of Toronto Press, 1968.

The American Presence: New Romans

4

1812

For almost two hundred years, Canadians have been defining themselves in a negative phrase: "No, we're *not* Americans!" That undefended (and undefendable) border may be a military joke; but ethically, culturally, and aesthetically it has been a real part of Canadian consciousness since 1776.

It was important in 1776 when Generals Montgomery and Benedict Arnold besieged Quebec City, and the Canadian soldiers celebrated their repulse in a popular song:

For the British boys have gained the day,
And the Yankees are retreating.[1]

It was important all through the last years of the eighteenth century when United Empire Loyalists drifted northwards into the Canadas and the Maritime colonies, rather than renounce their allegiance to Britain. The Loyalists celebrated that sad flight in elegant verse.

Then in 1812, the drums beat for the defence of the border. Again folk songs and legends emerged, idealizing General Brock, Laura Secord, and other Canadian heroes and belittling the Yankees.

The year 1837 carried American republicanism and revolutionary ideas back and forth from Buffalo to Toronto, and from Maine to Montreal. Again, many songs of the Rebellion of 1837 focus on the attitude to the United States and on Canadian response to the expansionist spirit in America.

Annexationist talk was loud in the States in the 1850's, particularly in the far West, where Oregon border dwellers raised the cry "54' 40" or fight!" The fighting never came, but songs about the border tensions in British Columbia did.

[1] E.F. Fowke, ed., *Canada's Story in Song* (Toronto, 1960), p. 58.

Confederation years, and again the border was tense—with
the underground railway for run-away slaves and with Fenian
raids organized by bands of Irish-Americans. Once again songs
caught the reaction to the American threat.

Annexationists mocked the border as an anachronism in
the 1870's and 1880's. The response was both political, in the
"Canada First" and the Imperialist movements, and cultural,
in the nationalist poems and essays of post-Confederation writers.

In the twentieth century, Uncle Sam's activities around the
Canadian border have remained cause for alarm, and stimulus
for art, in Canada. Today there is little intentional imperialism
or annexationism in the United States towards Canada. Americans
know too little about Canada to be interested in a political
take-over. But the pervasive cultural influences of the States
through television, magazines, and movies is felt as a form of
cultural invasion, paralleling economic take-over. And again, the
response of Canadians has generated a flurry of literary work,
crystallizing the Canadian feeling about the importance of the
border. Indeed, much of Canadian Literature right now consists of
response to the "new Romans". The American presence has
always been a staple of Canadian life and Canadian Literature.

United Empire Loyalists

In the 1770's, the Loyalists took the liberty *not* to believe
unreservedly in equality and fraternity. They weren't all wealthy,
and they weren't all cultured and elegant gentlemen. But gentility
became part of the Canadian legend of the Loyalists, because
the raw life of the Northern loyal colonies drew memorable
complaints from the more articulate Tories.

Jonathan Odell and Joseph Stansbury were typical examples:
clever writers who had sharpened their pens in political debates
back home in New Jersey and Philadelphia, they continued to
publish brilliant and bitter poems about the hardships of the
new life. Odell was an ardent and vigorous churchman, Stansbury

a jolly bon-vivant. Both brought unremitting resentment against the victorious Republicans into their new homeland. In Canada, they joined a society already consisting largely of losers in European causes: Highlanders who had come to the Maritimes after Bonnie Prince Charles' 1745 rebellion; other Highlanders who had been cleared out of the glens by sheep-minded landlords; Irishmen driven out by famine in Jonathan Swift's day. What could such people do but take up a gallant loser's stance?—mocking, ironic, unconvinced by success, but ready to add a little self-mockery as the realistic position of the loser. It is the stance of the righteous minority:

And see! how deluded the multitude fly
To arm in a cause that is built on a lie![2]

U.E.L. monarchism intensified in Canada when the United States celebrated a republican alliance with France in 1778:

Tho' ruin'd so deeply no Angel can save:
The Empire dismember'd: our King made a Slave:
Still loving, revering, we shout forth honestly
God save the King![3]

The Loyalist settlers in Upper and Lower Canada as well as in the Maritimes have become the subjects for later writers of historical romance. A modern American version of the life of the Loyalists is Kenneth Roberts' *Oliver Wiswell*, 1940; a modern Canadian example is Thomas Raddall's *His Majesty's Yankees*, 1942.

The Canadas continued to be a haven for American non-conformists: restless people simply drifting to another section of the frontier, crossing the Great Lakes to try their luck; other settlers moving by boat toward the Mid-West, and dropping off in Ontario counties en route; Methodist itinerants moving North to preach and teach. This growing ex-American population in Canada was not homogeneous. Tensions flared between Loyalists and post-Loyalists, as they had flared between Loyalists and pre-Loyalist pioneers. Strained and contentious, the

[2] Jonathan Odell, "A Birthday Song", in *Canadian Anthology*, eds. C.F. Klinck and R.E. Watters (Toronto, 1964), p. 8.
[3] Joseph Stansbury, "God Save the King", in *Canadian Anthology*, p. 12.

American portion of Canadian population grew and grew. By 1813
eighty per cent of Upper Canadians were of American origin—
only one quarter of these being of Loyalist stock. Yet in 1812
this group joined the British garrisons, the Scottish and Irish
immigrants, the Indian followers of Tecumseh and the French-
Canadian *habitants* to repel invasion by the United States armies.

The War of 1812

Out of the War of 1812 came early Canadian ballads, with
an anti-Yankee swing:

There was a bold commander, brave General Brock by name,
Took shipping at Niagara and down to York he came,
He says "My gallant heroes, if you'll come along with me,
We'll fight those proud Yankees in the West of Canadee!"[4]

Stories about Brock and other heroic people such as Laura Secord
and James FitzGibbon became part of Canadian folklore. A *Veteran
of 1812: the Life of James FitzGibbon* follows the gallant and peppery
FitzGibbon through his career in the War of 1812 and the
Rebellion of 1837.[5]

In the War of 1812, John Richardson, then only a fifteen-
year-old recruit, fought and was captured. Richardson would
draw upon his memories of 1812 when he came to write *Tecumseh*
in 1828, and later, when he recreated battle scenes in *Wacousta*
in 1832; he would return also to analysis of the politics and
campaigning in *War of 1812,* published in 1842, an important
bit of early Canadian historical writing.

All accounts of the campaigns are strained and distressing.
For many Canadians, they had the quality of civil war, of brother
against brother. In many contemporary records there appears more
hostility against the British than against the Americans. Supplies
were grudgingly sent to the armies in Canada, which seemed
to British commanders an insignificant area in the total perspective
of the Napoleonic wars.

[4] *Canada's Story in Song*,
p. 64.
[5] M.A. FitzGibbon, *A
Veteran of 1812*, facsimile
edition (Toronto, 1970).

The War ended and no one yet agrees as to "who won". After it ended, American ideas continued to invade Canada, principally through the American periodicals becoming commonplace in most homes. Canadian magazines like the *Literary Garland* could hardly compete; and they could only try to do so by including much popular American material.

The post-war era 1815-35 was socially distinguished by the presence of a British military force. Officers and their families added a note of internationalism and of protocol that gave Canadian garrison towns an air different from American cities. Yet the Monroe doctrine had offered to lay a protective American arm around Canada and a rebellion on American principles was fermenting. By the 1830's radical democratic ideals were seeping northward from Jackson's America, reinforcing the British strain of Chartism and the persisting Scottish sentiments of democracy immortalized by Burns. The rebellion of 1837 can be seen as a late version of the American Revolution.

Sam Slick: a Canadian Classic

In this era between 1812 and 1837, with its half-rueful, half-admiring recognition of the American spirit abroad in the land, *Sam Slick* was born. This book, *The Clockmaker, or The Sayings and Doings of Sam Slick,* by Judge Thomas Chandler Haliburton, a descendant of United Empire Loyalists, became Canada's first world-famous literary product. Sam Slick, salesman to Canada of Yankee goods, found a laughing, loving audience in Canada and in the United States. *And* (in spite of many a dig at British administrators in Nova Scotia), Sam Slick caught a chuckling audience in Great Britain several months before Charles Dickens stirred the same kind of laughter with the irreverent antics of *his* Sam—Sam Weller of *Pickwick Papers*. Dickens' comic masterpiece began appearing in British periodicals in 1836; *Sam Slick* had been featured in *The Nova Scotian* since 1835.

The pivot of the comic plots in the Sam Slick sketches
is Sam's Yankee ability to outsmart, outsell, outtalk and outthink
his Nova Scotia customers. But perhaps the real hero of the
stories is the "Squire", the Canadian narrator who watches Sam
operate, sometimes eggs him on—and laughs at him.

The range in humour is great. Whimsy, sardonic satire,
grim irony, innuendo to the borderline of good taste, clever
word play, parody, preposterous exaggeration, farce and romantic
fantasy—all can be found in the *Sayings and Doings* of Sam. But
besides particular bits of humour, there is the all-embracing fun
of the narrator's view-point.

The narrator suspends judgment on Sam. Is this Yankee
dishonest or just friendly? The narrator's attitude, like that of
many a Canadian confronted by an American operator, is
ambivalent. Haliburton is amused, and ruefully admiring. He is less
amused by the slow Nova Scotians who lay themselves open to
Sam's operations. Haliburton makes his comic hero comment
on the book:

It wipes up the blue-noses considerable hard, and don't let off
the Yankees so very easy neither, but it's generally allowed to
be about the prettiest book ever writ in this country. . . . It's nearly
all sold off, but jist a few copies I've kept for my old customers.
The price is just 5s 6d, but I'll let you have it for 5s.[6]

Sam Slick was an important book in its time because of
its pioneering use of dialect humour. "They all know me to
be an American citizen here, by my talk," says Sam. Scottish
writers in the Edinburgh magazines had experimented with dialect
for comic effect; but the Canadian book was the first to focus
centrally on this device, in a fashion that would become standard
in American humour. The book is also a pioneer in regional
realism. Place names, local details of landscape, houses, inns,
and public buildings, conveyances, food, and furniture all appear
in sharp recognizable detail. Structurally, the book is in the
form of anecdotes—a kind of sub-genre important as predecessor

[6] T.C. Haliburton, *The Clockmaker*, New Canadian Library edition (Toronto, 1958), p. 2.

of the short story, soon to flourish in the hands of Dickens and
Poe.

One of Sam's prime ideas is pride in American freedom.
This pride is answered by the Canadians, "*We* have no slaves!"
But Sam argues that all colonists are slaves, slaves to British
administrators. Haliburton's satire was designed to stir Nova
Scotians not only into seeing how they were being exploited
by Americans, but also into seeing themselves drained by Britain.
But as Sam Slick says, Canadians are "curious critters"; Haliburton
himself after a prominent career in Canadian law and legislation
capped his career by moving to England.

In his writings, Haliburton had followed Sam Slick from
Nova Scotia to the British court (*The Attaché*, 1843) back to
America (*Sam Slick's Wise Saws and Modern Instances*, 1853) and
aboard a coaster (*Nature and Human Nature*, 1855). In all, he
discriminates between American, British, and Canadian attitudes
and manners and speech, satirizes all three—and enjoys all three.
Out of the first half-century of American commercial imperialism
in Canada had come the first classic of Canadian humour. Are
we Americans? Canadian writers, engaged with that question
in the years before and since Haliburton, have often answered
ruefully—and laughingly—with him, "Not really: we're not quite
slick enough."

Yankee Neighbours in the Early Settlements

Travellers and British immigrants in the 1840's and 1850's
were less concerned with the commercial inroads made by
Americans, more concerned with another kind of infiltration: the
"Yankeefication" of social manners. Susanna Moodie, who had
been Yankee-watching in the Canadian settlements since 1832,
published her memorable report on Canadian life in 1852,
Roughing It in the Bush. One principal concern was Yankee manners
—lack of manners, in her view. Mrs. Moodie was acid in her
account of those Yankee neighbours, Emily S—, Betty Fye,

Betty B—, Uncle Joe, and Old Satan.[7] Mrs. Moodie is witty at
the expense of these garrulous, borrowing, intrusive, insensitive,
prying fellow-settlers. She could not forgive them for failing to
accede to her genteel insistence on deference and formality.
Margaret Atwood, in a marvellous modern recreation of Mrs.
Moodie's attitudes, makes her complain, "The Yankees were
unforgivingly previous to us."[8]

Mrs. Moodie's work adds to the Canadian store of anti-
American feelings. But readers may be amused not only by Mrs.
Moodie's book, but also by Mrs. Moodie. Her prim refusal to
unbend, to reduce her notions of propriety in the face of
American ways of coping with the forest and its menaces, loneliness,
and privations, is irritating, pathetic, and funny. The reader must
take the part of Haliburton's "Squire", and act as amused observer
of Mrs. Moodie and her Yankee neighbours. We accept, as Mrs.
Moodie could not, the notion that the manners so shocking to her
were just frontier manners. She probably dubbed as "Yankees"
many of the Loyalists' descendants, who now considered themselves
thoroughly Canadianized.

Mrs. Moodie was not alone in finding it hard to distinguish
between Americans and Canadians. Travellers in the 1850's and
1860's found that a common type, with a common twang in
speech, and a common reductiveness in manners was emerging
throughout the American continent, in British North America
as well as in the States. The major difference, according to such
an observer as Anthony Trollope, was that Canada was a dimmer
version of American life:

> Up in those regions which are watered by the Great Lakes—
> and by the St. Lawrence—the country is divided between Canada and
> the States. . . . The States are advancing faster than Canada, and
> in fact doing better than Canada.[9]

Cultural infiltration, led by American teachers, preachers, actors,
musicians, and popular writers, had thoroughly Americanized
Canada, most writers agreed. From 1863 on, American Labour

[7] Susanna Moodie, *Roughing It in the Bush*, New Canadian Library edition (Toronto, 1962), chs. 5, 6, 7, 11, 13.
[8] Margaret Atwood, *The Journals of Susanna Moodie* (Toronto, 1970), p. 14.
[9] Anthony Trollope, *North America* (London, 1862), p. 56.

Organizations were penetrating the Canadian work force; in 1867
the purchase of Alaska reinforced West-Coast fingering of
Canadian rights.

All of these facts about American cultural infiltration of
Canada were sharply noted in the Canadian press. All the writers
mentioned in this chapter were great contributors to the periodicals:
Richardson, Haliburton, and Mrs. Moodie. The American
question, the American presence, the American pressure, the
possibility of annexation by the States—all these issues were
thoroughly aired by most Canadian journals of the early
nineteenth century.

Annexation was strongly urged in the fifties. The tide of
American empire was flooding westward: why not make the whole
continent part of the American dream? Fenian raids organized
by Irish agitators, working from American bases, heightened
the tension. And then in the sixties, the American imperial
movement into Canada was halted. The States were floundering
in Civil War; Canada was quietly settling into a separate
destiny, establishing Confederation.

If in the sixties Canadians had been asked "Are we
Americans?" they could answer in two ways. One: "No, thank
goodness. No Civil War here!" Two: "No, alas! No Walt
Whitman among us; no Emily Dickinson, Mark Twain, Hawthorne,
Melville, Emerson, nor Thoreau." At best the new Dominion was
producing poets like Charles Sangster, palely imitating
Longfellow and Whittier. Among the first generation of writers
after Confederation there were many cries for Canadian Literature,
and this was often defined as a literature recognizably different
from that of the United States.

"Canada First" was a political and intellectual movement
of the 1870's with literary overtones. Charles Mair appeared in
this group, attempting to write (a) great poetry, to show Canadian
powers, and (b) Canadian poetry, to distinguish Canada from
the States. It is interesting to note his revisions of poetry of
the 1860's: he builds in, through the process of Canadianizing,
some not-very-deft allusions to those old battles of 1812:

. . . Let roving Fancy delve
In the fields of "Eighteen-Twelve";
In her dreams recall the sward
Where the wife of lame Secord,
Knowing Boerstler's subtle plan
To surprise the British van
In the far camp where it lay
Roused her cows at break of day . . .
Till at night, with heart aflame
To the British camp she came.[10]

Terrible poetry—but the message is clear. For Canada to be first,
the drums of 1812 must beat again . . . and maybe a few cows
must be roused.

The Imperial Theme

The slogans of "Canada First" shifted and shaded into those
of the Imperialist Movement. Now it was a cry for a strengthened
British Empire. As counterbalance to the American appeal, the
cry of empire, monarch, old homeland was raised.

The dream of a British imperial federation was doubly based
in Canada, rooted in the Loyalist sentiments of fidelity to the
British heritage, and rooted equally in the sentiment of antagonism
to the American republic. Carl Berger, in *The Sense of Power*,
a fine study of Canadian ideas in the years between 1867 and 1914,
surveys the charges laid against the United States by Canadians:
aggressions, swindles, political corruption, domestic instability
(a horrifying divorce rate), lynch laws, materialism, undignified
social patterns, "mobocracy". Berger emphasizes that this "critique
of the republic" was not merely malicious or sterile; it was part
of the growth of Canadian nationalism.[11]

On the negative side, the Imperialist movement resulted
in denunciations against the American way of life in poetry,
essays, and editorials. It produced also some rather vapid patriotic
effusions about the mystic power of the northern climate, for

[10]Charles Mair, "Dream-
land", revised version, 1901,
in *Canadian Anthology*,
p. 82.
[11] Carl Berger, *The Sense of
Power* (Toronto, 1970),
p. 176.

example, William Kirby's *Canadian Idylls*, 1886. But its
permanent achievement, from a literary point of view, was its
stimulus of the amusing novel by Sara Jeannette Duncan, *The
Imperialist*, published in 1904.

Sara Jeannette Duncan was deeply indebted as a writer to
the American William D. Howells and to the expatriate American
Henry James. But when she came to write *The Imperialist*,
she developed a tone, a style and a theme all delicately
Canadian. Perhaps an important part of the Canadian quality
inheres in the careful discrimination of feelings toward the
United States.

The Imperialist begins with a mild monarchism, on the
twenty-fourth of May. It moves deftly into the story of the political
aspirations of a young man in an Ontario town, wanting to
bring to Canadian politics his own ideal of the British Empire.
With gentle irony, Duncan touches in the details of the cultural
imperialism against which Lorne's politics are set. But her irony
touches also the British alternative, in the person of Lorne's English
friend Hesketh. Finally she turns the irony of plot against Lorne
himself, the young Canadian. He has voiced all the anti-American
sentiments of his own time, and ours:

We often say we fear no invasion from the south, but the armies
of the south have already crossed the border. American enterprise, American capital, is taking rapid possession of our mines
and our water power, our oil areas and our timber limits.[12]

But when Lorne fails to win an election with this cry, his only
avenue for success seems to be clear: to join a friend in a law
firm in Milwaukee. So Sara Jeannette Duncan, having dextrously
brought this plot and the secondary story of Lorne's sister's
romance to a gently reductive end, turns her Canadian humour
where Canadian humour has always been turned: on ourselves.

Are we Americans? Duncan implies, "We may well become
so—and the Americans won't even notice!"

[12] S.J. Duncan, *The
Imperialist*, New Canadian
Library edition (Toronto,
1961), p. 232.

Resistance to the New Romans

Among more recent novels, Hugh MacLennan's *The Precipice*,
1948, plays most subtly with the ironies of American unawareness
of our agonizing. The American hero of this novel is an emotional
imperialist, a man building his own power at the expense of his
Canadian wife. MacLennan carries the story to a positive conclusion.

Most contemporary uses of the American-Canadian encounter
offer no such idyllic hope. Stephen Leacock briefly sentimentalized
on the fun of being near the Americans so we could watch them
push the world around and relish the action,[13] but few Canadians
have re-sounded that positive note. Satire, ranging from light
caricature to caustic attack, has been the mode. Robertson Davies'
Fortune My Foe, 1949, focuses on the problem of a young Canadian
intellectual trying to resist the attraction of the American milieu.
The darkest and saddest of these comments has come from George
Grant, grandson of one of the leaders of the Canada First and
Imperialist Movements. Grant's *Lament for a Nation*, 1965, assumes
the hopelessness of the effort to withstand absorption into the
American orbit.

Curiously, another strong body of satire of the United States
is found in the writings of the large group of young American
writers who have come to Canada in recent years—draft-driven,
many of them, but bringing promise of literary strength.[14] Douglas
Fetherling's *The United States of Heaven*, 1968, is representative
of this group. Much of the attack on the States in such books
is attack not on American actions in Canada, but on American
actions in the world.

The best of recent comment on the U.S. presence is gathered
in a book that puts a new tag on their imperialism: *The New
Romans*, edited by Al Purdy. *The New Romans* includes poems
and prose by established, as well as by the rising writers from
all across Canada: Purdy himself, Margaret Atwood, Eric Nicol,
Robin Mathews, Peter Newman, Laurier LaPierre, Larry Zolf.
The tone of the attack is biting, ironic, furious, often witty, but

[13] Stephen Leacock, "I'll
Stay in Canada", in
Canadian Anthology, p. 203.
[14] Poems by many of these
new Canadians from the
United States are included
in *Made in Canada*, an
anthology edited by Douglas
Lochhead and Raymond
Souster (Toronto, 1970).

rarely funny. The Haliburton touch, the Duncan control have gone; the manner is closer to Mrs. Moodie. Only in a few instances—in Earl Birney's "Billboards", for example, is the explosion a laughing one. Birney gives us in dialect the intolerance of the American truck driver on the Oregon throughway:

yegotta choose fella yegotta
choose between
        AMERICA and UN-
between KEE-RISPIES and KEE-RUMPIES
between KEE-RYEST and KEEROOST-SHOVE
and brother if you doan pick
        RIGHT
you better
git this heap
tahelloffn
our
        TRUWAY[15]

[15] Earle Birney, "Bill Boards", in *New Romans*, ed. Al Purdy (Toronto, 1968), p. 89.

Are we American? Most writers in the seventies can only answer, savagely or sadly, depending on their natures, "Not yet!"

For Further Study

United Empire Loyalists

In Print:

Brebner, J.B. *The Neutral Yankees of Nova Scotia*. Toronto: McClelland and Stewart, 1937.
French, M.P. *Boughs Bend Over*. Toronto: McClelland and Stewart, 1943.
Raddall, Thomas. *His Majesty's Yankees*. Toronto: McClelland and Stewart, 1942.
Tyler, M.C. "Joseph Stansbury, Tory Song-Writer and Satirist" and "Jonathan Odell, Satirist". In *The Literary History of the Revolution*. New York: Ungar, 1957.

The War of 1812.

In Print:

FitzGibbon, M.A. *A Veteran of 1812*. Toronto: Coles, 1970.
Fowke, Edith. *Canada's Story in Song*. Toronto: Gage, 1960.
Pacey, Desmond. "A Colonial Romantic: John Richardson". *Canadian Literature*, Autumn 1959, Winter 1960.
Richardson, John. *The War of 1812*. Toronto: Historical Publishing, 1902.

On Record:

"Come All ye Bold Canadians". In *Canada's Story in Song*. Sung by Allan Mills. Toronto: Gage, 1960.

Other Media:

The Battle of Queenston Heights, 1812; *The Battle of York*, 1813. Dateline Series Collection. Toronto: McGraw-Hill.

Sam Slick: A Canadian Classic

In Print:

Baker, R.P. *A History of Canadian Literature to Confederation*. Cambridge: Harvard University Press, 1920.
Chittick, V.L.O. *Thomas Chandler Haliburton*. New York: Columbia University Press, 1924.
Haliburton, Thomas. *The Clockmaker*. Toronto: McClelland and Stewart, 1958.

Other Media:

Jeffreys, C.W. *Sam Slick in Pictures*. Ed. Lorne Pierce. Toronto: Ryerson, 1956.

Yankee Neighbours in the Early Settlements

In Print:

Moodie, Susanna. *Roughing It in the Bush*. Toronto: McClelland and Stewart, 1964.

On Record:

"Mrs. Moodie's Journal". Canadian Broadcasting Corporation. 1969. CBC, Box 500, Terminal A, Toronto. A recording of poems by Margaret Atwood, read by Mia Anderson.

The Imperial Theme

In Print:

Berger, Carl. *The Sense of Power*. Toronto: University of Toronto Press, 1970.
Duncan, Sara Jeannette. *The Imperialist*. New Canadian Library edition. Toronto: McClelland and Stewart, 1961.

Shrive, Norman. *Charles Mair, Literary
Nationalist*. Toronto: University of Toronto
Press, 196

Resistance to the New Romans

In Print:

Davies, Robertson. *A Voice from the Attic*.
Toronto: McClelland and Stewart, 1960.
Davies, Robertson. *Fortune My Foe*. Toronto:
Clarke, Irwin, 1949.
Fetherling, Doug. *The United States of Heaven*.
Toronto: Anansi, 1968.
Godfrey, Dave and Mel Watkins. *Gordon to
Watkins to You*. Toronto: New Press, 1970.

Gordon, Walter. *A Choice for Canada*.
Toronto: McClelland and Stewart, 1966.
Grant, George. *Lament for a Nation*. Toronto:
McClelland and Stewart, 1965.
MacLennan, Hugh. *The Precipice*. Toronto:
Macmillan, 1948.
McNaught, Kenneth and Ramsay Cook.
Canada and the United States. Toronto: Clarke,
Irwin, 1963.
Purdy, Al, ed. *The New Romans*. Edmonton:
Hurtig, 1968.
Redekop, John, ed. *The Star Spangled Beaver*.
Toronto: Peter Martin, 1971.
Williams, Roger. *The New Exiles*. New York:
Liveright, 1971.

Canadian Lady:
Swamp Angel

5

1841

Frances Brooke and Rosanna Leprohon chronicling French-English romances in Quebec; Pauline Johnson and Isabella Valancy Crawford poeticizing the Indian experience; Susanna Moodie and Sara Jeannette Duncan recording Canadian response to the American presence: so many women already noted among Canadian writers! Their number reminds us of another presence consistently pressing on the consciousness of the Canadian artist: the presence of the Canadian lady.

The lady coped with life in the bush. The lady struggled to stay lady-like, bush or no bush. The lady scribbled stories, or painted, or made music to keep up her spirit and to keep open an imaginative channel to a different life. All these ladies were a significant part of the Canadian scene.

Life in the Canadas was generally harder for women than in the States. The climate was worse, and the British government was less likely to respond quickly to the needs of the ordinary settler. Of the women who came to Canada in the nineteenth century, more had aspirations to gentility than in the United States. The Loyalist women who had come from the American colonies had come largely from the propertied class. After the Loyalists, came the half-pay officers, gentlemen disbanded after the Napoleonic wars, bringing their wives to the Canadas to take up land offered in lieu of severance pay. As long as the British army manned the Canadian garrisons, the women of the garrison added their touch of decorum, worldliness, and gentility to the social scene.

The Canadian woman, as reflected in early Canadian Literature, emerges as genteel, inhibited by her social ambitions and her sense of propriety. She was bound by a code that was strangely at odds with the necessities of the wilderness. Doggedly, the women of Canada tried to maintain their gentility. In the wilderness, in loneliness, in the urgencies of daily survival, Canadian "ladies" set the tea-table, hung the lithographs, put pinafores on the little girls and insisted that the men wipe off their boots and their moustaches. They might be roughing it in the bush, but they roughed it as elegantly as they could. Swamp angels, we might call them, mired but aspiring.

When the time or the place proved too frustrating, the aspiration might sour into simple defiance. There are many portraits in Canadian Literature of women in unbearably arid situations, stubbornly resisting the pressure to lower standards and to conform to the environment. The literary image of the Canadian woman has been one of integrity and tense fidelity to a code (often a foolish one) rather than one of sweetness, passion, or charm. The aspirations and the inhibitions of the Canadian lady have added important tones to Canadian Literature.

Garrison Ladies

Women came into prominence in Canadian publishing in the pre-Confederation era, particularly in the 1840's and 1850's. Mrs. Brooke had shown the possibility of good work in a light elegant vein way back in the Conquest period. She had established a style and an audience in English literary circles long before she came to Canada; so she pushed her Quebec frivolities into a form that would be acceptable to publishers "back home". Julia C. Hart of Fredericton produced a first novel both written and published in Canada: *St. Ursula's Convent, or the Nun of Canada,* printed in Kingston in 1824; but she too imported style, plot tricks, and character stereotypes from the Gothic novel then dominating best-sellers in Europe.

In 1848, Anna Jameson, another woman already established
as a serious writer in England, published *Winter Studies and Summer
Rambles*, a sensitive commentary on life in and around York in
Upper Canada. With Mrs. Jameson the literary content became
more Canadian. Her book's charm however lies in its revelation
of the life led by a gallant woman in Canada, morassed in an
unhappy marriage, but making forays both inward into her own
sensitivity, her world of books and studies, and outward to the
Indian camps at Port Credit, the dangerous rapids around Sault
Ste. Marie, the political gatherings in the pre-1837 rebellious
days.

Another young woman stirred to write was Rosanna Mullins
(later Mrs. Leprohon). Her poetry, short stories, and sketches
appeared in the *Literary Garland*, a magazine publishing elegant
and elevating reading material for women, and *The Family Herald*.
Mrs. Lephrohon, like Mrs. Brooke, was prolific and professional as a
writer—a determined producer of popular fare. She was also a
specialist in stories involving difficult decisions for intense,
conscientious girls, for example, *Antoinette de Mirecourt*, whose
sub-title is *Secret Marrying—Secret Sorrowing*.

The women in Mrs. Brooke's *History of Emily Montague*
represent the garrison life: social codes of aristocratic England
acted out with no attempt to adjust to the new life. The virtues
of garrison life, of the soldier's wife, remain high in Canadian
ideals. Mrs. Leprohon's *Antoinette de Mirecourt* is also involved in
romance with a soldier—two soldiers, in fact. Her great achievement consists in having a noble English Colonel love her
sincerely, and disentangle her from her foolish secret marriage
to a dashing but corrupt junior officer. The role of the heroine
here consists of submission to a father, passive acceptance of a
hero's help, and resistance to a charming but unprincipled villain.
This Canadian heroine will never be a Jane Eyre, defy propriety
or feel swept by impetuous passion. Antoinette remains a proper
lady, following a genteel code.

Roughing it with Mrs. Moodie

In the official circles of town and garrison, conventions of conversation, courtship, dress, and intellectual pursuits had clearly been established: ideals toward which the well-bred Canadian lady could strive. Outside the garrison, in the clearings and in the bush, the striving was more difficult. Books by Mrs. Moodie, her sister Mrs. Traill, Anne Langton, and other pioneering gentlewomen show variations of the portrait of the Canadian lady. [1]

In *Roughing It in the Bush*, 1852, Mrs. Moodie hovers between documentary report and a sense of sequential plot. She works events of her actual life into a suggestive developing order: a pattern of storms, fires, births, visits and travels. But for all her honesty, Mrs. Moodie does not expose a full emotional life to us. She reveals her social indignation, her maternal devotion, her sentimental sensitivity to scenery, but we are never sure that she is growing and learning from the complexities of mental and emotional voyage. The sense of propriety that gave her strength and reassurance in the clearings of backwoods Ontario inhibited her full growth as a person and as an artist. She could not let down her barriers when she was writing, any more than when she was entertaining a brash Yankee neighbour.

Nevertheless her book is important as a Canadian document. The great nineteenth century American novels tended to focus on a male cast of characters and to delve into metaphysical profundities. Mrs. Moodie followed a different line. Her work is realistic, sociological, personal, and centred in a feminine point of view. This line proved viable to generations of later Canadian novelists who couldn't, or wouldn't, sound the grander tones of Melville and Hawthorne.

Mrs. Moodie's anti-heroic self-portrait also served as a model for later Canadians, an acceptable Canadian substitute for the passionate intensities of Charlotte or Emily Brontë, Mrs. Moodie's great contmporaries. No Canadian has yet written a great novel of passion; but many have followed Susanna Moodie in

[1] See Audrey Miller, *Gentle Pioneers* (Toronto, 1968); Anne Langton, *A Gentlewoman in Upper Canada* (Toronto, 1971).

presenting the serio-comic story of aspiration and frustration
of everyday life "roughing it in the bush".

Latter-day Ladies

Many a gentlewoman, besides Mrs. Moodie, was still roughing
it in the later part of the nineteenth century. Visiting travellers
made a special point of commenting on the refinement of
manners even in the roughest parts of the country. Lady Dufferin,
Lady Monck, and Lady Aberdeen, among many other well-born
English travellers, made a point of comparing the Canadian lady
with the American girl and the English woman—a nice
exercise in feminist geography![2] In the States, travellers noted a
greater discrepancy between the manners of town and farm; in
Canada there was surprising universality in the straining for
civility. A great many of these ladies harboured literary aspirations.

Agnes Machar was one of a whole army of women hovering
midway between professional competence and amateurish effusions.
She had published much poetry as "Fidelis" before going on
to produce a serious novel, *Roland Graeme, Knight,* in 1892.
This is an honest and troubled confrontation of labour troubles,
and of the hypocrisy of churchmen in coping with new social
and industrial problems.

Many of the literary ladies produced historical fiction. Much
good historical research was done by these writers, but once
the tales got underway, fidelity to human norms of behaviour
disappeared. Details of dress and events were painstakingly
accurate, but plots were romantic and sentimental. They were very
readable, though, and there is still excellent swash-buckling
adventure in the novels of Agnes Laut, *Lords of the North,* 1900,
Heralds of Empire, 1902, or of Jean McIlwaith, *The Curious Career
of Roderick Campbell,* 1901, and *A Diana of Quebec,* 1912.

Most Canadian men, writing novels in the Victorian period,
also by-passed the reality of the contemporary life of women.
They too turned instead to historical romance, mostly choosing
exotic heroines like the French-Canadian Angélique in William

[2] Lady Dufferin, *My
Canadian Journals* (London,
1891); Lady Aberdeen,
*Through Canada with a
Kodak* (Edinburgh, 1893).

Kirby's *The Golden Dog,* 1855, and Alixe in Gilbert Parker's
Seats of the Mighty, 1896.

A student of the lives of late nineteenth century women
in Canada might better turn to Sara Jeannette Duncan's *The
Imperialist,* 1904. This author cut through the contemporary
conventions of best-selling silliness and historical romances to
write an honest study of a young girl coping with a restrictive
code of courtship. The heroine, Advena, is revealed to us as rich in
her emotional responses and fine in her intellectual energy. But
like Susanna Moodie and Anna Jameson, she is sadly inhibited
by her social environment. She is hampered by her own idealism.

Post-Victorians

Suffragism and the First World War released Canadian
women from many of the restrictions that hampered Victorian
Advena. But novelists in the 1920's continued to picture their
heroines as muffled, baffled, or battered by community, family,
or their own ideals.

Martha Ostenso wrote in *Wild Geese,* 1925, a powerful study
of loneliness, love, harsh land, and harsh family life in the North
West. Ostenso's heroine, unable to infuse her own ideals into an
angular remote community, withdraws from it, without changing
her own notions.

L.M. Montgomery, in *The Blue Castle,* 1926, created an
interesting heroine: an imaginative, rebellious girl who sets herself
against unimaginative conformity, family propriety, and a dreary
work ethic. At the end of this book Montgomery pulls her strong-
minded young heroine back into a childish fairy-tale ending.

The continuing portrayal of one special kind of woman—
ambitious, convention-ridden, sensitive, anxious, aesthetically gifted,
yearning for liberation from the restraints of her environment—is
significant. It marks the recognition by Canadian writers of the
Canadian lady as a particular complex, a force straining the already
complicated web of Canadian life. For something closer to a

documentary on this type, we have available a series of very readable autobiographies, including those of Emily Carr, Laura Salverson, and Nellie McClung.[3] A collection of biographies titled *The Clear Spirit* adds documentation of these lives and others.[4]

Women novelists of the Second World War seized on the war itself as a way of solving dilemmas of the women characters. In Gabrielle Roy's *The Tin Flute*, 1947, for instance, both mother Rose-Anne and daughter Florentine are momentarily released from tragic tensions by the coming of war. The same effect of by-passing crucial decisions appears in Gwethalyn Graham's *Earth and High Heaven*, 1944.

No such romantic evasion is doled out to the heroines of novels of the forties and fifties written by men. The nervous, aesthetic wife of a prairie preacher in Sinclair Ross's *As For Me and My House*, 1941, the heroine in Morley Callaghan's *The Loved and the Lost*, 1951, the artist in Hugh MacLennan's *The Watch that ends the Night*, 1959, are among many studies in idealism and aspiration. And all are defeated. The Canadian woman's lot is not a happy one—at least in the eyes of male novelists.

Poets of the fifties explored the theme of frustration in a new range of types and situations. In "The Stenographers", P.K. Page finds an image for the edginess of office-workers:

In the felt of the morning the calico-minded sufficiently starched, insert papers, hit keys.[5]

Another of Page's ladies is "Marina", walking "forever antlered with migraines".[6] Miriam Waddington focuses on women in a modern city setting:

Here kindness is pruned, and love
Torn up by the roots.[7]

Jay Macpherson uses the image of the northern wilderness, "to the level mild World locked and lost" as a metaphor for a woman, harsh and smouldering.[8] Variations on the theme of the new wilderness of modern life are sounded in poems from *Poetry by Canadian Women*, 1972, edited by Dorothy Livesay.

[3] Emily Carr, *The Book of Small* (Toronto, 1922); Laura Salverson, *Confessions of an Immigrant's Daughter* (London, 1959); Nellie McClung, *Clearing in the West* (Toronto, 1935).
[4] M.Q. Innis, ed., *The Clear Spirit*, (Toronto, 1967).
[5] P.K. Page, "The Stenographers", in *Canadian Anthology*, eds. C.F. Klinck and R.E. Watters (Toronto, 1966), p. 421.
[6] Page, "Portrait of Marina", in *Canadian Anthology*, p. 434.
[7] Miriam Waddington, "Portrait", in *Canadian Anthology*, p. 430.
[8] Jay Macpherson, "True North", in *Canadian Anthology*, p. 479.

Angel in a Modern Swamp

Cultural ideals based on a garrison situation inhibited the pioneer woman in Canada; climate and terrain locked her into a restricted life. In a sense, modern city economics have tightened those restraints. Today, when libertarian ideals have pushed into a feminist phase, Canadian women are caught in a contemporary sense of strain and change; but the desire for "liberation" takes a characteristic ironic twist in the Canadian context.

Among the younger poets, Margaret Atwood probes the intensities of personal relations:

Marriage is not
a house or even a tent
it is before that, and colder . . . [9]

Atwood strains in her poetic forms and in her themes against easy conformity; yet she circles from her own life back to the haunting puzzle of Susanna Moodie, going mad in the constricting settlements of early Canada.[10] Another intense young poet, Gwendolyn MacEwen, probes the "singular self" caught in the commonplace patterns of modern life—cooking, sewing, eating breakfast, making love, travelling.[11] In *Rings,* Daphne Marlatt explores the experience of childbirth as the ultimate reach of a woman's freedom—and her constraint.[12]

Writers of fiction are beginning to convert the rhetoric of "Women's Liberation" into experimental novels, such as Marian Engel's *The Honeyman Festival,* 1970. But in most fiction by modern Canadian women the old note of desire for decorum, even on the edge of a personal wilderness, still sounds. In the title story of the Alice Muntro Collection *Dance of the Happy Shades,* 1968, there is a poignant picture of Miss Marsalles, a music-teacher—old, poor, strange, simple-hearted, hopeful—going through the absurd and pathetic ritual of a recital and a tea-party, still believing in a possible miracle of music.[13] Alice Munro's novel, *The Lives of Girls and Women*, 1971, focuses the problem of

[9] Margaret Atwood, "Habitation", in *Procedures for Underground* (Toronto, 1970), p. 60.
[10] Margaret Atwood, "Further Arrivals", in *Fifteen Canadian Poets*, eds. Gary Geddes and Phyllis Bruce (Toronto, 1970), p. 174.
[11] Gwendolyn MacEwen, "Green with Sleep", in *Fifteen Canadian Poets*, p. 185.
[12] Daphne Marlatt, *Rings* (Vancouver, 1972).
[13] Alice Munro, "Dance of the Happy Shades", in *The Narrative Voice*, ed. John Metcalfe (Toronto, 1972), pp. 171 ff.

women's roles, women's status, and women's potential through
the device of setting different generations of women in contrast
to each other. Here, as in other modern novels, the relations
of mother and daughter emerge as a major Canadian theme.

Margaret Laurence has picked up this theme in her fine
studies of women characters. In *The Stone Angel,* 1964, Laurence
presents the last days in the life of a strong-minded, fiercely
self-disciplined prairie woman, Hagar. Tense, abrasive, she has
never achieved easy relations with her father, her brother, her
husband, her sons—or with herself. As a woman, she is a stoney
being, moving on stoney ground. Yet Hagar, like all the women
in Margaret Laurence's books, has great integrity, great vitality.
She is arrogant, irritating, ridiculous, but never petty, never
pretentious, never predictable.

The same strength of character appears in the younger heroine
of Margaret Laurence's *A Jest of God,* 1966. In this novel, Rachel's
mother, with her rigid sense of propriety, appears as a late example
of the would-be lady. Rachel strains against this code; she yearns
for vital experience, but is stifled by the mores of her small
prairie town, by the expectation of her mother, and most of
all by her own intensity. Rachel maintains toward her own
dilemma the sardonic realism of a Susanna Moodie; toward herself
the astringent wit of a Sara Jeannette Duncan. In the end, Rachel
proves herself capable of freedom. She is not, however, free to
achieve passionate flight and social independence; instead she
is free to accept the care of her mother and to move westward
into a quiet new life.

A novel written in 1954 encases all these versions of the
Canadian lady in its gentle wit. Ethel Wilson's novel *The Swamp
Angel* watches one heroine move out to the wilderness setting
to find herself; a second heroine slips from old age to death,
while her daughter moves decorously into marriage and maternity.
Mrs. Wilson writes beautifully of the wilderness setting in the
British Columbia interior. She writes beautifully also of the spirit
of her central character Maggie Vardoe. Maggie has cut away
from her small-minded husband, her job, her home in Vancouver

to "rough it in the bush". Here she can grow in freedom; here
she can begin new relationships—with a child, with an old man,
with her employer. But eventually her flight becomes anti-social.
She must cut away the affection of the boy, reject the job offered
by the old man, move away from her employer's marital problems,
throw away even the "swamp angel", the little gun that is her
souvenir of an old and gallant friend. [14]

Maggie's is a triumph of withdrawal rather than of
commitment. She is presented in a book admirable in an artistic
sense, elegant, sophisticated, and modern. In her, we have a
modern version of the perilous flight of the Canadian lady—the
"swamp angel". But where is the portrait of the Canadian woman
as a young, free, passionate person? Still to come . . . perhaps
from the new world of Women's Liberation—where angels may
well fear to tread.

[14] Ethel Wilson, *Swamp Angel* (Toronto, 1954).

For Further Study

Garrison Ladies

In Print:

Brooke, Frances. *The History of Emily Montague.* Toronto: McClelland and Stewart, 1961.
Jameson, Anna. *Winter Studies and Summer Rambles.* New Canadian Library edition. Toronto: McClelland and Stewart, 1965.
Leprohon, Rosanna. *Antoinette de Mirecourt.* Montreal: Lovell, 1864.
Miller, Audrey, ed. *The Journals of Mary O'Brien, 1828-1838.* Toronto: Macmillan, 1968.

Roughing It With Mrs. Moodie

In Print:

Atwood, Margaret. *The Journals of Susanna Moodie.* Toronto: Oxford, 1970.
Campbell, Grace. *Thorn Apple Tree.* Toronto: Collins, 1943.
Innis, M. Q., ed. *The Clear Spirit.* Toronto: University of Toronto Press, 1967.
Langton, H. H., ed. *A Gentlewoman in Upper Canada: The Journals of Anne Langton.* Toronto: Clarke, Irwin, 1966.
Moodie, Susanna. *Roughing It in the Bush.* New Canadian Library edition. Toronto: McClelland and Stewart, 1962.
Moodie, Susanna. *Life in the Clearings.* New Canadian Library edition. Toronto: McClelland and Stewart, 1959.
Morris, Audrey. *Gentle Pioneers.* Toronto: Musson, 1968.
Traill, Catherine Parr. *The Backwoods of Canada: Being the Letters From the Wife of an Immigrant Officer.* New Canadian Library edition. Toronto: McClelland and Stewart, 1966.

Traill, Catherine Parr. *A Canadian Settler's Guide.* Toronto: McClelland and Stewart, 1969.

Latter-day Ladies

In Print:

Aberdeen, Lady. *Through Canada with a Kodak.* Edinburgh: White, 1893.
Abrahamson, Una. *God Bless Our Home.* Toronto: Burns and McEachern, 1966.
Cram, Mrs. George. *A Woman in Canada.* London: Milne, 1910.
Dufferin, Lady. *My Canadian Journal.* London: Murray, 1891.
Duncan, Sara Jeannette. *The Imperialist.* New Canadian Library editon. Toronto: McClelland and Stewart, 1961.
Harper, Russell, ed. *Notman Photographs of an Era.* Montreal: McGill-Queen's University Press, 1967.
MacRae, Marion. *The Ancestral Roof.* Toronto: Clarke, Irwin, 1963.
Stewart, Don R. *A Guide to Pre-Confederation Furniture of English Canada.* Toronto: Longmans, 1967.

Post-Victorians

In Print:

Atwood, Margaret. *The Edible Woman.* Toronto: McClelland and Stewart, 1969.
Buckler, Ernest. *The Mountain and the Valley.* Toronto: McClelland and Stewart, 1952.
Callaghan, Morley. *The Loved and the Lost.* Toronto: Macmillan, 1970.

Carr, Emily. *The Book of Small*. Toronto:
Clarke, Irwin, 1971.

Coburn, Kay. *Grandmothers*. Toronto:
Oxford, 1949.

de la Roche, Mazo. *Jalna*. Toronto:
Macmillan, 1927.

Graham, Gwethalyn. *Earth and High Heaven*.
New Canadian Library edition. Toronto:
McClelland and Stewart, 1969.

Livesay, Dorothy, ed. *Poetry by Canadian
Women*. Montreal: Inglavit, 1972.

MacLennan, Hugh. *The Watch That Ends the
Night*. New York: New American Library,
1959.

McClung, Nellie. *Clearing in the West*.
Toronto: Thomas Allen, 1935.

Montgomery, L.M. *The Blue Castle*. Toronto:
McClelland and Stewart, 1926.

Munro, Alice. *Lives of Girls and Women*.
Toronto: Ryerson, 1971.

Ostenso, Martha. *Wild Geese*. New Canadian
Library edition. Toronto: McClelland and
Stewart, 1971.

Roy, Gabrielle. *The Tin Flute*. Trans.
Hannah Josephson. Toronto: McClelland
and Stewart, 1969.

Salverson, Laura. *Confessions of an Immigrant's
Daughter*. London: Faber, 1939.

Angel in a Modern Swamp

In Print:

Clarkson, Adrienne. *Hunger Trace*. Toronto:
McClelland and Stewart, 1971.

Atwood, Margaret. *Surfacing*. Toronto:
McClelland and Stewart, 1972.

Engel, Marian. *The Honeyman Festival*.
Toronto: Anansi, 1970.

Laurence, Margaret. *A Jest of God*. Toronto:
McClelland and Stewart, 1966.

Laurence, Margaret. *Stone Angel*. Toronto:
McClelland and Stewart, 1964.

Marlatt, Daphne. *Rings*. Vancouver:
Georgia Straight, 1972.

Sinclair, Sonja. *I Presume You Can Type*.
Toronto: Canadian Broadcasting Corporation,
1969.

Watson, Sheila. *The Double Hook*. Toronto:
McClelland and Stewart, 1959.

Wilson, Ethel. *Swamp Angel*. Toronto:
McClelland and Stewart, 1954.

On Tape:

Conversations with Margaret Laurence,
Dorothy Livesay, Gwendolyn MacEwen,
Miriam Waddington. Produced by Ontario
Institute for Studies in Education, and available
from Van Nostrand Reinhold Ltd., 1410
Birchmount Road, Scarborough, Ontario.

National Identity:
Made in Canada

6

1867

People of the Confederation period firmly believed that the new nation would not be truly established until Canada had found a voice in a national art. E.H. Dewart had written in 1864, when formal Confederation conferences were just beginning:

A national literature is an essential element in the formation of national character. It is not merely the record of a country's mental progress: it is the expression of its intellectual life, the bond of national unity, and the guide of national energy.[1]

Confederation built two motifs into the theme of national identity. First, because the nation was born not in blood and revolution and not in violent overthrow of government, there emerged a notion of Canada as a peaceful place, slow to change. Second, the guarantees of biculturalism built in the idea of a nation that is a mosaic of peoples rather than a melting-pot, with the emphasis on the preservation of differences. This was a notion of introspection and persistence, rather than of adaptation and change.

To these two staid ideas of Canada settled in Confederation, a contrary vision of energy and enterprise was added in the 1870's: a vision of Canada as a huge young country, a half-continent, bound by the "steel of empire"—the East-West bands of rail. Peaceable kingdom, conservative mosaic—suddenly energized by the railroad: the sense of Canadian identity became tense with contradictions. Conflicting images of the nation appear in the first generation of Dominion of Canada writers of the 1860's and 1870's.

When a new generation of writers, such as C.G.D. Roberts,

[1] E.H. Dewart, "Introduction to Selections from Canadian Poets", in *Canadian Anthology*, eds. C.F. Klinck and R.E. Watters (Toronto, 1966), p. 75.

Bliss Carman, Archibald Lampman, and Duncan Campbell Scott emerged in the 1880's, they all revealed not only the conflict between conservation and change, wilderness and technology, but also the tension between poetic integrity and the patriotic impulse. Working to perfect their craft and to write in the best modern style of their day, they wanted also to "write Canadian". This combination of intentions proved difficult to handle.

Later Canadian writers have shared this difficulty. Many have been willing in theory to create a sacrament of praise for their country, but few have found themselves able to raise simple-hearted hymns.

Patriots and Poets

E.H. Dewart and other patriots stood ready to point out to Confederation poets the available ingredients for the "subtle but powerful cement" of a national literature:

We have the inspiring spectacle of . . . grand and gloomy forests . . . brilliant skies and varied seasons . . . magnificent lakes and rivers . . . hoary mountains and fruitful valleys . . . while human nature . . . still presents an exhaustless mine of richest ore.[2]

The Canadian forests, the men of the Canadian past: both silent, both needing a voice in Canadian art—this was a popular, if conservative, thesis. And from 1867 on, a batch of rather timid national poetry began to appear.

In 1867, Alexander Muir, writing "The Maple Leaf Forever", symbolized the continuity of the past in the Canadian emblems:

The thistle, shamrock, rose entwine
The maple leaf forever!

[2] Dewart, "Introduction", in *Canadian Anthology*, p. 75.

Charles Sangster, whose elegant polish made him a great hero in the 1870's with Dewart and other editors of nationalistic

magazines, produced for *Canadian Monthly and National Review*
poems about the Canadian woods, poems about Canadian sailing-
ships, poems about Tecumseh, always idealizing the past. Of
Tecumseh he says:

Vainly they strive, the toiling years,
No greater on the scroll appears
Than this wise warrior of the wood.[3]

Charles Mair wrote rather vapid "dreamland poems" to prove
that a Canadian could imitate well the poetry of Spenser and
Milton. Later he became a member of the "Canada First" movement, a small group of ardent patriots banded to foster a sense
of national identity separate from both great Britain and the
United States. As a "Canada First" stalwart, Mair revised his
poems to add Canadian content—which he took to mean references
to Canadian history.[4] In a similarly retrospective vein, Isabella
Valancy Crawford "wrote Canadian" by recreating the life of
pioneers in "Malcolm's Katie" and by incorporating Indian
metaphors.[5]

Outside Canada, the respected poets of the 1870's were also
oriented to history, concerned like Browning with people from
past eras, or like Tennyson and Longfellow with myths and
legends. But Canada's past offered little except the Acadian exodus
(already "done" by Longfellow) and Wolfe's assault on the cliffs
of Quebec (a touchy subject in a shaky confederation of conquerors
and conquered). Nature was more interesting than history in
Canada.

Contemporary British and American poets like Swinburne,
Whitman, Dickinson, and Rossetti were exploring exotic varieties
of experience, celebrating intensities and perversions and
obscurities in their own souls. But the Canadian soul seemed
to be either very well-adjusted or very self-concealing. Halifax
and Kingston in the 1870's didn't seem to foster decadence,
exoticism, or mysticism. Changes in nature appeared more
dramatic than changes in the Canadian soul.

[3] Charles Sangster,
"Tecumseh", in *Canadian
Monthly and National
Review*, II, 1872, p. 9.
[4] Charles Mair, "Summer",
in *Canadian Anthology*,
pp. 80-82.
[5] I.V. Crawford, "Malcolm's
Katie", in *Canadian
Anthology*, pp. 83 ff.

Therefore, most Canadian poets of the sixties and seventies settled for the landscape. Their style was modelled on Tennyson and Longfellow. Twenty years of Confederation landscape poetry culminated in one artistically satisfying poem by Wilfred Campbell of Kitchener, published in 1889:

Along the line of smoky hills
The crimson forest stands . . . [6]

This poem is sad and private, rather than enthusiastic or patriotic. The description swings from crimson glory to mist, from hills to river's mouth, from the call of a single bird to the continuous exodus of flocks. It presents a wilderness scene, a picture of a land untouched by man, and in particular untouched by technology.

The same delicate, careful play of sound and the same wilderness note of melancholy and mutability runs through the early work of Frederick George Scott.

There's a lonely spot in the soul of man
More lone than the moonless sea, [7]

he wrote in "Isolation", 1882. At about the same time, George Frederick Cameron was writing in more bitter tones of "gloom and desolation and dark hours",[8] as if joining a quiet conspiracy of resistance to the politician's optimism and affirmation in the early Canadian years.

In fiction, the first major novel after Confederation was William Kirby's *Golden Dog*, 1877. This historical novel turned away from contemporary Canada, not merely to the years before Confederation, but to the time before British settlement.

Meantime the nation was taking on new strength. Poets had been writing of gentle, melancholy, pastoral scenes; but in fact an era of power politics had opened, an age of business empire-building and of railway construction. And the first generation of Dominion of Canada writers was dissolving. G.F. Cameron

[6] W.W. Campbell, "Indian Summer", in *Canadian Anthology*, p. 97.
[7] F.G. Scott, "Isolation", in *Poems* (London, 1910), p. 144.
[8] G.F. Cameron, "With all my Singing", in *Canadian Anthology*, p. 93.

died in 1885, Isabella Crawford in 1887; Charles Mair moved
permanently to Prince Albert in the new North West in 1886;
F.G. Scott acted as official laureate in Quebec, celebrating royal
visits and jubilees, and gradually became absorbed in his work
in the church; Wilfred Campbell settled into a flurry of effort
on travel books, tourist guides, Canadian ethnic histories, and
historical romances. The first era was over.

Melancholy Masters

In the late 1880's a new generation of writers appeared.
They were anxious to "write Canadian", but they also failed
to create an image of a new nation of growth, enterprise, and
construction. Instead they followed the previous generation of
writers and produced reveries on landscape and on the life of
the past.

Charles G.D. Roberts, Bliss Carman, Archibald Lampman,
and Duncan Campbell Scott were all born around 1860.
Consequently they were school children during the Confederation
decade. In 1880, Charles Roberts, still only twenty years old,
published *Orion,* a book of poems, in Fredericton. His equally
young contemporary in Toronto, Archibald Lampman, wrote of
his tremendous excitement at the thought that *Orion* was Canadian
poetry:

I sat up all night reading and re-reading Orion in a state of the wildest
excitement and when I went to bed I could not sleep. It seemed to
me a wonderful thing that such work could be done by a Canadian,
by a young man, one of ourselves.[9]

[9] Archibald Lampman,
"Two Canadian Poets", in
Masks of Poetry, ed. A.J.M.
Smith (Toronto, 1962),
p. 30.

What Lampman admired was the poetic technique. Poems in
Orion were in the Pre-Raphaelite style, delicately sensuous. They
were well made poems, but not noticeably Canadian in content,
diction, or rhythm.

When Roberts moved from Fredericton to Toronto for a
brief hectic session as editor of *The Week,* the two young poets
met. Later Lampman in turn, having moved to Ottawa to join
the Civil Service, met and encouraged young Duncan Campbell
Scott, a clerk in the Department of Indian Affairs. Lampman
and Scott together made friends with Wilfred Campbell, who
had also moved to Ottawa. From Ottawa, Lampman, Scott, and
Campbell contributed a column of literary chit-chat to the Toronto
Globe in the 1890's. Bliss Carman, Roberts' cousin, came to know
and appreciate all these other poets. These young men formed
a kind of coterie, pacing each other.

Charles G.D. Roberts in his early poems was most exact
and photographic. Opening lines of the sonnets published in
In Divers Tones, 1886, and in *Songs of the Common Day,* 1893,
specify: "A little grey hill-glade . . ." or "These are the fields of
light . . ." or "Winds here, and sleet . . .".[10] Each poem watches
a rural scene of pioneer action, providing a severe and sober
vignette of the land and the workers on it.

In his major early poem, "The Tantramar Revisited", the
poet describes the Maritime shore scene in an off-season, when
the nets are stowed away to dry, the reels stand idle and the
"wide red flats, above tide-mark/(are) Pale with scurf of the salt,
seamed and baked in the sun". Then the poet, relishing the
"old-time sweetness" of the scene, writes of his dread of change:

Yet will I stay my steps and not go down to the marshland,
Muse and recall far off, rather remember than see . . .[11]

This is an ominous note of escapism in a young poet, still only
twenty-five, in a young country very much in the process of
change.

In his non-poetic work, Roberts also preferred to "rather
remember than see". His earliest prose publication was a translation
of Phillippe Aubert de Gaspé's *Les Anciens Canadiens,* translated
as *Canadians of Old* in 1890. Roberts' own major novels, appearing
from 1895 on, were mostly re-creations of old-time Acadian life.

[10] C.G.D. Roberts,
"Sonnets", in *Poets of the
Confederation,* ed. M.M. Ross,
(Toronto, 1960), pp. 6-8.
[11] C.G.D. Roberts, "The
Tantramar Revisited", in
Poets of the Confederation,
p. 3.

His travel books, such as *The Land of Evangeline,* 1889, emphasized romantic archaic features. His animal stories can be seen as a retrogression to a wilderness fast disappearing in the mechanizing turn-of-the century years.[12]

A second part of the reminiscent image of Canada appears in the work of Duncan Campbell Scott. The French-Canadian village of quaint old ways is the scene of many of his short stories. His poems feature the world of the Indian or half-breed in remote outposts, "On the Way to the Mission"; in scenes of past eras, "At Gull Lake, 1810"; or in the wilderness itself, "The Forsaken".[13] D.C. Scott later became one of the editors of the *Makers of Canada Series.* This series climaxed a great deal of interest in historical research in Canada, presenting volume after volume of well-written accounts of great figures of the Canadian past. William Kingsford had set the pace for academic historians in *History of Canada,* 1887, and Roberts presented a softer and more dramatic version in *A History of Canada,* 1902.

Meanwhile another poet meditated on his own responses to nature. Archibald Lampman painted poetic scenes in which the modern city appeared only distantly as a delicate line of towers on the horizon. In "Morning on the Lièvre", Lampman moves through a soft, silvery, misty world, where

> the forest and the stream
> In the shadow meet and plight
> Like a dream . . .[14]

Lampman had moments of revulsion against these dreamy pastels. In one poem, he wrote of a far different world, in a far different tone: of noon, "the bleached crossing of two streets . . . hags, a lean dog";[15] he called this poem "Reality". In another poem he presented a nightmare vision of a city of machines: "City of the End of Things".[16] Lampman certainly knew the pressure of the modern world, the machine, and the city. Yet most of his poems are delicate withdrawals from that pressure. This is not to say that his poems are escapist. They are penetrations

[12] C.G.D. Roberts, *The Last Barrier and other Stories*, NewCanadian Library edition (Toronto, 1958).
[13] D.C. Scott, *Poets of the Confederation*, pp. 98, 99, 107.
[14] Archibald Lampman, "Morning on the Lievre", in *Canadian Anthology*, p. 123.
[15] Archibald Lampman, "Reality", in *Canadian Anthology*, p. 133.
[16] Archibald Lampman, "City of the End of Things", in *Poets of the Confederation*, p. 75.

of his own responses to the quiet stimulus of moments in nature.
Carefully he shapes stimulus and response into pale, polished
lyrics. And carefully he leaves in each a touch of corrosion—a
note of fear, grief, or panic.

Fourth of this group of writers was Bliss Carman. In his
poetry, also, there are scenes of remote and poignant beauty. In
"Low Tide on Grand Pré", Carman catches a moment in nature
and fuses it with a moment in every life—a moment of regret
for the elusiveness of time and happiness, the impermanence
of youth and love. The poem frames a remembered summer of
scented meadows, gliding canoe, sunset gold, within a barren
present, a tidal waste.[17]

Carman does many other things in his poetry. He writes
for fun, rollicking vagabond songs, rather aggressively jaunty;
poems for children reminiscent of Robert Louis Stevenson (one
of Carman's literary models); also husky, panting, self-conscious
love poetry and philosophical poems which hostile critics dub
"pseudo-profound". But "Low Tide on Grand Pré" remains a
fine, pleasing poem. It causes the wheel of time and thought to
hover briefly, before circling from remembered "inelusive glory"
into the reality of loss and grief, end of day, flood-tide, and
autumn.

Travellers through Canada were already experiencing the
more grand, more sublime, more angular forms of the Laurentian
Shield, the prairie stretch, the Rockies, the West Coast canyons
and fiords and totemed islands. The railroads of the 1890's were
making such experiences available more and more readily to
Canadians. But the writers we have been considering stayed in
the East—or moved away to the States or to England. In 1889,
Carman drifted away, over the border to New England, away
from the flood-tide of the new Dominion. Roberts joined the
exodus in 1897. Lampman died in 1899. Only D.C. Scott
remained a permanent resident of Canada.

The first made-in-Canada portfolio was complete. No epics,
no five-act dramas, but small poems produced by young poets,
most of them not destined to move on to deeper soundings.

[17] Bliss Carman, "Low
Tide on Grand Pré", in
Poets of the Confederation,
p. 26.

Canadian Trademark

The new nation was soon to be bombarded by potentially disintegrative forces. Some Canadians at the turn of the century urged renewing ties with Britain in a strengthened British Imperial Federation. Other Canadians followed Goldwin Smith's lead in urging that Canada accept her "destiny" as inevitably part of the North American continent, and thus ultimately one of the United States of America. The Boer War strained French-English solidarity, as the Riel Rebellion had done.

To resist these forces, journalists and politicos pounded the patriotic drums. The cry for support from artists was raised. Canadian content should appear in work made in Canada in the twentieth century, "Canada's century" as Sir Wilfred Laurier hopefully called it. Patriots again urged artists to celebrate Canada's enormous potential in natural resources and in vigorous manpower.

A considerable national literature began to pile up. Anthologists could soon collect volumes with titles such as *A Treasury of Canadian Verse,* 1900. Critics could begin to generalize about Canadian Literature in works such as L. J. Burpee's *A Little Book of Canadian Essays,* 1909. But as the years went by, anthologists and critics alike found themselves more and more hard put to define the Canadian element in the work under consideration.

What constitutes the Canadian trademark? What themes and techniques stamp poetry today as "made in Canada?"? A modern anthology bearing the title *Made in Canada: New Poems of the Seventies,* 1970, shows the curious persistence of many of the notes struck by the Confederation poets.

The anthology contains few direct confrontations of the question of national identity. Tom Marshall writes one of the few poems in the volume that actually name the country. His phrase is

[18] Tom Marshall, "The Return", in *Made in Canada: New Poems of the Seventies*, eds. Douglas Lochhead and Raymond Souster (Ottawa, 1970), p. 134.

Canada, where things
are so intensely themselves.[18]

The intense though quiet individuality of people and things in
Canada stirs the poets. Severe and sober scenes, half lights, small
serious animals, all appear in careful and precise detail. A universe
emerges: a poet's Canada not so very different from that of the
earlier writers in spite of differences in diction and technique.

Genevieve Bartole in "Breakup" focuses on "ice and brown
weed water".[19] John Newlove notes "crisp shards of leaves",
and Doug Jones adds goldenrod, dried wild flowers, and
"sharp/split pods of milkweed".[20] Fireflies flicker in poems by
George Amabile, and Milton Acorn; and the city's brighter lights
are caught fitfully in Amabile's "windshield light", or Ron
Bates' "rear-view mirror sunset".[21] Shaggy hoofed animals are in a
poem by Margaret Atwood, but dimmed, caught in a film.[22] Not
many people in these scenes. The poets focus on their own lonely
experiences, and many of the poems study the ultimate isolation
of a dream world: John Newlove, P.K. Page, Michael Ondaatje,
and J. Michael Yates all appear in dream poems.[23]

Taken together, these topics cover a range of experience not
so very different from that of Roberts or Lampman. A dominant
note in both generations has been anxiety or melancholy
suppression. The heartier, gutsier mood of Carman sounds only
in Milton Acorn. The first major note of Confederation continues,
then: an insistence on the preservation of individual shades of
response.

The second note—persistent interest in the past—appears,
but with a difference. Poets of the 1970's turn back not for
reassurance, but in puzzlement, guilt, and disturbance. R.G.
Everson surveys "a field of Ontario Quaker graves".[24] Don
Gutteridge calls up the ghost of Riel.[25] Bill Howell conjures:

the well-appointed Red of my forefathers marching
in strict time toward my time.[26]

The question asked by Douglas Lochhead, addressing the ghost
of Etienne Brulé, characterizes the stance of the modern poet,
probing the past: "What in hell happened?"[27]

[19] Genevieve Bartole,
"Breakup", in *Made in
Canada*, p. 29.
[20] John Newlove, "Dream",
in *Made in Canada*,
p. 152,; D.G. Jones, "These
Flowers", in *Made in
Canada*, p. 112.
[21] George Amabile,
"Fireflies", in *Made in
Canada*, p. 15; Milton
Acorn, "Live with me on
Earth", in *Made in Canada*,
p. 14; Ronald Bates,
"Driving East on Cheap-
side", in *Made in Canada*,
p. 33.
[22] Margaret Atwood,
"National Film Board:
Shorts Before Features",
in *Made in Canada*, p. 18.
[23] John Newlove, "Dream",
in *Made in Canada*, p. 151;
P.K. Page, "Another Space",
in *Made in Canada*, p. 161;
Michael Ondaatje, "Black
and Gold", in *Made in
Canada*, p. 157; J. Michael
Yates, "The Great Bear
Lake Meditations", in
Made in Canada, p. 189.
[24] R.G. Everson, "The
Chance-Taking Dead", in
Made in Canada, p. 73.
[25] Don Gutteridge, "Riel",
in *Made in Canada*, p. 94.
[26] Bill Howell, "The
Handle of Tomorrow", in
Made in Canada, p. 100.
[27] Douglas Lochhead,
"Canadian Jollies", in
Made in Canada, p. 128.

Lochhead, one of the editors of *Made in Canada,* continues in "Canadian Jollies" the historic reminiscent strain of Canadian poetry. Raymond Souster, his co-editor, epitomizes the nature lyrics. In "Queen Anne's Lace" he sees

the shyest filigree of wonder
born among grasses.[28]

In the wild flower he sees a model for poems: spare, brief, "natural with themselves". Queen Anne's Lace" provides also an appropriate metaphor for all the best work in this volume—and in its predecessors among Canadian anthologies. They, too, are "shyest filigree of wonder".

Made in Canada responds to the recurring patriotic appeal for Canadian poetry. "Here it is—not blatant, not flamboyant, but worthy of notice. Poetry that is made, and well-made, by writers of a peaceable country." Such poems quietly attest to the intellectual life of the country, and to the national character, the unity, and the energy dreamed of in 1867.

[28] Raymond Souster, "Queen Anne's Lace", in *Made in Canada*, p. 170.

For Further Study

Patriots and Poets

In Print:

Careless, J.M.S. *Brown of the Globe*. Toronto: Macmillan, 1959.

Careless, J.M.S. and Craig Brown. eds. *The Canadians Part One*. Toronto: Macmillan, 1967.

Cheadle, Viscount and W.B. Milton. *The Northwest Passage by Land, 1865*. Facsimile edition. Toronto: Coles, 1970.

Cook, Ramsay, ed. *Confederation*. Toronto: University of Toronto Press, 1967.

Creighton, Donald. *Dominion of the North*. Toronto: Macmillan, 1944.

Kilbourne, William, ed. *Canada: A Guide to the Peaceable Kingdom*. Toronto: Macmillan, 1970.

Klinck, C.F. *William Wilfred Campbell*. Toronto: Ryerson, 1942.

Lampman, Archibald. "Freedom". In *Listen! Songs and Poems of Canada*, ed. Homer Hogan. Toronto: Methuen, 1972.

Lapointe, Gratien. "Your Country". In *Listen! Songs and Poems of Canada*, ed. Homer Hogan. Toronto: Methuen, 1972.

McInnis, Edgar. *Canada: A Political and Social History*. Toronto: Holt, 1969.

McDougall, R.C., ed. *Our Living Tradition*. Toronto: University of Toronto Press in association with Carleton University, 1959, 1962, 1965.

Morton, W.L. *The Canadian Identity*. Toronto: University of Toronto Press, 1971.

Ross, Malcolm, ed. *Our Sense of Identity*. Toronto: Ryerson, 1954.

Sinclair, David, ed. *Nineteenth Century Narrative Poems*. Toronto: McClelland and Stewart, 1972.

Other Media:

Hutton, C., Ivan Owen and William Toye. *A Picture History of Canada*. Toronto: Oxford, 1956.

Melancholy Masters

In Print:

Collin, W.E. *The White Savannahs*. Toronto: Macmillan, 1936.

Gnarowski, Michael, ed. *Archibald Lampman*. Toronto: McGraw-Hill Ryerson, 1971.

Lighthall, W.D, ed. *Songs of the Great Dominion, 1889*. Toronto: Coles, 1971.

Pacey, Desmond. "C.G.D. Roberts". In *Our Living Tradition*, fourth series. Toronto: University of Toronto Press, 1962.

Pacey, Desmond. *Ten Canadian Poets*. Toronto: Ryerson, 1958.

Roberts, C.G.D. *King of Beasts*. Toronto: Ryerson, 1947. Canadian Author Pictures Series. Chamainus, B.C., P.O. 74.

Roberts, C.G.D. *The Last Barrier and Other Stories*. New Canadian Library edition. Toronto: McClelland and Stewart, 1958.

Ross, Malcolm, ed. *Poets of the Confederation*. Toronto: McClelland and Stewart, 1960.

Smith, A.J.M. "D.C. Scott". In *Our Living Tradition*, first series. Toronto: University of Toronto Press, 1959.

Smith, A.J.M. ed. *Masks of Poetry*. Toronto: McClelland and Stewart, 1962.

Stephens, Don. *Bliss Carman*. New York: Twayne, 1966.

On Film:

Morning on the Lièvre. National Film Board. 1961. Colour. 13 minutes.

Canadian Trademark

In Print:

Canadian Writers and their Works Series:
Toronto: Coles.
Canadian Writers Series. Toronto: McClelland
and Stewart.
Canadian Writers and Critics Series. Toronto:
Copp Clark.
Critical Views of Canadian Writers Series.
Toronto: McGraw-Hill Ryerson.
Dawe, Alan, ed. *Profile of a Nation*. Toronto:
Macmillan, 1969.
Dudek, Louis and Michael Gnarowski, eds.
The Making of Modern Poetry in Canada.
Toronto: Ryerson, 1967.
Frye, Northrop. *The Bush Garden*. Toronto:
Anansi, 1971.
Fulford, Robert, Dave Godfrey, and
Abraham Rotstein, eds. *Read Canadian*.
Toronto: James, Lewis and Samuel, 1972.
Grant, George. *Lament for a Nation*. Toronto:
McClelland and Stewart, 1965.

Lochhead, Douglas, and Raymond Souster,
eds. *Made in Canada*. Ottawa: Oberon, 1970.
Ludwig, Jack, and Andy Wainwright, eds.
Soundings. Toronto: Anansi, 1970.
Mandel, Eli, ed. *Contexts of Canadian Criticism*. Toronto:
University of Toronto Press, 1971.
Pacey, Desmond. *Essays in Canadian Criticism*.
Toronto: Ryerson, 1969.
Purdy, Al, ed. *Storm Warning*. Toronto:
McClelland and Stewart, 1971.
Richler, Mordecai, ed. *Canadian Writing
Today*. London: Penguin, 1970.
Smith, A. J. M. , ed. *Masks of Poetry*. Toronto:
McClelland and Stewart, 1962.
Wainwright, Andy, ed. *Notes for a Native
Land*. Ottawa: Oberon, 1969.
Whalley, George, ed. *Writing in Canada*.
Toronto: Macmillan, 1956.
Woodcock, George, ed. *Choice of Critics*.
Toronto: Oxford, 1966.

On Tape:

The Canadian Imagination. Toronto: CBC
Learning Systems. 1970.

Interlude:
Canadian Railroad Trilogy

1885

"What is Canada?" we asked at the outset, and temporarily
answered by focusing on some geographic facts. But Canada is
also a man-made nation. The 1860's cemented our political founda-
tion; the 1870's wrestled financial structures into a great skeletal
framework; the 1880's threw across the connecting iron girders
of the man-made structure. From Atlantic to Pacific, natural
forms sprawled and sloped and heaved and stretched; the railway
was a man-made geometric answer to those menacing shapes
and humps and horrors of geography.

After the railroad had become not just a dream but a fact,
writers in Canada continued to work that fact into their art. Some,
like E. J. Pratt, retold the epic story of the movement of the
railroad builders in "Towards the Last Spike". Others, like Stephen
Leacock, used scenes at a railway station or on a train as crucial
settings for Canadian experience. Still others, like Frank Scott,
used the railway system as a symbol of economic exploitation.

Today the railroad age is perhaps over. Air travel replaces
the train, and our sense of space, national travel, and of nationality
itself changes in this age of astronauts and moon walks. Yet
the image of Canada and the national sense of Canadian identity
seems still bound in with the memory of the railroad. Sense of
conflict between wilderness and technology still infuses references
to the railroad with symbolic intensity. The railroad as
menace, as dream, and as memory has bonded and branded the
Canadians' image of their own nation.

When the modern Canadian writer looks back at that great
synthesizing feat, the building of the railroad, he expresses his
response in forms that differ from the mid-Victorian lyrics, essays,
and romances that served the Confederation writers. Somewhere

toward the end of the nineteenth century, the Dominion settled
into her own ways: her own political patterns, her own technology,
and her own style of dress and landscaping and social manners
and speech—and her own ways of writing. Modern accounts
of the railroad era appear in fact-packed narrative poems, in tense
sardonic epigrams, in vigorous documentary prose, and in popular
song in the new folk style. These new styles, like the new fact
of a steel-bound Canadian confederation, ocean to ocean, carry
us from early days in the Canadas to a new era of Canadian
nationality.

The Railroad as Fact

In 1871, a transcontinental railway was promised by the Canadian
Parliament to the distant province of British Columbia as an
inducement to that western colony to link with the British North
American confederation. By 1885, that transcontinental railway
was complete. In spite of "impassable" land north of Lake Superior,
in spite of the timberless prairies, in spite of the "impregnable"
defenses of the Rockies, the Selkirks, and the Coastal Ranges, the
Canadian Pacific Railway advanced arrogantly across the country.
Local lines had been laid much earlier, from 1836 on.
Junctions and branch lines linked most of these to the central
system, the CPR, in a second era of major construction, 1880-1910.
As the twentieth century began, the Canadian railway drew an
east-west line across the continent. The United States' railway
system spread like a great complex spiderweb; but in Canada all
branch lines fed sooner or later into the single transcontinental.
By 1917, amalgamation of several railway companies produced a
second transcontinental line, Grand Trunk, Grand Trunk Pacific,
Canadian Northern, National Transcontinental, and Intercolonial
fusing into the Canadian National Railway. This second all-Canadian
line ran parallel to the CPR double-bonding east-to-west the
strips of terrain that nature had seemingly designed to drift in a
north-to-south axis.

Historically, the railways had been funded partly because of military need, transporting men to the Red River to cope with the Riel Rebellion in 1870. In the Boer War, 1899, troop movement to the imperial battles in South Africa again turned the railroad into a military highway. From 1914 to 1918, the young men of the nation flowed from section to section, back and forth across the continent in troop trains. The Second War would repeat the pattern. This fact, too, became part of the image of Canada, another weaving of the railroad into the sense of Canadian identity.

The Railroad and Art

The actual experience of railroad building stirred a range of autobiographic uses. Charles Horetzky wrote *Canada on the Pacific*, 1874, an account of the urgent effort to find an easy northern route through the Rockies. George Munro Grant in *Ocean to Ocean*, 1873, dramatized the story of his journey west with Sandford Fleming, chief engineer of the CPR. Sandford Fleming later added his own retrospective account, *England and Canada: A Summer Tour between Old and New Westminster*, 1884.[1]

The general manager of the Canadian Pacific Railway, William Van Horne, made a direct connection between the arts and the railroad by commissioning artists to go West in the new Canadian Pacific, to paint scenes of grandeur in the foothills, the prairies, and the Rockies. Furthermore, the CPR's massive purchases of paintings and prints to decorate stations and hotels gave an impetus to native production. Railway stations included some rather charming little buildings, fanciful in design, and enhanced by romantic pictures of Lake Louise, Banff, Murray Bay, etc.

The initial excitement of using the railway brought travellers as well as settlers. The most entertaining account of these early trips along the new line of rail was Lady Dufferin's *My Canadian Journal*, 1891. Other excellent accounts include Douglas Sladen's

[1] Charles Horetzky, *Canada on the Pacific* (Montreal, 1874); G.M. Grant, *Ocean to Ocean*, facsimile edition (Toronto, 1970); Sandford Fleming, *England and Canada* (London, 1884).

On the Cars and Off, 1895, and Stuart Cumberland's *The Queen's Highway*, 1887.[2]

The railway trains and the stations that served them furnished settings for critical Canadian experiences. Canadian writers turned the spotlight on such settings, in scenes such as the humourous and nostalgic train ride described in the opening and closing chapters of Stephen Leacock's *Sunshine Sketches of a Little Town*, 1912, the exciting train ride used in the central flashback of Hugh MacLennan's *The Watch that Ends the Night*, 1959, and the sight of a train disappearing which makes a melancholy climax in Ernest Buckler's *The Mountain and the Valley*, 1952.[3] An amazing number of Canadian war novels contain scenes set in a railway station or a troop train, scenes of separation or of sad return. The memory of the railroad and of the men who built it still laces the country together, and runs as recurring motif through Canadian art.

Canadian Railroad: Trio and Trilogy

Twentieth-century Canadian writers have produced samples of work in almost every traditional genre, inspired by stories of the railroad builders. For instance, E.J. Pratt's "Towards the Last Spike" is blank-verse narrative on epic scale; Frank Scott's "All the Spikes but the Last" is sharp, witty, social verse; Pierre Berton's *The Last Spike* is vivid prose.

Pratt's "Towards the Last Spike", 1952, condenses the drama of the railroad into vignettes of the heroes: Sir John A. Macdonald, sleepless, scheming; his political opponent Edward Blake, dismayed at the Conservatives' skullduggery; William VanHorne, indomitable, taciturn; Donald Smith and his cousin George Stephen, the financiers. Interspersed are glimpses of the army of work-gangs assaulting the prairies, the Rockies, the land North of Superior. Pratt's epic celebrates all three: heroic leaders, the gangs of workers, and the grim land they battled,

[2] Lady Dufferin, *My Canadian Journals* (London, 1891); Douglas Sladen, *On the Rails and Off* (London, 1895); Stuart Cumberland, *The Queen's Highway* (Chicago, 1887).
[3] Stephen Leacock, *Sunshine Sketches of a Little Town* (Toronto, 1912), chs. 1 and 12; Hugh MacLennan, *The Watch that Ends the Night* (New York, 1959), Part V, ch. 1; Ernest Buckler, *The Mountain and the Valley* (Toronto, 1952), Part VI.

Until the cliffs delivered up their features
Under the civil discipline of roads.[4]

In "All the Spikes but the Last", 1954, Frank Scott, poet
of social protest and satirist, resists the super-man images of
Pratt's epic. For Scott, the coming of the age of rail opened an
age of exploitative capitalism:

Slowly forming, with steel syntax,
The long sentence of its exploitation.[5]

For Scott, the story of the railroad should be remembered in
this perspective: "Where are the coolies in your poem, Ned?"
he asks. "Did they get one of the 25,000,000 CPR acres?"[6]

Scott's poem, sour, condensed, penetrating, anti-epic,
represents the controlled counter-heroic strain of Canadian irony.
His attitude toward the railroad is echoed in such recent poems
as Earle Birney's "Transcontinental", and bill bissett's "The
Canadian".[7]

The Last Spike, 1971, by Pierre Berton amplifies. It retells
in full the story condensed and high-lighted by Pratt, and implied
and undercut by Frank Scott. Pierre Berton, in strong, flashing
prose, moves from the national dream of the 1870's to the achievement of the 1880's. His book is massive; the facts he gathered
are extensive and complex.[8] For such a writer, facts are themselves
art. It is ironic to read this energetic modern book about the
railroad age in conjunction with the fragile landscape poetry
actually produced during that age.

The three modern artists, Pratt, Scott, and Berton, in their
acceptance of the notion that art can be concerned with machines,
with technology, with politics, with commercial concerns, show
how the twentieth century notion of what belongs in art differs
from earlier assumptions.

As we shift from the nineteenth to the twentieth century
in Canada, we define the country increasingly in terms of

[4] E.J. Pratt, "Towards the Last Spike", in *Poets Between the Wars*, ed. Milton Wilson (Toronto, 1967), p. 67.
[5] F.R. Scott, "Laurentian Shield", in *Poets between the Wars*, p. 91.
[6] F.R. Scott, "All the Spikes but the Last", in *Poets between the Wars*, p. 98.
[7] Earle Birney, "Transcontinental", in *Listen! Songs and Poems of Canada*, ed. Homer Hogan (Toronto, 1972), p. 11; bill bissett, "The Canadian", in *Listen!* p. 12.
[8] Pierre Berton, *The Last Spike* (Toronto, 1971). See also Pierre Berton, *The National Dream* (Toronto, 1970).

technology, of a construct effected by man. Appropriately, we
shut the book of lyric poems, and turn on Gordon Lightfoot,
singing his "Railroad Trilogy".[9] This is not private art, meant
for a lonely reader. It is mass art, for a participating public
audience. The guitar accompaniment is part of its multi-sense
impact. The rough, insistent voice, the dramatic change in singing
pace is part of the composition.

Lightfoot presents a trilogy, a compound of three voices,
three phases of the railroad construction in the artist's mind.
Memory of the green dark forest, "too silent to be real" is followed
by the energy, the cries of the young vigorous organizers of
the railway, with their dream of "the iron road running from
the sea to the sea". Then comes the evening of workers' exhaustion.
Finally, the human costs of building the railway are framed by
the recurring memory of the forest and the dead men, whose
lives have paid for progress.

Why a trilogy? Perhaps to suggest the three levels of time:
the dream, the actualization, and the memory retained by the
artist. Perhaps to suggest the three part co-operant art of today:
the artist, the technology, the participating audience.

The age of rail is over. The jumbo jet, the skyliner bus on
the highway, rather than the pullman and the colonist car, have
become the norm of travel experience in the twentieth century.

And perhaps the traditional literary genres are dissolving
too. In art, man re-creates nature: his own, the God-given landscape, and the technical universe resulting from the assault on
nature by human intelligence. The forms of art reflect the progress
of that assault.

[9] Gordon Lightfoot, "The
Canadian Railroad Trilogy",
in *Listen! Songs and Poems
of Canada*, p. 3.

For Further Study

The Railroad as Fact

In Print:

Butler, William Francis. *The Great Lone Land, 1872.* Edmonton: Hurtig, 1968.
Dufferin, Lady. *My Canadian Journal.* London: Murray, 1891.
Fleming, Sandford. *England and Canada: A Summer Tour Between Old and New Westminster.* London: Low Marston, 1884.
Glazebrook, G.P. *A History of Transportation in Canada.* Toronto: McClelland and Stewart, 1964.
Grant, George M. *Ocean to Ocean, 1873.* Facsimile edition. Toronto: Coles, 1970.
Harper, Russell. *Painting in Canada.* Toronto: University of Toronto Press, 1966. See especially paintings by Homer Watson, Lucius O'Brien, Mower Martin and J.W. Morrice.
Horetzky, Charles. *Canada on the Pacific.* Montreal: Dawson, 1874.
Lorne, Marquis of. *Canadian Pictures.* London: Religious Text Society, 1886.
Shaw, Charles Aeneas. *Tales of a Pioneer Surveyor.* Ed. Raymond Hull. Toronto: Longmans, 1970.
Stanley, G.F.G. ed. *Mapping the Frontier.* Toronto: Macmillan, 1970.
St. John, F.E.M. *The Sea of Mountains.* London: Day, 1877.

Other Media:

Harper, Russell, ed. *Portrait of a Period.* Montreal: McGill-Queen's University Press, 1967. Photographs.
Posters developed from old railroad pictures, available from Cole-Pavey Academic Aids, 463 Ellerslie Ave., Willowdale.

The Railroad and Art

In Print:

Birney, Earle. "Transcontinental". In *Listen!*

Songs and Poems of Canada, ed. Homer Hogan. Toronto: Methuen, 1972.
bissett, bill. "The Canadian". In *Listen! Songs and Poems of Canada,* ed. Homer Hogan. Toronto: Methuen, 1972.
Jonas, George. "The C.N.R. Virgin". In *Made in Canada,* ed. Douglas Lochhead and Raymond Souster. Ottawa: Oberon, 1971.
Lane, Red. "Marchlands V". In *Listen! Songs and Poems of Canada.* Toronto: Methuen, 1972.
Purdy, Al. "Transient". In *Fifteen Canadian Poets,* ed. Gary Geddes and Phyllis Bruce. Toronto: Oxford, 1970.
Stevens, Peter: "Coming Back". In *Made in Canada,* eds. Douglas Lochhead and Raymond Souster. Ottawa: Oberon, 1971.

On Film:

Helicopter Canada. National Film Board. 1966. Colour. 50 minutes.
The Railroader. National Film Board. 1965. Colour. 25 minutes.

Canadian Railroad: Trio and Trilogy

In Print:

Berton, Pierre. *The Last Spike.* Toronto: McClelland and Stewart, 1971.
Berton, Pierre. *The National Dream.* Toronto: McClelland and Stewart, 1970.
Lightfoot, Gordon. "Canadian Railroad Trilogy". In *Listen! Songs and Poems of Canada,* ed. Homer Hogan. Toronto: Methuen, 1972.
Pratt, E.J. "Towards the Last Spike". In *Poets Between the Wars,* ed. Milton Wilson. Toronto: McClelland and Stewart, 1967.
Scott, F.R. "All the Spikes but the Last". In *Poets Between the Wars,* ed. Milton Wilson. Toronto: McClelland and Stewart, 1967.

Regionalism:
The Mountain and the Valley

7

1900

One response to the presence of the railway in the nineteenth century was the sense of mobility in local regions. When railways began linking small towns into a national system, dwellers in those small towns felt less strained and isolated. Small towns seemed less like traps, more like points on an open line. Writers enjoyed regional detail when they had a possible point of comparison. By the 1890's, romances of small towns flourished in an affectionate regional treatment.

The regions of Canada were originally a series of geographic pockets, clearly defined by natural barriers. But because of the unique patterns of ethnic settlement in Canada, immigrants into these pockets brought customs of work, art, worship, and politics which made it possible to define the regions in cultural terms. Since Canada, unlike the older-settled nations, grew in the age of technology, her regions also became defined by man-made lines: railways, road systems, newspaper circulations, and educational centrifuges.

Although some early Canadian writers wrote of their own regions because they knew little else but the local scene, most recorded local details, both physical and social, because of a feeling that these regional realities had unique significance in the Canadian federation. In the late nineteenth century, regional realism became the literary style in many countries. Thomas Hardy in England and Hamlin Garland in the States used local peculiarities of terrain, climate, and folk culture to present a tragic vision of life. In Canada, at the turn of the century, regional realism took the opposite tack. *Sunshine Sketches of a Little Town*, Stephen Leacock's title for his 1912 book, could be the title affixed to a whole shelf of regional realists of Canada in the years before

the First World War. Why should this be so? Were the local
communities of Canada from coast to coast as idyllic as they
appear in *Anne of Green Gables*, *Glengarry Schooldays*, *Sunshine
Sketches*? We should speculate about the personal and national
factors that encouraged the sunshine view in the pre-war period.

In later years, even when the local community appeared
in less charming colour, Canadian writers continued to accept
regional realism as a major objective. The lay of the land, the
mountains, the valleys, the local architecture, the folkways, the
religious festivals, and the political rituals continue to be recorded
with documentary care.

Idyllic Escape

By the time of Confederation, Maritime writers had piled
up a sizeable library of stories and poems reporting what life
was like in Nova Scotia, New Brunswick, and Prince Edward
Island, in part to capitalize on the market established by Haliburton
with *Sam Slick*. The poetry of Roberts and Carman, in particular,
specified Maritime details: marshland, sea-flats, and old-time
ways of fishing and farming. Prince Edward Island entered the
imaginary map of many readers soon after, when L.M.
Montgomery published *Anne of Green Gables*, 1907, first of a
long series of gentle, imaginative stories set against the red roads,
white sands, and proud, though threadbare, people of "The
Island". In contrast, a male world of storm and stress and heroic
endeavour appeared in Norman Duncan's Newfoundland stories,
Dr. Luke of the Labrador, 1904, and *The Cruise of the Shining
Light*, 1907. In these books, the "Newfie" joined the ranks of
the lovable, laughable poor, doomed to a low economic and social
position by his dialect, but idealized in literature for his simple
virtues.

A Quebec regional poet who won world audiences in the
early days of the century was William Henry Drummond. His

poems in *The Habitant*, 1897, *Johnny Courteau*, 1901, and *The Voyageur*, 1905, provided happy, folksy, rhythmic escape, and an account of the scenery and folkways of rural Quebec. Before Drummond died in 1907, he had established his dialect verse as easy, accessible, undisturbing pleasure. *Habitant* country was bathed in glamour and fond amusement.

Ralph Connor's Ontario stories also found a wide audience. Ralph Connor had begun by publishing two "local colour" stories of the Far West, *Black Rock*, 1897, and *The Sky Pilot*, 1898. Then he swung into retrospective romance of Ontario in *The Man from Glengarry*, 1901, and *Glengarry Schooldays*, 1902.

Ralph Connor was born in 1860. It is the 1860's that he pictures in his "Glengarry". The manse, the school and the church in the frontier community are set against the turbulent life of the lumber-drives down the river to Quebec, and the terrors of encounter with natural ferocities such as a bear-hunt or a sudden fire. *The Man from Glengarry* preaches of quiet courage, motherly love, church-going piety, defense of the weak, and sportsmanship in defeat. The honest young man from Glengarry becomes manager of a company, prominent clubman, social worker among derelict young boys. The book is morally affirmative and optimistic. It preserves the memory of values and attitudes in old Ontario. It ends with romantic happiness, and the echo of an old cry, "Heard long ago on the river . . . 'Glengarry forever!' "[1]

Ralph Connor's was only one of many books recreating life in rural Ontario, "long ago on the river". Marian Keith's *Duncan Polite*, 1905, and *The Silver Maple*, 1906, William Fraser's *The Lone Furrow*, 1907, and R.E. Knowles' *Saint Cuthbert*, 1905, are all of the same kind. Though academic critics scorned them, these authors wrote stories for the rural newspapers, for the farm papers such as *The Family Herald and Weekly Star* and *Farmer's Advocate*, and for the publishers supplying literature to a large, non-genteel audience. Local libraries, many funded by Carnegie grants, opened in the small centres and added to the demand for light fiction. Since many writers were ministers, teachers,

[1] Ralph Connor, *The Man from Glengarry*, New Canadian Library edition (Toronto, 1969), p. 287.

or ministers' wives, their life experiences were narrow and the range of permissible materials was small. Passion was inhibited; inebriation was considered tragic or pathetically funny; death-bed scenes were treated with lingering piety.

As new communities developed, particularly on the prairies, Canadian artists began exploring a further range of social material. Certainly in the new neighbourhoods one would find all the material for a local colourist: eccentric characters, pathetic and amusing incidents, landscapes with regional features, rituals of courtship, sports rivalry, and work. But once again, writers between 1900 and 1920 chose to bathe this new life in the colour of romance. Nellie McClung, for instance, wrote the very popular *Sowing Seeds in Danny* in 1908, and *The Second Chance* in 1910. She dealt with the hard life of Western homesteaders. But there was no note of despair or bitterness in her books. Family troubles were dissolved in love. Poverty was endured without either hopelessness or revolt.

Sociologists would decry this as a false picture of a period seething with political and economic unrest, leading to the agitations out West in the pre-war period, and to such out-breaks of dissatisfaction as the Winnipeg strike. Psychologists might feel that *Sowing Seeds in Danny* is an unreal view of family life. In all such works, local colour helped readers swing away from central political and theological issues, into imagined places on the fringe of Canadian life. Whether such escapism is a sensible way to ease stress, or whether it is a dangerous, debilitating, and false use of art remains an open question. Contemporary best-sellers in England included H.G. Wells and his science fiction fantasies, sentimental romances such as *Peter Pan* by J. M. Barrie and exotic Oriental stories by Rudyard Kipling. Most best-sellers in the States also provided romantic escape to far-away places.

In the most remote of Canadian regions, Robert Service found enough colour to make his work immensely popular in the years just before the War. The Scottish-born Service, drifter

along the British Columbia Coast from 1895 to 1904, hovered
in the Yukon long enough to establish a repertoire of bar-room
ballads, tall tales of the midnight sun and rag-time romances—
funny, macabre, fantastic, swinging to an infectious rhythm.
Audiences around the world loved the "Shooting of Dan McGrew",
the "Cremation of Sam McGee", and all the other *Songs of a
Sourdough*, 1907, *Songs of a Cheechako*, 1909, and *Rhymes of a
Rolling Stone*, 1912. These songs of the Yukon by-passed propriety,
domesticity, and sobriety. They celebrated raw, vigorous life.
The humour is rough, the rhyme and rhythm unsubtle, the
plots preposterous, but they gave enormous pleasure to audiences
living the tame and decorous existence in pre-war society.

Were you ever out in the Great Alone, when the moon was awful clear,
And the icy mountains hemmed you in with a silence you most could hear?[2]

Writers such as Service offered romance in the wider sense
of escapist stories, re-constituting life closer to dreams than to
waking realities.

Twentieth century reality in Canada, as everywhere in the
West, included economic troubles and financial scandals, natural
disasters in bad harvest years, family disruptions in the first
bitterness of woman's suffragism, labour troubles, city malaise,
and the tense and confused movement toward the First World
War. But literature of Canada between 1900 and 1914 was
oblivious to all this tension. Darwin, Marx and Freud might never
have written, for all they are reflected in the works of Ralph
Connor, William Henry Drummond, Robert Service, Nellie
McClung, or Stephen Leacock.

Stephen Leacock knew the Canadian novels of this period
well enough to parody them in *Nonsense Novels*. He knew the
political and economic theories of his time and held a professorship
at McGill University. He was a subtle psychologist as appears
in his discussion of the cruel basis of humour, in his essay on
"The Nature of Humour". He had grown up in a small town in

[2] Robert Service, "The
Shooting of Dan McGrew",
in *Canadian Anthology*,
eds. C.F. Klinck and
R.E. Watters (Toronto,
1966), p. 219.

rural Ontario in the Carman-Lampman-Roberts era. He gathered
all these bits of awareness together, tucked his tongue into
his cheek, and in 1912 wrote *Sunshine Sketches of a Little Town*.

Sunshine Sketches is both spoof of the romantic fiction of
the small town, and essential defense of that romantic illusion.
Leacock's language has small town flavour, chatty, anecdotal,
with a little chuckle in the turn of the phrases. His posture is that
of the rather shy, rather sly old duffer—the village story-teller.
He pokes fun at foibles, and he helps the town improve by
laughing at those foibles. Since he has no strong alternative ideal,
he produces no strong condemnation.

We drift away from Darwin, Marx, and Freud, aboard the
Mariposa Belle.

The Mariposa Belle sailed off in her cloud of flags, and the band
of the Knights of Pythias, timing it to a nicety, broke into "The Maple
Leaf for Ever!"[3]

Revelation of Truth

Regional literature in the United Kingdom and the United
States struck darker and sharper notes in the war years and the
twenties. The British writer D. H. Lawrence led the way into
novels in which local forces elicit troubled aspects of the soul.
The American Sinclair Lewis did a sour exposé of dusty, dreary
little communities which erode the lives of ordinary people. Some
traces of both these kinds of regionalism appeared in Canadian
Literature. But on the whole, the affirmative note of affection
and humour prevailed.

Robertson Davies wrote a series of penetrating satiric novels
in which character is revealed in the ordinary man's response
to local social pressures. Davies writes with a sociologist's care
of a small Ontario town in a regional vein reminiscent of Leacock.
"Salterton", in *Tempest-Tost*, 1951, *Leaven of Malice*, 1954, *A
Mixture of Frailties*, 1958, joins the imaginative map of Canada

[3] Stephen Leacock, *Sunshine
Sketches of a Little Town*,
New Canadian Library
edition (Toronto, 1952),
p. 42.

somewhere in the vicinity of "Mariposa". In his later novels, including *Mixture of Frailties* and also *Fifth Business*, 1971, and *The Manticore*, 1972, Davies has added scenes in Europe to balance and sharpen the Canadian scenes.

Hugh MacLennan achieves something of this effect of posing different regions against each other. MacLennan's regions are all within Canada however; he uses a kind of mythic Canadian geography to suggest levels of experience. Eastern scenes appear in studies of troubled youth, while the Montreal area acts as setting for complex tensions of middle-age in *The Watch That Ends the Night*, 1959. Similar symbolic use of regions characterizes *Each Man's Son*, 1951, a primitive moral drama set in Nova Scotia, and *The Return of the Sphinx*, 1967, a sophisticated political and familial study set in the heart of Montreal. It would be interesting to compare the symbolic polarizing of Maritime and Montreal settings with that of the younger novelist Hugh Hood, in *White Figure, White Ground*, 1964. Hood, like MacLennan, is faithful to the social and physical realities of Canadian scenes and uses these to reveal universal truths of character. Hood's range, like MacLennan's and Robertson Davies, is limited to Eastern Canada.

Canadian regionalism is still strongest in the area where it first began: the Maritime provinces. Will Bird's stories and Elizabeth Brewster's stories, Charles Bruce's *The Channel Shore*, 1954, Thomas Raddall's *The Nymph and the Lamp*, 1950, and Ernest Buckler's *The Mountain and the Valley*, 1952, represent the range of achievement in fiction. Fred Cogswell, Alden Nowlan, Dorothy Roberts, and others produce poetry strong in Maritime flavour.

One might expect Western regionalists to present the prairie area as a place of freedom and energy. On the contrary, the prairie provinces appeared early in darker tones, as in Frederick Philip Grove's novels of the twenties. Gwen Pharis Ringwood's *Still Stands the House* is an early play exploring prairie loneliness.[4] Sinclair Ross continues this strain in *As For Me and My House*, 1941, acidly real in its presentation of western scenes as

[4] G.P. Ringwood, "Still Stands the House", in *Encounter: Canadian Drama in Four Media*, ed. Eugene Benson (Toronto, 1973).

menacing to nerves and to moral fibre. Anne Marriott repeated
this motif in a strong narrative poem, "The Wind our Enemy":

Wind raises dead curls of dust and whines
under its breath on the limp dragged wires.[5]

Among younger poets, John Newlove catches and intensifies
this dark strain in Western realism. Most prairie regionalism,
however, is less dour. In *Who has Seen the Wind* the shimmering
land, the silver willows and the alkaline-white edges of the little
stream soften the life of the prairie town. In a French-Canadian
variant, *Where Nests the Water Hen*, Gabrielle Roy presents a gentle
study of family warmth in a remote Northern Manitoba farm
setting. In such works, the regional life in the West, both cultural
and physical, enhances and encourages moral and emotional
growth of the individual. But the western sense of fun prevents
prairie people from taking even their own regional mystique
too seriously. In many ways the most "western-flavoured" book
in Canada is Paul Hiebert's spoof, *Sarah Binks—Sweet Singer of
Saskatchewan*, 1947.

Farther West, the intensities of the Rocky Mountain country
seemed more apt to encourage a vision like that of D.H. Lawrence,
of the wilderness in the human soul, capable of harmonizing
with the passionate moods of nature. Earle Birney's early poem
"David" shows such a world of extremes, both moral and
geographic. But Birney's mature work, from "Vancouver Lights"
and "Dusk on English Bay" to "November Walk Near False
Creek Mouth", adds to his strong sense of locale a reductive
note of wit and irony.[6] Lawrence's intensities are reduced in
Birney, as they are in other West Coast regional writers, including
Ethel Wilson and Roderick Haig-Brown.

Mystique of Facts

A reaction against moralizing has helped produce a final
kind of regionalism in Canadian Literature. Young writers affirm

[5] Anne Marriott, "The
Wind Our Enemy", in *The
Book of Canadian Poetry*,
3rd ed., ed. A.J.M.
Smith (Toronto, 1957),
p. 419.
[6] Earle Birney, "November
Walk near False Creek
Mouth", in *Fifteen Canadian
Poets*, eds. Gary Geddes
and Phyllis Bruce
(Toronto, 1970), p. 15.

that they must record the sights and sounds of their own regions not because regional reality provides escape, nor because it provides reflection of character or enhances moral values, but simply for its own sake, because it exists as fact.

West Coast Seen is the suggestive title of one little magazine growing out of this new regionalism. It implies the value of simply *seeing*. Patrick Lane struck the new West Coast note:

Now moving to Hazleton B.C. Lost city—great north where I can dig into my old pure scene of god/people/mountains . . .[7]

London, Ontario, has been a scene of such localism, in graphic arts as well as as in poetry and fiction. The Western Ontario cult of regionalism has led to a revived interest in Indian artifacts and in the more recent historical strata recorded in Orlo Miller's *The Donnellys must Die* and Kenneth Galbraith's *The Scotch*.

Similar regional flurries occur in Fredericton, Montreal, Sherbrooke, Kingston, Toronto, Winnipeg, Edmonton, and in any number of other centres. Some of this new regionalism is rather grim, as in the short stories of the self-styled "Montreal Story Group", including John Metcalf and Clark Blaise. Some is strangely intense, like the curious novel by Graeme Gibson, *Five Legs*, 1969. Some is wistful and delicate, like the *Civil Elegies* of Toronto poet Dennis Lee. But a good deal of it still has something of the affectionate tone of acceptance of Stephen Leacock.

From the Valley to the Mountain

Ernest Buckler's *The Mountain and the Valley* is a regional novel—a beautifully detailed study of the Annapolis Valley in Nova Scotia. But *The Mountain and the Valley* is also a novel *about* regionalism. It analyses the hold of a familiar locale over a valley man. It shows the tragic consequences as well as the value to him of his local affiliation. It offers a symbolic alternative:

[7] Patrick Lane, biographical note in *Made in Canada*, eds. Douglas Lochhead and Raymound Souster (Ottawa, 1970), p. 115.

the idea of the mountain. This is the place to climb away from
the valley.

The Mountain and the Valley has the conviction of a documentary. Even if we have never experienced the sights, smells, sounds
of this locale, the writer convinces us of his accuracy. The author
shows us the contours of the land and its seasons. He also reports
the language, the acts, and the jokes of the valley boys and
men along with their sensibilities and dreams. Animal life and
the facts of slaughter appear along with the lyric poetry of the
growing season and the gentle love in a family.

The terms "mountain" and "valley" are used in the book
not only to report the two dominant landforms. They also suggest
two kinds of life—the social life of family, working life, and
society in the valley, and the elevated lonely life of contemplation,
creation, self-understanding on the mountain. Throughout the
book, David, the hero, tries to make his way to the mountain.
The book ends on the mountain, but in a pain-filled scene of
solitude and snow.[8]

The Mountain and the Valley poses the riddle of literary
regionalism. Doused in local colour, the regional writer easily
finds a local readership that enjoys home-town flavour. But he
may dim his power of communicating with readers outside his
own valley. He can play up eccentricities, mannerisms, and local
folkways, to attract the tourist interest in most readers; but he
of course risks narrowness. He can retreat into the recesses of
his own region in order to confront the essential mysteries of
the environment and of his own self; but he is in danger of
coming to general conclusions on the basis of insufficient evidence.
Canadian regionalists from Ralph Connor and Leacock on, have
created a vivid locale. But they run the risk of being cut off from
universal currents of change.

[8] Ernest Buckler, The
Mountain and the Valley,
New Canadian Library
edition (Toronto, 1961),
p. 301.

For Further Study

Idyllic Escape

In Print:

Connor, Ralph. *The Man From Glengarry*. New Canadian Library edition. Toronto: McClelland and Stewart, 1969.

Connor, Ralph. *Glengarry Schooldays*. Chicago: Revell, 1902.

Costain, Thomas. *Son of a Hundred Kings*. Toronto: Doubleday, 1950.

Creighton, Luella. *High Bright Buggy Wheels*. Toronto: McClelland and Stewart, 1951.

Drummond, W.H. *Johnny Courteau and Other Poems*. New York: Putman, 1901.

Duncan, Norman. *The Cruise of the Shining Light*. New York: Harper, 1907.

Duncan, Sara Jeannette. *The Imperialist*. New Canadian Library edition. Toronto: McClelland and Stewart, 1961.

Leacock, Stephen. *Sunshine Sketches of a Little Town*. New Canadian Library edition. Toronto: McClelland and Stewart, 1948.

McClung, Nellie. *Sowing Seeds in Danny*. New York: Doubleday, 1908.

Montgomery, L.M. *Anne of Green Gables*. Toronto: Ryerson, 1942.

Service, Robert. *Songs of a Sourdough*. Toronto: Briggs, 1907.

On Record:

Leacock, Stephen. *John Drainie Reads Stephen Leacock*. Toronto: Melbourne SMLP4015, 1966.

Leacock, Stephen. *Bernard Braden reads Stephen Leacock*. Malton: Capital, 1969.

Service, Robert. *The Spell of the Yukon*. Read by Frank Willis. Scarborough: Quality Records V1695. 1969.

Service, Robert. *Pierre Berton reads poems by Robert Service*. Toronto: Arc 704, 1954.

On Film:

Leacock, Stephen. *My Financial Career*. National Film Board. 1961. Colour. 7 minutes.

Revelation of Truth

In Print:

Bird, Will. *Sunrise for Peter and Other Stories*. Toronto: Ryerson: 1946.

Birney, Earle. "David". In *Canadian Anthology*, eds. C.F. Klinck and R.E. Watters. Toronto: Gage, 1966.

Bruce, Charles. *The Channel Shore*. Toronto: Macmillan, 1954.

Carr, Emily. *The Book of Small*. Toronto: Clarke, Irwin, 1942.

Carr, Emily. *Klee Wyck*. Toronto: Clarke, Irwin, 1941.

Davies, Robertson. *Leaven of Malice*. Toronto: Clarke, Irwin, 1954.

Davies, Robertson. *A Mixture of Frailties*. Toronto: Clarke, Irwin, 1958.

Davies, Robertson. *Tempest-Tost*. Toronto: Clarke, Irwin, 1951.

Grove, F.P. *Over Prairie Trails*. New Canadian Library edition. Toronto: McClelland and Stewart, 1969.

Haig-Brown, R.L. *Measure of the Year*. Toronto: Collins, 1967.

Hiebert, Paul. *Sarah Binks*. Toronto: Oxford, 1947.

Kreisel, Henry. *The Rich Man*. Toronto: McClelland and Stewart, 1948.

Lemelin, Roger. *The Town Below*. Trans. Samuel Putnam. Toronto: McClelland and Stewart, 1961.

MacLennan, Hugh. *Barometer Rising*. New Canadian Library edition. Toronto: McClelland and Stewart, 1969.

MacLennan, Hugh. *Each Man's Son*. Toronto:
Macmillan, 1951.
MacLennan, Hugh. *Return of the Sphinx*.
Toronto: Macmillan, 1967.
Marriott, Anne. "The Wind Our Enemy".
In *The Oxford Book of Canadian Verse,* ed. A.J.M.
Smith. Toronto: Oxford, 1965.
McCourt, E. A. *The Canadian West in Fiction*.
Toronto: Ryerson, 1949.
McCourt, E. A. *Home is the Stranger*. Toronto:
Macmillan, 1950.
Mitchell, W. O. *Who has Seen the Wind*.
Toronto: Macmillan, 1947.
Munro, Alice. *Dance of the Happy Shades*.
Toronto: McGraw-Hill Ryerson, 1968.
Niven, Fred. *The Flying Years*. London:
Collins, 1935.
Nowlan, Alden. *Bread, Wine and Salt*.
Toronto: Clarke, Irwin, 1967.
Purdy, Al. *Cariboo Horses*. Toronto:
McClelland and Stewart, 1965.
Purdy, Al. *North of Summer*. Toronto:
McClelland and Stewart, 1967.
Purdy, Al. *Wild Grape Wine*. Toronto:
McClelland and Stewart, 1968.
Raddall, Thomas. *The Nymph and the Lamp*.
New Canadian Library edition. Toronto:
McClelland and Stewart, 1963.
Richler, Mordecai. *Saint Urbain's Horseman*.
Toronto: McClelland and Stewart, 1971.
Richler, Mordecai. *Son of a Smaller Hero*. New
York: Paperback Library, 1955.
Ross, Sinclair. *As For Me and My House*.
Toronto: Macmillan, 1941.
Roy, Gabrielle. *Where Nests the Water Hen*.
Trans. H.L. Binsse. Toronto: McClelland and
Stewart, 1965.
Wilson, H. D. *More Tales From Barretts Landing*.
Toronto: McClelland and Stewart, 1967.

On Film:

Klein, A. M. *Autobiographical*. National Film
Board. 1965. Black and white. 11 minutes.
Carr, Emily. *Klee Wyck*. National Film Board.
1947. Colour. 15 minutes.

On Record:

Birney, Earle. Poems. *Canadian Poets I*.
Toronto: Canadian Broadcasting Corporation.
1966.
Newlove, John. Poems. *Canadian Poets I*.
Toronto: Canadian Broadcasting Corporation.
1966.
Purdy, Al. Poems. *Canadian Poets I*. Toronto:
Canadian Broadcasting Corporation. 1966.

On Video:

Birney, Earle. *Portrait of a Canadian Poet*.
Toronto: Metropolitan Educational Television.

On Tape:

Purdy, Al. *Poetry Readings*. Toronto: High
Barnet Cassettes. 1971.

The Mystique of Facts

In Print:

Buckler, Ernest. *Ox Bells and Fireflies*.
Toronto: McClelland and Stewart, 1968.
Connors, Stompin' Tom. "Sudbury Saturday
Night". In *Listen! Songs and Poems of Canada,*
ed. Homer Hogan. Toronto: Methuen, 1972.
Davey, Frank. *Weeds*. Toronto: Coach House.
1972.
Elliott, George. *The Kissing Man*. Toronto:
Macmillan, 1970.
Galbraith, J.K. *The Scotch*. Boston: Houghton
Mifflin, 1964.
Garner, Hugh. *Cabbagetown*. Toronto:
Ryerson, 1968.
Gibson, Graeme. *Five Legs*. Toronto: Anansi,
1971.
Hardy, W.G. ed. *Alberta: A Natural Hsitory*.
Edmonton: Hurtig, 1967.
Hood, Hugh. *Around the Mountain*. Montreal:
Peter Martin, 1967.
Jude, William and Murray Speirs, eds.
A Naturalist's Guide to Ontario. Toronto:
University of Toronto Press, 1964.
Lee, Dennis. *Civil Elegies*. Toronto: Anansi,
1968.
MacEwan, Grant. *West to the Sea*. Toronto:
Ryerson, 1967.

McWhirter, George. ed. *Contemporary Poetry of British Columbia.* Vancouver: Sono Nis, 1972.
Miller, Orlo. *The Donnellys Must Die.* Toronto: Macmillan, 1962.
Morton, W.L. *Manitoba: A History.* Toronto: University of Toronto Press, 1967.
Reaney, James. *Twelve Letters to a Small Town.* Toronto: Ryerson, 1962.
Robinson, Brad. "Before *Tish:* From *Oral History of Vancouver*". In *Open Letter.* Second series. Toronto: Winter, 1971-2.
Scammell, A.R. *My Newfoundland.* Montreal: Harvest House, 1966.
Souster, Raymond. *Ten Elephants on Yonge Street.* Toronto: Ryerson, 1965.
Trueman, Stuart. *An Intimate History of New Brunswick.* Toronto: McClelland and Stewart, 1970.
Warkentin, John. *The Western Interior of Canada.* Toronto: McClelland and Stewart, 1964.

Wiebe, Rudy. ed. *Stories from Western Canada.* Toronto: Macmillan, 1972.

On Tape:

Lee, Dennis. *Poetry Readings.* Toronto: High Barnet Cassettes. 1971.
Purdy, Al. *Al Purdy's Ontario.* Toronto: Canadian Broadcasting Corporation. 1920.

From the Valley to the Mountain

In Print:
Buckler, Ernest. *The Mountain and the Valley.* New Canadian Library edition. Toronto: McClelland and Stewart, 1961.
Cameron, Donald. *Conversations with Canadian Novelists.* Toronto: Macmillan, 1972.
Minshell, Robert. *Regional Geography—Theory and Practice.* London: Hutchison University Library, 1967.
Odum, H.W. and H.E. Moore. *Regionalism in America.* New York: Holt, 1938.

The Dark Side:
Tin Flute

8

1914

The First World War cast a sombre shadow on all the regions of Canada. In the twenties, "sunshine sketches" were replaced by a darker kind of literature.

Loneliness and physical hardship had been part of early Canadian experience; a literature of despair was not new in Canada. The "thrifty little heaps of civilized values" brought from Europe, as Northrop Frye says, "look pitiful beside nature's apparently meaningless power to waste and destroy".[1] Early settlers faced a climate and a terrain both strange and menacing. The drift of nineteenth century thought added a note of moral alienation; in Canada the riddles of nature encouraged spiritual despair and moral nihilism. Then, to the terrors of climate and terrain, the twentieth century added further shadows of mechanized war and city tensions.

E.J. Pratt, Morley Callaghan, and F.P. Grove began publishing in the early 1920's, flanked by Mazo de la Roche, Laura Salverson, Martha Ostenso, and Raymond Knister. All these authors opened their art to themes and scenes previously censored as unpleasant or improper. Reading these writers of the dark side leads to a vision of Canada as a bleak country. It has had more than its share of depressions and wars. The artist, a man of extra sensitivity, responds to the despair of his time. The Irish poet William Butler Yeats said "war" and "poetry" are contradictory terms; we might find "chaos" and "creativity" similarly opposed. Yet Canadian artists have had to make poetry out of war, creative order out of natural chaos.

Canadian writers have responded to darkness, not so much

[1] Northrop Frye, "Canada and its Poetry", in *The Bush Garden* (Toronto, 1971), p. 138.

with deep organ tones of tragedy, but with a thinner music
of ironic resistance and endurance. The title of Gabrielle Roy's
novel about depression days in a Montreal slum is *The Tin Flute,*
1947. This title suggests a metaphor for the kind of music raised
by Canadian writers working in the shadows—sometimes the
mad shadows—of modern life.

The Savagery of Nature

One human response to grief has always been the strange
instinct to create a song out of sadness. The two first songs
to drift back to Europe from English Canada were songs of sorrow.
Irish Tom Moore composed a "Canadian Boat Song" with the
urgent refrain:

Row brothers row! the stream runs fast;
The rapids are near—and the daylight past.[2]

A nameless Scot wrote of "The Lone Shieling":

From the lone shieling of the misty island
Mountains divide us and the waste of seas—
Yet still the blood is strong, the heart is Highland
And we in dreams behold the Hebrides.[3]

The Irish and Scots who sang such sad songs predominated
in the first group of settlers to Canada. They were the first of
a series of groups of immigrants, already saddened by life in
the "old country". Soon after came Loyalists from the States,
the losers in the War of Independence. Then came soldiers
disbanded from the Napoleonic wars, crofters put out of Scottish
glens by capitalist enterprise, Irish victims of the potato famine,
handloom weavers, and other agrarian workers exiled by the
coming of the machine age. One historian has dubbed Canada a
"nation of losers".

[2] Thomas Moore,
"Canadian Boat Songs", in
Songs for Canadian Boys
(Toronto, 1940), p. 24.
[3] "The Lone Sheiling",
in *Songs for Canadian Boys*,
p.26.

The first century of Canadian Literature is a literature of exiles. A journal like Mrs. Moodie's *Roughing It in the Bush* is typical in its account of the suicidal moods of people like Brian the Still-Hunter.[4] Typically, also, Alexander McLachlan wrote of his new life:

We live in a rickety house,
In a dirty, dismal street . . .[5]

But as settlement matured, such bitter notes were less often heard.

Then in the mid-nineteenth century, Europe experienced an intellectual crisis, stemming from the geological discoveries of people like Charles Darwin. Darwin had taught people to see nature as evolving through unimaginably long reaches of time, by bitter competition and through catastrophes such as earthquakes, volcanoes, and glacial drifts. The idea of evolution seemed to overthrow the notion of a benign, reasonable universe created and directed by an all-powerful, merciful God. Few Canadian writers of the Confederation period, however, introduced these new Darwinian ideas into their poetry or novels. Nature stirred them only to a mild melancholy; human forms of competition were romantically idealized. Only in Archibald Lampman's poems was there an occasional sharpening into pain at the November ravages of nature. Most of the turn-of-the-century Canadian Literature was pale and gentle.

In 1923, E.J. Pratt published his first volume of poetry. A young Newfoundlander, Pratt had come to Toronto to study theology, had shifted into the study of psychology and then into the teaching of English literature at the University of Toronto.

In Pratt's first verses, man confronts a savage nature and an inscrutable God.

Eternity
Had fashioned out an edge for human grief.[6]

[4] Susanna Moodie, *Roughing It in the Bush*, New Canadian Library edition (Toronto, 1962), ch. 10.
[5] Alexander McLachlan, "We Live in a Rickety House", in *The Blasted Pine*, eds. Frank Scott and A.J.M. Smith (Toronto, 1957), p. 81.
[6] E.J. Pratt, "Ground Swell', in *Canadian Anthology*, eds. C.F. Klinck and R.F. Watters (Toronto, 1966), p. 225.

Nature could produce the shark, menacing and metallic, like
the man-made destructive machines.[7]

As modern priest and psychologist, Pratt faced the fact of
terror and ravage in nature. As modern poet, he created clever,
stylish, imagist poems, converting the darkness of his observations
into a controlled aesthetic pleasure.

In 1925, Pratt observed the post-war age, the jazz age,
the years of wild parties. He concocted his "Witches' Brew",
a rollicking poetic joke which imagines the oceans turned into
a monstrous punch-bowl, the sea-beasts gripped in a cosmic
drunken brawl. This is a clever, terrifying chant of the twenties,
of the roaring end of decorum and propriety—Pratt's response
to the age of bootlegging, rum-running, the Canadian edge of
American Prohibition.

In more sober tones, Pratt published two poems in 1926,
thoughtfully received by his growing audience of students,
colleagues, and readers of magazines of experimental verse in the
States and Canada. "The Cachalot" plays with terrifying
scenes at sea: sperm whale, great squid, fragile human boat,
a *Moby Dick* pursuit and death, seen from the perspective of
the self-destroying whale: "a Titan's broken pride". "The Great
Feud" again draws from the terrible battles of the sea a lesson for
men. Primeval struggles between living things are complicated
by the fluke, the chance,

> an adverse Fate
> Running a self-destroying course . . .[8]

In 1932, Pratt gathered his shorter verse into *Many Moods*. Some
of the moods are gentler, more domestic than in *Newfoundland
Verses*. But most are still turbulent with sea, storms, and tidal
struggles. He still sings in chains of careful rhyme and stanza
schemes, and of carefully controlled sound and image patterns.

"The Titanic", 1935, seemed to gather all the themes and
facts that had hammered their way into the art of the post-war

[7] Pratt, "The Shark",
in *Canadian Anthology*,
p. 226.
[8] Pratt, "The Great Feud",
in *Poetry Between the Wars*,
ed. Milton Wilson
(Toronto, 1967), p. 2.

period. The scene was the dark incomprehensible universe. The time: contemporary, from the age of technology, not some long-ago time of romantic ruralism. The theme: man and his vanity; his moments of will, of sacrifice; pitted against chance, error, and fatality.

Later Pratt moved westward in his imagination, from the Newfoundland waters of "The Titanic", 1935, to Northern Ontario forests in "Brébeuf and his Brethren", 1940, and to the Laurentian Shield and the prairies and the Rockies in "Towards the Last Spike", 1952. In theme, he turned from human pride pitted against fate and the destructive or indifferent ocean, to the spectacle of religious conviction set against savagery in the forest, and then to human organizing ability conquering rock, space, and height.

Tension in the Family

The novelist Frederick Philip Grove shared Pratt's willingness to report the un-pretty, unkindly, raw, and ragged face of nature. In *Over Prairie Trails,* 1922, and *The Turn of the Year,* 1923, he recorded storms, waste places, and the erosion of human dignity, as observed on his lonely drives from Gladstone to Falmouth in Manitoba:

A burst, a cataract, a convulsion, a spasm of light breaks loose . . . .
And instantaneously, a thunderclap follows, short, rattling: a blasphemy
and an abomination of sound.[9]

The dream of a brave new world in the Canadian West to be conquered by the hard-working immigrant was fading in the twenties. The struggle to make crops, build housing, and raise families on the frontier seemed to heighten the loneliness of the newcomers to Canada. Grove wrote of the new Canadians, Balkan, Scandinavian, and Mediterranean groups, washed out of Europe by successions of persecutions and depressions.

[9] F.P. Grove, "A Storm in July", in *Canadian Anthology*, p. 212.

There were only three settlers in the bush so far, and they
were miles apart. The woman had become acclimated in speech and
thought; and as summer went by, this dumb Icelandic man became
a horror to her.[10]

For Grove, the plight of prairie farmers epitomized the wide-
spread problem of alienation in the post-war years. Strange
currents of human feeling—a sense of inadequacy, uncertainty,
awkwardness—came under his eye as he worked in lonely Western
communities. These currents fitted in with his vision of the
universal human condition which had emerged during his years
of wandering in Europe and America, and in his long bouts of
reading the works of modern Russian, Scandinavian, and French
realists. Grove's novels, like Pratt's poetry, are a double response:
to his immediate experiences in the uglier aspects of life, and
to modern artistic techniques, experiments with symbolism and
structure. But where Pratt was praised, Grove was condemned.

Settlers of the Marsh, 1925, traces Niels Lindstedt's lonely
pilgrimage from youthful hope and work as a Swedish newcomer
in a western marshland to neurotic loneliness, repression, and
finally to murder. Strong stuff! Grove depicted personal
exploitation, masochism, and dreadful poverty both physical and
spiritual. The subject matter seems sad to the reader of today
but not particularly shocking. But the 1920's in Canada were not
the free uninhibited jazz age of popular legend. *Settlers of the
Marsh* was fiercely condemned for its "pornography" and brought
an outcry against both the author and the publisher. Such an
outcry might have made a best-seller out of a similar book in the
United States; but in Canada this strong, strange, serious novel
found only a very small audience.

Grove's work explored some of the psychic tensions analyzed
by Sigmund Freud. Freud, like Darwin, had been one of the
great disruptive and creative thinkers deeply affecting all Western
thought. Freud unveiled fears and desires lurking within
conventional family relations. Following Freud, writers explored the
secret springs of actions and idealisms, and analyzed fetish and

[10] Grove, "The Sower",
in *Canadian Anthology,*
p. 214.

taboo, inhibition and sublimation. All these Freudian elements appear in Grove's novels.

Laura Goodman Salverson also explored some Freudian aspects of life in *The Viking Heart,* 1923. In recounting the story of an immigrant's life in Canada she particularized the rivalries between two sisters and the insane acts of a young mother. In her view, immigrant life represents deep dislocation. Her novel shows the plight of New Canadians—Icelanders, Finns, Mennonites, Serbs, Ukrainians, Poles—treated as "foreigners", refused a chance to assimilate with the earlier English-speaking communities, and hence drifting into neurotic hostility and into internal discord within the family. Salverson adds to the psychic analysis a vivid picture of the physical sufferings of the poor.

Other novels contributed further to the dour account of rural family life, particularly in the not-so-golden West: Martha Ostenso's *Wild Geese,* 1925; Arthur Stringer's *Prairie Wife,* 1915, *Prairie Mother,* 1920, and *Prairie Child,* 1922; and Robert Stead's *Grain,* 1926.

A Canadian writer need not go West to find a clutch of ugly facts. Nor need he turn to a new-Canadian family to find a Freudian tangle. Mazo de la Roche stayed in rural Ontario and told the same kind of truths about aspects of traditionally Canadian family and community life, once tabooed. Though Mazo de la Roche was very proud of her "old Canadian" lineage, when she wrote about an imagined family of WASP landowners, she revealed a torrent of jealousies, passionate attachments, sadism. In *Jalna,* 1927, and the later Whiteoaks novels, strange, intense characters clash in a series of effective theatrical scenes. Old society, old families: but a new dark view of family life, and a new professionalism and integrity in telling the story.

The Shabby City

Morley Callaghan dealt with no arrogant or dynamic figures in his early stories, but with shabby, unpretentious people in the crannies of city life. Yet here too he was breaking with

romantic tradition. The city as a place of light, an ideal to which
the rural dreamer turned in his ambition, was a theme of the
immigrant novels, as it had been of the rural romances of the
pre-war period. There had been in literature a general restriction
of permissible types: either genteel, articulate, literate heroes
or comic rural people with a certain peasant dignity. But Morley
Callaghan in his short stories introduced a cook at a quick lunch-
counter, a priest embarrassed by a drunk in the confessional
box, a small-time boxer muffing the chance to win a fight, a
young wife haggling with her husband over her purchase of an
expensive hat. All these realities—not so much ugly as unromantic—
would have been outside the permissible range of art in the
pre-war period. But out of these realities, Callaghan constructed
terse, ironic studies of the real city of 1920 and after.

While he was still a student at the University of Toronto,
Callaghan wrote a group of short stories which drew from Ernest
Hemingway, then a reporter on the Toronto *Star,* the comment,
"You're a real writer. You write big-time stuff. All you have to
do is keep on writing." Callaghan continued writing while he
finished a course in law, then made for Paris. There in the bright
cafés, Hemingway, and Fitzgerald, Ezra Pound, and James Joyce
were shaping up a new age in literary art to match the innovations
in graphic arts of Picasso, Miro, Roualt, and Modigliani. The
young Canadian might have stayed in that world of expatriates.
Certainly he developed there a cosmopolitan coolness and clarity.
But he came back, after "that summer in Paris" to produce
not passionate stories of exile in Spain or glittering tales of love
on the Riviera, but sharp clear accounts of people at home.

Callaghan's is an art of economy and intensity. *Strange
Fugitive,* a novel, appeared in 1928; *It's Never Over* in 1930,
and a novella *No Man's Meat* in 1931. But Callaghan worked
most and best in the short story form during the 1920's. In
1929 many of the short stories were gathered in *A Native Argosy,*
while many others appeared in the 1936 collection *Now That April's
Here.* Callaghan produced other novels in the 1930's: *Such is My*

Beloved, 1934, *They Shall inherit the Earth,* 1935, *More Joy in Heaven,* 1937. Then he dropped into broadcasting, playwriting, film-script writing throughout the years of the Second World War. Finally, after a fourteen-year hiatus, he began publishing novels again, adding *The Loved and the Lost* and others to his earlier novels. The novels concentrate on distrubing social and moral ironies. A released convict fails to live up to the faith of his sponsor; a girl who tries to make friends with a black man is brutally murdered; a young priest is broken because of his gesture of friendship to two young prostitutes. The early short stories imply the same range of concern and the same dispassionate acceptance of life, without hypocrisy or sentimentality.

Morley Callaghan's novel *The Loved and the Lost,* 1951, presents the story of a girl who tries to free herself from the conventions and attitudes of her background, and to create a life of energy and loving kindness. Callaghan's vision of such an ideal is dark. The girl is doomed to suffer from the forces she has tried to free. The narrator of her story lives in the modern city of Montreal, a city of snow and cold. It is a city of night-clubs, slums, and murder. In this city, the small church, once glimpsed as a haven, seems to have disappeared.

Other writers of stories about shabbiness and restlessness include Raymond Knister, an early acquaintance of Callaghan's, but a man who did not live long enough to explore his own powers fully. Knister, like Callaghan, spent a brief period as expatriate, this time in the middle Western States. But like Callaghan—and unlike most major American writers of the period—he came home, to work out in modern experimental forms his view of the often petty tensions of post-war life in Canadian terms. Knister's novel *White Narcissus* was published in 1929.

One reason such writers could stay in Canada was the emergence of several strong magazines, including *Canadian Forum* and the *Canadian Magazine,* which were willing to publish unromantic work as long as it was well-written. The Canadian

scene seemed darker in the 1920's than in the 1890's, when
Roberts, Carman and company, became expatriates; but it did
not impede the appearance of major writers like Pratt, Grove,
and Callaghan.

Two World Wars

The twentieth century brought a series of social and economic
disasters: crop failures, economic depression, and two World
Wars. In the First World War, Canada lost 60,000 men; another
180,000 were wounded. The proportion of strong, ambitious,
energetic men destroyed by the War was much greater than
in the States. The loss in material was devastating, too. French-
Canadian hostility to conscription brought a break in national
unity. The war broke down the assumption that technology is
a guarantee of progress: a century of technological miracles had
led to war between the most "civilized" and "sophisticated"
nations of the world.

Out of the Canadian war experience came one fine poem.
In "In Flanders Fields", John McCrae, speaking in the grim voice
of "the dead", presents a tragic sequence:

We . . . loved and were loved, and now we lie
In Flanders Fields.[11]

The grim warning "We shall not sleep" plays ironically into
the allusions to "poppies" (flame-coloured, free, but implying
death-like sleep) and "crosses" (rigid, man-made, but implying
Christian regeneration and life). Controlled, in a circular structure,
these sequences give the little poem a formality which is itself
a kind of testament against the destructive force of the guns.

When the Second War came, there was no poetry of poppies
and crosses and torches held high. Poetry of the Second World
War was a bitter mix of pain and inefficiency, guts on the pave-
ment, children "groping in gravel for knobs of coal",[12] "mad
transmitters [that] send impossible orders on crossed frequencies".[13]

[11] John McCrae, "In Flanders Fields", in *Canadian
Anthology*, p. 216.
[12] Earle Birney, "The Road
to Nijmegen", in *Canadian
Anthology*, p. 304.
[13] Douglas LePan, "The
Net and the Sword",
in *Canadian Anthology*,
p. 408.

The best war poems came from Earle Birney and Douglas
LePan, and from the young poets whose work was gathered by
John Sutherland into an anthology called *Other Canadians,* 1947.

There were war novels too. Canadian novels of the First
World War had appeared under such romantic and idealistic
titles as *The Sky Pilot in No Man's Land, The High Heart, Drums
Afar, All Else is Folly.* The Second World War novelists chose
harsher titles: LePan, *The Deserter*; Lionel Shapiro, *The Sealed
Verdict*; A.J. Elliott, *The Aging Nymph*; Hugh Garner, *The Storm
Below.*

Depression and Flute Music

Between the wars stretched years of unemployment and
disappointment, culminating in the Depression of the "dirty
thirties". The novel *Waste Heritage* by Irene Baird, 1939, is a
bitter picture of a strike situation. Dorothy Livesay's poems,
stories, and essays in the thirties are outstanding in their sympathy
with the factory workers, the outcasts in the hobo jungles, the
men on strike, the victims of the free enterprise system. The
best novel about the thirties, both in fidelity and in craftsmanship
was Hugh MacLennan's retrospective *The Watch that Ends the
Night*, 1959.

Darkest, and most haunting, was another retrospective story,
Adele Wiseman's *The Sacrifice*, 1966. This is a Winnipeg story,
focused on a region within the region: the ghetto of Ukrainian
Jews in the city. Winter in the prairie and poverty in a strange
land form a present overlaid with terrible memories of pogrom,
typhus, and flight. Over the years come adjustment and gradual
peace, gentle fading of old memories. Then the memory of ritual
killing, memory of the Biblical sacrifice confused with the memory
of persecutions, produces a manic scene of breakdown and murder.[14]

Most serious modern writers still show marks of that period's
strain and depression. Alden Nowlan writes cryptically grim lyrics

[14] Adele Wiseman, *The
Sacrifice* (Toronto, 1956).

on pain. Milton Acorn shouts "I've tasted my blood!" and
remembers his friends:

One died hungry, gnawing grey porch-planks;
One fell, and landed so hard he splashed.[15]

Irving Layton faces and voices all the evil and the suffering in
the world. His early poems are shocking in their brutality. "De
Bullion Street" presents the ugliest part of Montreal. "The Bull
Calf" is a scene of slaughter. Raymond Souster's poems still reflect
the thinness, the flatness, the disappointment of life in the city.
Georges Jonas combines in his poems the loneliness of Souster's
world of shabby rooming-houses with the slick phoniness of
high-rise apartment living. Miriam Waddington sees the sad city
of "Investigator":

The old houses running to seed, the grass grown tall,
The once mansion made into quaint apartments.[16]

In the works of some modern writers, the note of sadness
turns into bitterness and revolt. Earlier writers mostly voiced
middle-class griefs. Today's media encourage people of a less
privileged class to express the griefs of the proletariat. The writers
of the dark side today include prisoners, social outcasts, the
unemployed, and the unemployable. bill bissett adds another
darkness—in Oakalla Prison: when

th 10 pm curfew struck befor
this really great etc. movie was ovr.[17]

John Herbert's *Fortune and Men's Eyes* brings both prison abuse
and homosexuality into range.

Finally, Leonard Cohen sings his dark lyrics. "Stories of
the Street" and "Stories of Isaac" invoke all the old themes of
suffering, sacrifice, persecution.[18] But they *are* songs. Cohen shapes
his troubles. His rasping intense voice illustrates perfectly the
strained survival of song in a darkened world.

[15] Milton Acorn, "I've Tasted my Blood", in *Listen! Songs and Poems of Canada*, ed. Homer Hogan (Toronto, 1972), p. 54.
[16] Miriam Waddington, "Investigator", in *Canadian Anthology*, p. 431.
[17] bill bissett, "th average canadian nose-bleed", in *nobody owns th earth* (Toronto, 1971), p. 59.
[18] Leonard Cohen, "Story of Isaac", "Stories of the Street", in *Listen! Songs and Poems of Canada*, pp. 145, 147.

Canada seems newly dark because of the threats of Separatism, the threat of dissolution of the Confederation. In French-Canadian literature, the signs of tension have always been strong; contemporary work in French strikes a near-manic note. *Convergences*, a fine work of literary criticism, exposes some of the special sources of darkness in Quebec.

But in this phase of darkness, we remember that one French-Canadian novelist several years ago gave poignant testament to the power of the human spirit to survive a convergence of shadows. Gabrielle Roy's *The Tin Flute*, published in French in 1945 and in English in 1947, is set in pre-war days. In this moving study of life in the Saint Henri district, Gabrielle Roy recognizes the fact that the war temporarily relieved the most disturbing symptoms of Montreal poverty. Moral difficulties and the erosion of family solidarity and of faith are suspended rather than resolved in the book's conclusion by the outbreak of war.

The small boy in the story has longed for a shiny tin flute. But his death comes before he can find even this cheap happiness. The French title of the novel was *Bonheur d'Occasion*—"bargain basement" or "chance-found happiness". There seems little chance of any happiness in this world. The city settings are shabby. The men are caught in war. They enlist, leaving family situations doomed by weakness, deceit, vanity, and poverty. Yet the final lines of the book present a vision of the stubborn persistence of hope:

. . . a tree deep in a courtyard, its foliage drooping with fatigue before it had come into full leaf, its twisted branches pushing bravely up through a network of electric wires and clotheslines towards the sky.[19]

[19] Gabrielle Roy, *The Tin Flute*, New Canadian Library edition (Toronto, 1958), p. 274.

Not a happy ending; but at least a thin flute song of resistance and survival.

For Further Study

The Savagery of Nature

In Print:

Frye, Northrop. *The Bush Garden.* Toronto: Anansi, 1971.
Grove, F.P. *Over Prairie Trails.* Toronto: McClelland and Stewart, 1969.
Pratt, E.J. *Collected Poems.* Toronto: Macmillan, 1958.
Scott, Frank and A.J.M. Smith, eds. *The Blasted Pine.* Toronto: Macmillan, 1957.

Pictures:

Spears, Borden, ed. *Wilderness Canada.* Toronto: Clarke, Irwin, 1971.
Mellen, Peter. *The Group of Seven.* Toronto: McClelland and Stewart, 1970.

Drama:

Ringwood, G.P. "Still Stands the House". In *Encounter: Canadian Drama in Four Media,* ed. Eugene Benson. Toronto: Methuen, 1973.

Tension in the Family

In Print:

Atwood, Margaret. "The Lifeless Wife". In *Listen! Songs and Poems of Canada*, ed. Homer Hogan. Toronto: Methuen, 1972.
de la Roche, Mazo. *Jalna.* Toronto: Macmillan, 1947.
Grove, F.P. *Settlers of the Marsh.* New Canadian Library edition. Toronto: McClelland and Stewart, 1966.
Hambleton, Ronald. *Mazo de la Roche of Jalna.* Toronto: General Publishing, 1966.
Ostenso, Martha. *Wild Geese.* New Canadian Library edition. Toronto: McClelland and Stewart, 1971.
Ross, Sinclair. *As For Me and My House.* Toronto: McClelland and Stewart, 1957.
Roy, Gabrielle. *Street of Riches.* Trans. Henry Binsse. Toronto: McClelland and Stewart, 1967.

Salverson, V.G. *The Viking Heart.* Toronto: McClelland and Stewart, 1947.

Drama:

Davies, Robertson. "Overlaid". In *Encounter: Canadian Drama in Four Media*, ed. Eugene Benson. Toronto: Methuen, 1973.

The Shabby City

In Print:

Callaghan, Morley. *The Loved and the Lost.* Laurentian Library edition. Toronto: Macmillan, 1970.
Knister, Raymond. *White Narcissus.* New Canadian Library edition. Toronto: McClelland and Stewart, 1962.
Mann, W.E. *Canada: A Sociological Profile.* Toronto: Copp Clark, 1968.
Mann, W.E. *The Underside of Toronto.* Toronto: McClelland and Stewart, 1970.
Richler, Mordecai. *Saint Urbain's Horseman.* Toronto: McClelland and Stewart, 1971.
Richler, Mordecai. *Son of a Smaller Hero.* Toronto: McClelland and Stewart, 1955.
Ross, Sinclair. *Whir of Gold.* Toronto: Macmillan, 1970.
Souster, Raymond. *Colour of the Times.* Toronto: Ryerson, 1964.

On Record:

Dudek, Louis. Poems. *Six Montreal Poets.* New York: Folkways, 9805. 1958.
Souster, Raymond. Poems. *Six Toronto Poets.* New York: Folkways, 9806. 1958.

On Tape:

Souster, Raymond. *Poetry Readings.* High Barnet Cassettes. 1970. 503 Merton Street, Toronto 7, Ontario.
Mandel, Eli. *The Canadian City seen through the Eyes of the Poet.* Toronto: Canadian Broadcasting Corporation. 1970. 1 hour.
Callaghan, Morley. *The Short Stories.* Toronto: Canadian Broadcasting Corporation Learning Systems. 1971. 11 tapes. 30 minutes each.

Two World Wars

In Print:

Acorn, Milton. "I've Tasted My Blood". In
Listen! Songs and Poems of Canada, ed. Homer
Hogan. Toronto: Methuen, 1972.
Baird, Irene. *Waste Heritage.* Toronto:
Macmillan, 1939.
Birney, Earle. "The Road to Nijmegen". In
Canadian Anthology, eds. C.F. Klinck and
R.E. Watters. Toronto: Gage, 1966.
Child, Philip. *God's Sparrow.* London:
Butterworth, 1937.
Garner, Hugh. *Storm Below.* Toronto:
Ryerson, 1949.
Hénault, Gilles. "The Prodigal Son". Trans.
F.R. Scott. In *Listen! Songs and Poems of Canada,*
ed. Homer Hogan. Toronto: Methuen, 1972.
LePan, Douglas. *The Deserter.* Toronto:
McClelland and Stewart, 1964.
McCrae, John. "In Flanders Fields". In
Canadian Anthology, eds. C.F. Klinck and
R.E. Watters. Toronto: Gage, 1966.
Portal, Ellis. *Killing Ground.* Toronto: Peter
Martin, 1968.
Shapiro, Lionel. *The Sealed Verdict.* New York:
Doubleday, 1947.
Stanley, F.G. *Canada's Soldiers.* Toronto:
Macmillan, 1954.
Sutherland, John, ed. *Other Canadians.*
Montreal: First Statement Press, 1947.

On Tape:

Mandel, Eli. *The Poetry of War.* Toronto: CBC
Learning Systems. 1970. 2 talks. 30 minutes
each. 1970.

Depression and Flute Music

In Print:

bissett, bill. *nobody owns th earth.* Toronto:
Anansi, 1971.
Bliss, Michael and Linda Grayson, eds. *The
Wretched of Canada.* Toronto: University of
Toronto Press, 1972.
Dewdney, Selwyn. *Wind Without Rain.*
Toronto: Copp Clark, 1946.
Dooley, P.J. *Contemporary Satire.* New York:
Holt, 1971.
Graham, Gwethalyn. *Earth and High Heaven.*
New Canadian Library edition. Toronto:
McClelland and Stewart, 1969.
Horn, Michael, ed. *The Dirty Thirties.* Toronto:
Copp Clark, 1972.
Livesay, Dorothy. Selections in *Poets Between
the Wars,* ed. Milton Wilson. Toronto:
McClelland and Stewart, 1967.
Roy, Gabrielle. *The Tin Flute.* Trans. Hannah
Josephson. New Canadian Library edition.
Toronto: McClelland and Stewart, 1958.
Salverson, Laura G. *Confessions of an
Immigrant's Daughter.* Toronto: Ryerson, 1939.
Wiseman, Adele. *The Sacrifice.* Toronto:
Macmillan, 1956.

On Tape:

Frye, Northrop. *Northrop Frye on Evil.*
Toronto: CBC Learning Systems. 1971. Box
500, Station A, Toronto 1, Ontario. Catalogue
no. 693.
Herbert, John. *Fortune and John Herbert's Eyes.*
Toronto: CBC Learning Systems, 1971.

World Arena:
New Ancestors

9

1930

The question, "Should an ambitious writer remain in Canada?" was answered one way by Carman and Roberts, another way by Callaghan and Pratt. The same question is being answered again today by Mordecai Richler, Leonard Cohen, and others, who alternate between expatriatism and Canadian home. The question is related to another one. At home or abroad, should the Canadian try to keep his Canadian accent? Some feel that straining for a Canadian accent, working on Canadian materials, may limit a writer's potential.

Discussion of these topics was very intense in Canada in the 1930's. British imperial ties were weakening. America was withdrawing into an isolationist position in politics and in art. In Europe, the rising menace of Fascism and Nazism made visits abroad less and less pleasant for Canadians. But in the thirties there appeared a group of Canadian writers who pleaded that Canada should not accept the drift into isolationism. They urged Canadians to break out of narrow nationalism. Join the world! Face its issues, march in its causes, experiment in new techniques of art. This was the gospel of Frank Scott, A.J.M. Smith, A.M. Klein, Dorothy Livesay—the generation of the thirties:

. . .The tissue of art is torn
With overtures of an era being born.[1]

In 1935, E.J. Pratt and Robert Finch of Toronto joined the young Montreal poets Scott, Smith, and Klein to issue a volume of poetry titled *New Provinces*. The title did not imply a poetic effort to hymn the Maritimes or the Prairie provinces. Instead, the "new provinces" were parts of the universe of modern poetry—

[1] F.R. Scott, "Overture", in *Poets Between the Wars*, ed. Milton Wilson (Toronto, 1967), p. 83.

a universe that these Canadian poets wanted to join. Battle
was waged against the patriotic efforts of earlier writers to "write
Canadian". Canadianism, the poets of the thirties suggested, was
a kind of "provincialism" and that seemed not much better than the
still older "colonialism." Substitute, they suggested, some other
world-wide "ism": socialism, Zionism, pacifism, Catholicism,
communism, expressionism, surrealism. The key to all the "isms"
was "cosmopolitanism", the sense of belonging to the society
of mankind.

Today, the question of whether or not we should "join
the world" has become almost academic. Modern technology has
created a "global village". The world has joined us. We cannot
live in isolation even if we want to. Contemporary Canadian
writers set their work in Ghana, Kyoto, or Colombia as these
far-away places become part of their experience. In turn, Canadian
writing today includes work from newcomers from Hungary, from
the West Indies and from Ceylon, as well as from Britain and
the States.

Today, the globe itself seems too restrictive an arena for
man's imagination. In the space age, Canadian writers, like their
contemporaries all over the earth, have begun to draw images
and ideas from the voyages of the astronauts. The moonscape
is added to the landscape; the world is imaginatively seen from
the spaceship perspective. "Canadian accent" again becomes
problematic when the human voice sounds by telestar. In such
an age, Canadian writers, with a long tradition of argument
about provincialism, nationalism, and universalism, should have
something useful to say. The arguments of the writers of the
thirties, raising the issue of native versus cosmopolitan art, are
newly relevant.

New Provinces

Historically, Canada has never been isolationist. Even before
the Conquest her allegiance and ideals centred beyond the

American continent. As part of the British Empire she had inevitable ties with world events. Her history was affected by a game of diplomacy and war played on a world scale. Her boundaries were set by conferences held in distant places. Her constitution was subject to tinkering in capitals across the ocean. Her economy depended on whims of boardrooms thousands of miles away. Three times she was involved in wars that began with no invasion of her physical territories.

The comings and goings within the Empire kept a lively current of ideas flowing into the outposts. Garrisons, manned by officers and men in transit within a world empire, kept a defense against provincialism. Many nineteenth century writers, such as Judge Haliburton and Sir Gilbert Parker, considered it their greatest privilege to retire to the "mother country".

As the Empire weakened, the Dominions suffered culturally. By the time the Statutes of Westminister were passed in 1931, the ex-colonies were in danger of becoming rather old-fashioned, smug, and stagnant culture-pockets. It was against such a danger that the younger writers raised their protest.

In Montreal, a group of undergraduates and young faculty members published the *McGill Fortnightly Review* in 1926-7. McGill University was an exciting intellectual milieu at this time. The world-famous scientist Rutherford was there, Osler had made the medical faculty world-famous, and Leacock kept a devoted following. At McGill, people were reading both the American satirists, like Sinclair Lewis and H.L. Mencken, and the bright young Englishmen, like Aldous Huxley and Evelyn Waugh. In Montreal one could hear a variety of languages and dialects to stimulate one's sense of the excitement of words. The city itself was visually exciting—a mix of old and new architecture, of wealth and poverty, of mountain and harbour-front.

But the young poets of the McGill group did not want to chronicle local life. They wanted "to be involved in the whole complex life of our time—its politics, its society, its economics".[2] A.J.M. Smith, Frank Scott, Leo Kennedy, and A.M. Klein began a literary friendship at McGill. By 1936, their poetry had developed

[2] A.J.M. Smith, "Introduction", in *The Book of Canadian Poetry*, 3rd ed. (Toronto, 1957), p. 30.

interesting differences in subject and method but a common desire
to write poetry of ideas: *modern* ideas.

For A.J.M. Smith, joining the world meant experimenting
in modern techniques of poetry. When Smith set his verse free from
punctuation, capital letters, and conventional syntax, he was
aligning his work with new writing outside Canada: the work
of Gertrude Stein, e e cummings, Edith Sitwell and others. His
strange precision of images and his subtle rhythms marked him
consciously the contemporary of T.S. Eliot. Like the painters
of the Group of Seven who were also working at this time,
Smith used short jagged strokes:

this smoky cry
curled over a black pine.[3]

Smith's modernism included a revival of interest in classical
myths in the fashion established by T.S. Eliot's "Waste Land".
Smith also admired such early English poets as Donne and Blake,
and he worked in the light of their methods rather than in any
native Canadian tradition. In many of his poems he voiced the
central philosophical concern of contemporary Europe: the theme
of death, a universal topic in an age moving toward existential
philosophy.

For Frank Scott, another Montreal poet of the thirties,
involving oneself in modern ideas meant taking a stand on
socialism, communism, fascism, capitalism. He showed the
unadmirable side of Canada in "Summer Camp", "Efficiency, 1935",
and in "Ode to a Politician". In the name of modernism Scott
attacked the conventional patriotism of the Canadian Authors'
Association for too much "painting the native maple",[4] but he
himself drew Canadian scenes into the vortex of imagist poems,
in "old song", "North Stream", "Abstract", and other poems.[5]

The youngest of the Montreal group was A.M. Klein. Klein's
images and allusions were drawn from the Old Testament, modern
science, and world history. Klein added to the political interests

[3] A.J.M. Smith, "The
Lonely Land", in *Poets
Between the Wars*, p. 106.
[4] F.R. Scott, "Canadian
Authors Meet", in *Poets
Between the Wars*, p. 82.
[5] F.R. Scott, selections in
Poets Between the Wars.

of Frank Scott and the metaphysical subtleties of A.J.M. Smith
a special richness of experience and language from the Jewish
tradition. He explored the legends, the biblical cadences, and
the pungent irony of his ancestry.

Klein's Jewish birth led to vicarious suffering in the period
of Nazi persecution of European Jews—witness *Hath not a Jew,*
1940, and *The Hitleriad,* 1944. Relating to international Jewry
and involved in the Zionist movement, Klein nevertheless wrote
with sympathy about other cultures such as the French Canadians
and the Canadian Indians. Several of his early poems reappeared
in *The Second Scroll,* 1951, linked with the moving story of a
Montreal man's search for a missing relative, in Italy, Morocco,
and Israel. Here Klein literally stretched his art beyond Canada.
The book is cosmopolitan also in its experimental method and
its blend of poetry and prose, narrative and meditation.

Fourth member of the Montreal group was Leo Kennedy.
His prominence in Canadian art did not last as long as did that
of the others. Kennedy left the university circle and Canada to
move to the United States.

A second glance at the careers of the Montreal group leads
to the question of Canadian domicile as one mark of the Canadian
writer. A.J.M. Smith moved to the University of Michigan, and
remained there through the major years of his teaching career.
He has nevertheless continued to be regarded as a leader among
Canadian poets. His anthology, *The Book of Canadian Poetry,*
contains an important preface, articulating controversial theories
about nationalism versus cosmopolitanism. Frank Scott stayed in
Montreal, as Dean of Law at McGill. He also continued to take
a prominent role in Canadian politics, and has also been a staunch
advocate of exchange between English- and French-Canadian
poetry. His interests thus seem more parochial than Smith's.
A.M. Klein remained in Montreal, though not at the University;
he exerted a quiet influence on younger poets.

The two Toronto poets whose work was included in *New
Provinces* were E.J. Pratt and Robert Finch—both Professors

at the University of Toronto. Critics of the volume could claim
that although it strove to escape from nationalistic narrowness,
it was in danger of slipping into another kind of narrowness—
that of an academic coterie. Finch's poetry in particular roused
the hostility of anti-academic critics for its learned urbanity. But,
in fact, the poets of *New Provinces* were most anxious not to retreat
to an ivory tower. They desired to use modern styles to create
consciousness in Canada of the central issues of a difficult period.

Joining a World of War

The capitalist system seemed to have become incurably
corrupt and inadequate in the Depression period. Many writers of
the thirties urged the need for social and political reforms. They
discussed the dangers and attractions of extreme systems—
socialism, communism, fascism—constructed to combat or
substitute for the free enterprise system.

Short stories showing the tragic consequences of the
break-down of responsibility, and studies of poverty, crime,
unemployment, and other social problems filled the pages of
Canadian magazines such as *Canadian Forum, Masses,* and *The New
Frontier.* There is a sense in all these writings of a world-wide
movement and of a beginning of universal class warfare. Magazines
carried the burden of publishing most of the serious work of the
period, because publishers in those hard times were hesitant
to print long serious novels because of the financial risk.

Social and political uneasiness crystallized in the time of
the Spanish Civil War. Many Canadian writers, like their contemporaries in the United States and Britain, went to Spain to fight
on the communist side. The Canadian units in the "Mac-Pap
Brigade" (named for William Lyon Mackenzie and Louis-Joseph
Papineau) included many writers. Other writers who remained
at home wrote in sympathy. Raymond Souster's poem "Spain",
for instance, describes:

Bomb after dropping bomb, death-nosed,
. . .thunders Spain, Spain, Spain,[6]

Even a "retiring academic" like L.A. Mackay wrote a "Battle Hymn of the Spanish Rebellion".[7] The Anthology *Spirit of Canadian Democracy*, 1945, gathered many writings that allude to what Norman Bethune called "Spain's War, Canada's war, England's war, the war of the workers of the world".[8] The sense of involvement in world politics, crystallized in the Spanish confrontations, is reflected in Hugh MacLennan's novel *The Watch that Ends the Night*. The character of Dr. Jerome Martell in this novel is thought to be modelled in part on the personality of Dr. Norman Bethune, the self-sacrificing Canadian doctor who has since become a national hero of the Chinese communists.

Going to Spain was "joining the world" in a literal sense. Hard on the heels of this experience, shared by a very few Canadians, came the experience of World War II, a movement from Canada to Europe shared by hundreds of thousands. One light-hearted novel on this serious subject, Earle Birney's *Turvey*, 1949, follows an absurd hero who moves through the war without comprehension of its issues. But most war novels were subtle studies of different life-styles in the occupied countries, particularly Italy. Douglas LePan's *The Deserter*, 1964, and A.J. Elliott's *The Aging Nymph*, 1948, typify the impact on Canadian consciousness of wartime experience abroad. The sense of having been touched by tense and sophisticated older societies lingered in post-war memories, demanding complex techniques for expression.

Returns from Europe

In the years following the war, the movement was reversed. Waves of immigration brought a new mix of ideas. To Montreal came Brian Moore and Patrick Anderson; to Vancouver came Malcolm Lowry—just to mention a few writers from abroad who had major impact on Canadian Literature. These writers, whether they remained or merely stayed briefly, became part of the heritage of later generations of writers.

[6] Raymond Souster, "Spain", in *Spirit of Canadian Democracy*, ed. Margaret Fairley (Toronto, 1945), p. 176.
[7] L.A. Mackay, "Battle Hymn of the Spanish Rebellion", in *The Book of Canadian Poetry*, p. 304.
[8] Norman Bethune, "Our War", in *Spirit of Canadian Democracy*, p. 171.

Patrick Anderson, a poet who came to Montreal in 1940, helped stimulate a revival of excitement among the now older poets, Scott, Klein, and company, and the formation of a new group of writers including Irving Layton and Louis Dudek. Anderson added his own tense and exciting kind of imagery and imported some of the new styles of W.H. Auden and Stephen Spender plus the new lyricism of Dylan Thomas.

Brian Moore, a novelist who came from Ireland in 1948, had a similar stirring effect on Montreal writers. His wit, his sympathy, the breadth and openness of his interest in off-beat and eccentric characters were all stimulating to young novelists, such as Richler and Hugh Hood, just beginning to emerge. Brian Moore wrote *The Lonely Passion of Judith Hearne,* 1955, and *The Luck of Ginger Coffey,* 1960, while he was in Montreal. The stories are set in Dublin; the people are as Irish as can be. Can such a book be considered as part of Canadian Literature? Surely such a question is itself parochial. What matters is the quality of the book and the fact that Montreal proved a stimulating setting for the novelist during his creative period.

Similarly, in Vancouver, Malcolm Lowry briefly worked in a frenzied revision of his great novel *Under the Volcano,* 1947. Again, the presence of this dynamic, disturbed, ferociously conscientious artist had an immeasurable effect on young West Coast writers. The book itself is set in Mexico; Lowry was an itinerant Englishman residing only briefly in British Columbia. But again this book should be considered Canadian by assimilation: it became deeply important to the next generation of Canadian writers interested in difficult experimental techniques.

Of newcomers to Canada during the post-war era who came and stayed, Henry Kreisel might be mentioned in particular. Here is an example of a novelist bringing from Europe a sense of style and construction different from the native tradition. In *The Rich Man,* 1948, Kreisel not only enlarged the Canadian novel to include scenes abroad, but also added the cosmopolitan touch in style and attitude so earnestly desired twenty years earlier by the *New Provinces* people.

In the post-war world, Canada joined the nations as an independent power. The quiet leadership of Lester Pearson helped launch the United Nations era of peace-keeping. It seemed that many Canadian doors were open to the world—doors of political influence and economic growth. And the traffic through these doors was at last two-way.

The Newest Ancestors

Canada has continuously absorbed writers from a very wide range of countries. To name only a few recently arrived Canadians who contribute significant work to current publications, we might mention George Jonas who came to Canada from Hungary in 1956 when he was twenty-one, and George Faludi and Robert Zend who also came from Hungary. These writers had already established themselves in the old country. Kenneth McRobbie came from England in 1954 at the age of twenty-five; Michael Ondaatje arrived from Ceylon in 1962 at the age of nineteen. There are many more newcomers of equal stature, including of course the recent wave of Americans coming North because of the Vietnam war. Wherever they come from, these writers will be the literary ancestors of future generations of Canadian writers. With them, Canada moves into the new world—the global village of the 1970's.

The old puzzle of "What is a Canadian book?" is now doubly compounded. Consider Michael Ondaatje, for instance. Born in Ceylon, Ondaatje's major publication so far is *The Collected Works of Billy the Kid,* 1970, a curious book based on the life of a folk-hero—or anti-hero—of the United States. It was produced in Canada; and for this work the author received the Governor-General's Award for poetry. Such poetry assimilates into Canada the temper of the time.

A different kind of service is performed by Austin Clarke. His fine book of short stories, *When He was Free and Young and He Used to Wear Silks,* 1971, discloses a new Toronto—Toronto

of the Barbadians and other newcomers, a warm, dangerous,
frightening, and funny city. George Jonas's Toronto is also a
revelation. Suddenly the city that was the archetype of provincialism,
and parochialism, the city that most Canadians hated because of
its banality and blandness, glows in literature as an exciting
place, because new Canadian writers have realized its life.

As for the "old Canadians", more and more they move out
into the world arena. Writers who stay at home in a physical
sense may swing up and away in imagination. Gwendolyn
MacEwen has produced a volume of poems on the moon walk, in
Armies of the Moon, 1971. Margaret Avison speaks for all moderns
when she writes:

> To walk the earth
> Is to be immersed
> Slung by the feet
> In the universe . . .
>
> shored on a crumb
> whether in hinterland or town
> It's all one.[9]

In this age of easy travel, other Canadian writers like Mordecai
Richler, P.K. Page, Leonard Cohen, and Norman Levine travel
back and forth across the Atlantic both in person and in literary
topics. Still more Canadians travel briefly farther afield, and use
exotic materials for subject matter. Earle Birney meets a "Bear
on the Delhi Road", and writes a poem for his Canadian audience
about it. Irving Layton watches an elephant scratch himself on
a tree in India, and writes a poem about *that*—and incidentally
about Northrop Frye's theory of poetry. Leonard Cohen's "The
Only Tourist in Havana" catches most effectively the new
Canadian stance: ironic, interested, ready to move.

World issues and a cosmopolitan outlook rather than provincialism predominate in fiction especially. Margaret Laurence
depicts our involvement with the third world countries through
her short stories in *Tomorrow Tamer,* 1963, and through her novel

[9] Margaret Avison,
"Civility a Bogey", in
Canadian Anthology, eds.
C.F. Klinck and R.E.
Watters (Toronto, 1966),
p. 436.

This Side of Jordan, 1961. David Knight followed with *Farquhar's Physique and what it Did to his Mind,* 1971.

Dave Godfrey, encouraged by Laurence, extended this vein of exploration in his *New Ancestors,* 1970. *New Ancestors* is set not in Canada but in a fabulous country, an African country, the "Lost Coast". Its characters are not Canadians but Africans, Englishmen, Americans, Russians, and Chinese, playing out national manoeuvres on the political surface of life. Here our new political ancestors create the world of tomorrow for us.

Godfrey shows in his experimental style the enlarging effect of his own foray abroad. Like all the new literary ancestors working today toward a world-oriented modernism, he presents radical disruptions of style. Violent events—murder, political coup, rape, drowning—are all filtered in a strange nightmare form through the consciousness of his characters. The time sequence in the book is disrupted. The sense of normal cause and effect is disturbed. The sense of boundaries, limits, and exclusions dissolves. And the Canadian reader is pulled, pushed, shocked, and ejected out of the castle of his own skin, his own home, nation, colour, and age.

Such writing represents Canadian contribution to a world of sensitivity. Its author will claim place as ancestor of future writers as the world webbing tightens. Young authors like Godfrey may in turn acknowledge among their literary antecedents those writers of the thirties, Smith, Scott, and Klein, who led Canada into the new provinces of modernism in thought and art.

For Further Study

New Provinces

In Print:

Brown, E.K. *Canadian Literature Today.* Toronto: University of Toronto Press, 1938.
Callaghan, Morley. *That Summer in Paris.* Toronto: Macmillan, 1963.
Collin, W.E. *The White Savannahs.* Toronto: *Macmillan, 1936.*
Klein, A.M. *The Second Scroll.* New York: Knopf, 1951.
Scott, F.R. "Preface to *New Provinces*". In *The Making of Modern Poetry in Canada*, eds. Louis Dudek and Michael Gnarowski. Toronto: Ryerson, 1967.
Scott, F.R., ed. *New Provinces.* Toronto: Macmillan, 1936.
Smith, A.J.M. ed. Preface to *The Book of Canadian Poetry.* Toronto: Gage, 1943.
Stevens, Peter. *The McGill Movement.* Toronto: Ryerson, 1969.
Wilson, Milton, ed. *Poets Between the Wars.* Toronto: McClelland and Stewart, 1967.

On Record:

Scott, F.R. Poems. *Six Montreal Poets.* New York: Folkways, 9805. 1958.
Smith, A.J.M. Poems. *Six Montreal Poets.* New York: Folkways, 9805. 1958.

On Film:

Klein, A.M. *Autobiographical, The World of A.M. Klein.* National Film Board. 1965. Black and white. 11 minutes.

Joining a World of War

In Print:

Birney, Earle. *Turvey.* New Canadian Library edition. Toronto: McClelland and Stewart, 1949.

Elliott, A.J. *The Aging Nymph.* Toronto: Collins, 1948.
Fairley, Margaret, ed. *The Spirit of Canadian Democracy.* Toronto: Progress Books, 1945.
Le Pan, Douglas. *The Deserter.* Toronto: McClelland and Stewart, 1964.
Mackay, L.A. "Battle Hymn of the Spanish Rebellion". In *The Book of Canadian Poetry*, ed. A.J.M. Smith. Toronto: Gage,1943.
MacLennan, Hugh. *The Watch That Ends the Night.* Toronto: Macmillan, 1958.
Souster, Raymond. "Spain". In *Spirit of Canadian Democracy*, ed. Margaret Fairley. Toronto: Progress Books, 1945.

On Film:

Bethune. National Film Board. 1964. Black and white. 1 hour.

Other Media:

Jackdaw Kit. Canada and the Great War. Toronto: Clarke, Irwin.

Returns From Europe

In Print:

Dudek, Louis and **Michael Gnarowski,** eds. *The Making of Modern Poetry in Canada.* Toronto: McGaw-Hill, 1967.
Godfrey, David and **William McWhinney.** *Man Deserves Man.* Toronto: McGraw-Hill, 1968.
Kreisel, Henry. *The Rich Man.* Toronto: McClelland and Stewart, 1948.
Lillard, Charles and **J.M. Yates,** eds. *Volvox: Poetry From the Unofficial Languages of Canada in English Translation.* Vancouver: Sono Nis, 1972.
Lowry, Malcolm. *Under the Volcano.* New York: Reynal, 1947.

Moore, Brian. *Judith Hearne.* New Canadian Library edition. Toronto: McClelland and Stewart, 1964.

Moore, Brian. *The Luck of Ginger Coffey.* New Canadian Library edition. Toronto: McClelland and Stewart, 1972.

Richler, Mordecai. *A Choice of Enemies.* London: A. Deutsch, 1957.

Richler, Mordecai. *Cocksure.* Toronto: McClelland and Stewart, 1968.

On Tape:

Birney, Earle. *Poetry Readings.* High Barnet Cassette. 1970. 503 Merton Street. Toronto 7, Ontario.

On Record:

Birney, Earle. *Six Poems. Canadian Poets I.* Canadian Broadcasting Corporation. 1966.

The Newest Ancestors

In Print:

Birney, Earle. "The Bear on the Delhi Road". In *Fifteen Canadian Poets*, eds. Gary Geddes and Phyllis Bruce. Toronto: Oxford, 1970.

Clarke, Austin. *When He Was Free and Young and He Used To Wear Silks.* Toronto: Anansi, 1971.

Cohen, Leonard. "The Only Tourist In Havana". In *Five Modern Canadian Poets*, ed. Eli Mandel. Toronto: Holt, Rinehart and Winston, 1970.

Godfrey, Dave. *The New Ancestors.* Toronto: New Press, 1970.

Jonas, George. *The Absolute Smile.* Toronto: Anansi, 1967.

Jonas, George. *The Happy Hungry Man.* Toronto: Anansi, 1970.

Knight, David. *Farquharson's Physique and What It Did To His Mind.* New York: Stein and Day, 1970.

Laurence Margaret. *This Side Jordan.* Toronto: McClelland and Stewart, 1961.

Laurence, Margaret. *The Tomorrow Tamer.* Toronto: McClelland and Stewart, 1963.

MacEwen, Gwendolyn. *Armies of the Moon.* Toronto: Macmillan, 1971.

MacEwen, Gwendolyn. *King of Egypt, King of Dreams.* Toronto: Macmillan, 1971.

Ondaatje, Michael. *The Collected Works of Billy the Kid.* Toronto: Anansi, 1970.

On Tape:

Jonas, George. *Poetry Readings.* High Barnet Cassettes. 1970. 503 Merton St. Toronto 7, Ontario.

Myths:
Colours in the Dark

10

1950

By 1950 there had been two hundred years of attempting to produce art in Canada—an aim sometimes, but not always, equated with trying to produce Canadian art. Critical catch-phrases had cancelled each other out. "Let's be cosmopolitan!" had given way to "Let's sound the native note!" "Art should spread sunshine!" had been replaced by "Art should throw harsh light on dark corners!" and now "Explore the world!" was being countered with a new slogan. Since 1950 or so a new cry had been heard: "Not external reality, but imaginative vision. Write not of the political world of practical affairs but of the inner world of dreams and desires. Not manners, but myths." A new phase of Canadian art began.

Pioneer Canadians had brought with them some memories of traditional myths. Myths of Greece and Rome were taught in schools, while the stories of Old and New Testament were taught in the churches. Fairy-tales and folk stories reamined half-remembered from childhood. English and Scottish ballads, Scandinavian lore, French Provincial tales, or mid-European folk stories were brought from the various homelands. But we would expect that as a new nation grew up in Canadian terrain a new mythology would shape itself. Terrors of the wilderness, unsatisfied desires, awe and reverence aroused by unfamiliar objects, pressed upon the consciousness of men and women in the Canadian settlements. New stories were told, or old ones told in a new way. So the archetypal parts of Canadian experience began to coalesce as a Canadian mythology— a Canadian way of retelling the universal story of birth, growth, and death.

Canadian writers such as Roberts and Lampman

experimented with localized versions of classical myths. Carman,
furthermore, explored the basis of myths in his essay "Subconscious
Art". This essay pre-dated Carl Jung's scientific explanation of the
psychic basis of myths, and the connections between primitive
myths and more sophisticated literature.

In Canada Professor Northrop Frye has been the chief pro-
ponent of the theory that all art inculcates mythic patterns and
archetypal allusions, and can best be understood if read in that
light. In *Fearful Symmetry*, 1947, and in *Anatomy of Criticism*, 1957,
Frye worked out a full theory of myths and genres of literature.
Through these books, and through his work in the class rooms
of the University of Toronto, Professor Frye stirred a generation
of college students. These students in their turn moved into the
network of English departments at Canadian universities, and
preached the theory of myth and archetype as aesthetic gospel.

The archetypal critic observes Canadian art as a set of local
variants on the universal human story. This story follows man
through four principal ages: birth, quest or apprenticeship,
marriage and maturity, and decay. Certain plot motifs seem to
be connected with phases of the journey from birth to death. A
voyage under water, a flight through burning air, a fall from a
high tower, a tortured passage through a maze: these are archetypal
plot motifs. They stir memories, desires, and fears connected
with the inevitable patterns of human lives.

Among Canadian writers who caught fire over some of these
ideas about myths and archetypes were James Reaney, Ronald Bates,
Eli Mandel, Jay Macpherson, Douglas Jones, George Johnston,
Coleen Thibaudeau, Wilfred Watson, and Sheila Watson. Other
contemporaries, outside the direct range of Professor Frye's
influence, responded to the stimulus of their fellow-poets—or
perhaps to the tendencies in the age, to which Northrop Frye
had given critical voice. In this sense, Irving Layton, Miriam
Waddington, Leonard Cohen, Anne Wilkinson, Margaret Avison,
Robertson Davies, Mordecai Richler, Ernest Buckler, Margaret
Laurence and other writers of the fifties can be seen as exploring

myths and archetypes, even when they reject the critical position
of Professor Frye.

Colours of the "real" Canadian world, pulled into the darkness
of the Canadian author's subconsciousness, flash into his work
in the form of imagery or of twists in the archetypal plot motifs.
From studying these local variations of universal myths we learn
something about the creative process, something about the myths
themselves, and something about Canada.

Archetype of the Child: the Spring-time Phase

All stories of childhood reflect universal human concern with
beginnings, with innocence, with morning. Myths of the child
preserve a memory of a green world of vitality. The young sun-God
Apollo, or the infant Hercules, are associated with the fire and
strength of childhood desires. But Canadian stories of childhood
show some surprising variants of these birth-myths.

Perhaps a "young" country, a country of hope rather than
of memory, places special emphasis on its children. Certainly
early Canadian writers had established a penchant for writing
books about children. One of Mrs. Moodie's sisters, Catherine
Parr Traill, had written *Adventures of Little Downy, the Field Mouse*
in 1844, and followed it with *Lady Mary and her Nurse: Stories
of the Canadian Forest,* in 1856. R.M. Ballantyne's books about
the Hudson Bay country, for example *The Young Fur Traders*,
1856, added that adventurous and open part of the world to
English boy's fantasies. Then came Marshall Saunders, whose
Beautiful Joe, 1894, became a child's classic among animal stories.
L.M. Montgomery's Island became a part of the adolescent dream-
world, a magic-island world of imaginative freedom.

Books about children rather than for children were written
by many other Canadians, including Nellie McClung and Mazo
de la Roche. Increasingly, the child was seen as "eye among the
blind," perceiver among a world of adult hypocrites. *The Mountain*

and the Valley, partly focused on a boy's consciousness, and *Who
has Seen the Wind,* entirely so focused, are among the best
novels yet produced in Canada.

More recent stories and poems about childhood in Canada tend
to invert some of the archetypal associations of innocence, freedom,
light-heartedness. Raymond Souster in his poems "Beautiful
Children" sets these adolescents sadly into a longer cycle of
despair, in a landscape of "useless swamp/or lakes reflecting empty
skies".[1] Dorothy Livesay speaks of the child's "small thankless
growing place,"[2] and Miriam Waddington sees birth as entry
into "morning, morning—/full of problems and sorrow";[3]
Douglas Jones presents the image of little girls as butterflies,
"as though" under a "benignant sun"[4]—but the title of his volume
of poems is *The Sun as Axeman.* James Reaney shows a crisis of
alienation, terror, rejection, in "Antichrist as a Child": reversing
the archetypes of cherished and innocent childhood.[5] The child
here stands terrified in his mother's garden, where even weeds
wither at his touch.

A surprising archetype of the child as hindered and hampered
emerges in the writings of the fifties. Recurring metaphors
reinforce this bias. James Reaney uses an important image: the
kite. In "The Two Kites", the free life of childhood is imaged
not as really free but as flying on a string, ready to be pulled
down into the toy-box coffin of age and death.[6] Souster uses the
same image: the kite is like the prophecy of the child's life,

> . . .the fall to earth
> Or almost earth—but the both of them are hell.[7]

W.O. Mitchell's haunting novel of return to a boyhood world
of country innocence is called *The Kite,* 1962. Perhaps Leonard
Cohen has these associations of kites with childhood in mind
when he writes, "A kite is a victim you are sure of" and lets his
mind swing to the real travelling purity of the "cordless moon".[8]
Certainly in *The Favourite Game,* 1963, he presents childhood
in an anti-idyllic mood.

[1] Raymond Souster,
"Beautiful Children", in
Canadian Anthology, eds.
C.F. Klinck and R.E.
Watters (Toronto, 1966),
p.466.
[2] Dorothy Livesay, "The
Child Looks Out",
in *Canadian Anthology,*
p.355.
[3] Miriam Waddington,
"Night in October",
in *Canadian Anthology,*
p.432.
[4] Douglas Jones,
"Beautiful Creatures Brief
as These", in *Canadian
Anthology,* p. 478.
[5] James Reaney, "Antichrist
as a Child", in *Canadian
Anthology,* p. 474.
[6] James Reaney, "The Two
Kites", in *Canadian
Anthology,* p. 474.
[7] Raymond Souster,
"Kites", in *Canadian
Anthology,* p. 464.
[8] Leonard Cohen, "A Kite
is a Victim", in *Selected
Poems* (Toronto, 1968), p. 37.

Only occasionally does a Canadian poem strike a happy note of childhood. One of these is A.M. Klein's "Pastoral of the City Street".[9] Here the children's innocent pleasure converts the concrete world of stairs, curbs, and streetlights into an idyllic realm of games, friendship, and family love. But images of childhood as tied and troubled outweigh the occasional affirmation of such poems. One might ask if the sad image of childhood reflects the experience of the individual authors, or if it is a revelation of some nightmare quality in modern Canadian childhood.

Archetype of the Young Hero: the Quest Motif

According to pyschologists, all stories of the young hero are mythical workings of the human desire to rise, to command, to control. The Canadian "apprenticeship" or "quest" story will show the unique way Canadian experience has modified the human power drive—the drive to learn, to find a kingdom, to oust the old ruler, and to be initiated into maturity.

The portrait of the hero as a young man in Canada as painted in the fifties and sixties was certainly tinted in tones of irony rather than of tragedy or romance. In myths and legends, the young hero attains either a crown or a cross. That is, he either succeeds and becomes the new god or ruler, or he fails to conquer the established order and is sacrificed to it. Young heroes in recent Canadian stories rarely achieve either heroic death or epic victory. In novel after novel, the ending is ironic or absurd; in poetry, the poet presents himself as wryly compromised and compromising. Mythopoeic critics would suggest that this reflects an inhibition or a diffidence in Canadian drive for power.

For example, *The Apprenticeship of Duddy Kravitz,* 1959, by Mordecai Richler is a wasteland apprenticeship: the story of a motherless, loveless hero, downing a series of opponents in order to take the place of his youthful idol, "the Boy Wonder", only to find himself like the "Wonder" crippled, exploited and rejected.

[9] A.M. Klein, "Pastoral of the City Streets", in *Canadian Anthology*, p. 335.

It is a bleak plot, although filled with tremendous energy, and gusto, and with the joy of effort for its own sake, and for the achievement of a goal—even if the author feels bound to point out the emptiness of the hero's final achievement. [10]

The image of heroic effort for Duddy is the mountain. In Buckler's *The Mountain and the Valley* the same image recurs, but there, too, the mountain is delusive or impossible. Other "young hero" poems and novels substitute the image of a stairway for the mountain. Running upstairs to school, climbing stairs to an altar, leaping upward like salmon up the waterfall, dreaming of flight like Icarus—all these images recur in Canadian poems of young manhood. But many show the leap or the climb as abortive. The ironic note prevails. Jay Macpherson watches the rite of initiation:

The dove descended on my brother . . .
    the glory of the bird scorched his roses. [11]

Portraits of the Canadian as a young man: not much of a hero!

What about the archetypal Canadian as a young lover? The recurring image in Canadian love poems seems to be that of a prison or a cage. P.K. Page in her poem "The Condemned" sets the tone: "In separate cells they tapped the forbidden message". [12] Few love songs in Canada suggest that love is open, strong, sane, or sweet. Erotic fantasies seem full of pain or of resentment. Leonard Cohen, prophet of the new love poets, writes in essential loneliness, and in a desire to maintain the right to "say good-bye", "as the mist leaves no scar." [13] Love in many of his poems is linked with death, or with religious rituals which entail sacrifice. Love is captivity, love is limitation.

Other poets pick up the theme: Dorothy Livesay in "Bartok and the Geranium", [14] Al Purdy in "Song of the Impermanent Husband", [15] Irving Layton in "Berry-Picking". [16] James Reaney saw the paradox of the lovers' relation as an archetypal image of the human condition. In "The Heart and the Sun", Reaney used the metaphor of the troubadour, lyrically serenading the

[10] Mordecai Richler, *The Apprenticeship of Duddy Kravitz* (Toronto, 1959).
[11] Jay Macpherson, "Ordinary People in the Last Days", in *Canadian Anthology*, p. 481; see also Alden Nowlan, "I Icarus", in *Listen! Songs and Poems of Canada*, ed. Homer Hogan (Toronto, 1972), p. 29.
[12] P.K. Page, "The Condemned", in *Canadian Anthology*, p. 420.
[13] Leonard Cohen, "As the Mist Leaves No Scar", in *Selected Poems*, p. 63.
[14] Dorothy Livesay, "Bartok and the Geranium", in *Canadian Anthology*, p. 357.
[15] Al Purdy, "Song of the Impermanent Husband", in *Fifteen Canadian Poets*, p. 26.
[16] Irving Layton, "Berry Picking", in *Fifteen Canadian Poets*, p. 53.

imprisoned lover. By analogy, the soul imprisoned in the body, eternal energy imprisoned in particular experience, wears away the receiving lover:

> the gold prisoner within her . . .
> Wore away her red, russet walls.[17]

Modern Canadian poets have erupted into frankly erotic poetry, in part as rebellion against the long hold of the genteel and puritan tradition. But when Irving Layton collected a set of Canadian love poems in *Love Where the Nights are Long,* 1962, the dominant mood seemed less one of celebration, more one of exploitation or ferocity.

Archetype of Maturity: the City

> I have not been unhappy for ten thousand years.
> During the day I laugh and during the night I sleep.[18]

That is Leonard Cohen, in "I have not lingered in European Monastries", hymning the happiness man is capable of. Man in maturity, man in control, man at his creative best enjoying himself, expressing himself. Irving Layton sounded this same note of triumphant achievement in "And me happiest when I write poems", and in "Composition in Late Spring".[19] In such poetry, the artist pictures himself as lord of the city, striding through crowded avenues, famous, strong, and good. Layton sometimes sees himself as Theseus, the dragon-killer and the archetypal hero in glorious maturity.

Much more frequently modern Canadian writers present the adult world as a terrifying city, a labyrinth in which some terrible monster lurks to defeat them. This is the archetype of experience in Canadian art. The beast in the city may well defeat the hero.

The city has always appeared to artists either as a "city of dreadful Night", a place of archetypal evil, confusion, chaos;

[17] James Reaney, "The Heart and the Sun", in *Canadian Anthology,* p. 473.
[18] Leonard Cohen, "I Have Not Lingered in European Monastries", in *Fifteen Canadian Poets,* p. 80.
[19] Irving Layton, "Composition in Late Spring", in *Collected Poems* (Toronto, 1965), p. 63.

or as a "City of God", a new Jerusalem of divine order and form,
the height of social achievement. In the Jewish and Christian
tradition, the city had appeared as paradisal: a sharp contrast from
pagan ideas that heaven consists of "Elysian fields" or a "happy
hunting-ground". Early treatments of the city in Canadian poetry
tended to emphasize the dæmonic aspects. Lampman's "City
of the End of Things" is a powerful example. [20] But in the early
twentieth century, the city was a goal, an ideal. The lights of
Vancouver for Birney symbolized the height of human achievement.

In the 1950's the nightmare city recurs. One of Layton's
early poems presents the city as a reptile, a monster. "De Bullion
Street" is apostrophized:

O reptilian street whose scaly limbs
Are crooked stairways. [21]

Miriam Waddington internalizes the city streets:

hot streets . . .
Pouring from the city like coiled intestines. [22]

Louis Dudek imagines a city as a fossilized monster:

Gather together the broken teeth of light scattered
From Rockefeller's skyscrapers and the bones of numb neon. [23]

The myth of the city as monster posing a terrible riddle is
implied in Hugh MacLennan's novel of this period, *The Return of
the Sphinx*, 1964. The city as maze, hiding its secret heart, is also
a motif in *The Loved and the Lost*. Brian Moore tells Irish
stories, but his life in Montreal contributes special labyrinthine
tones to his novels. The metaphor of the maze is linked with
the feeling of being menaced as artist in many of these poems
and novels.

The archetype of the city man is Souster's "Roller-Skate Man".
Here man is diminished, crippled, moving on a skate-board

[20] Archibald Lampman,
"City of the End of
Things", in *Canada
Anthology*, p. 129.
[21] Irving Layton, "De
Bullion Street", in
Collected Poems, p. 14.
[22] Miriam Waddington,
"Investigator", in *Canadian
Anthology*, p. 431.
[23] Louis Dudek, "O
Contemporaries", in
Canadian Anthology, p. 441.

through the debris of city streets, "flotsam in the jetsam of their lives".[24] Eli Mandel, in his Minotaur Poems used the labyrinth motif to suggest universal alienation.[25]

In short, the image of the city-maze becomes a central ironic motif of much Canadian Literature, especially in the fifties. Each mature man moves into his own "city"—an adult world of power and responsibility. He may live in benign order; but he may find himself trapped in the labyrinth of his own organization, lost in a city of terror. What myth of adult fears lurks behind Canadian novels and poems about city life?

Curiously enough, most of the artists who exploit this motif are themselves city-dwellers. Most of this group are downtown people including Layton, Waddington, and Souster. We may take their insistence on the labyrinth motif as an example of their desire and readiness to voice general rather than private attitudes. Malaise, alienation and dread of the city find voice in these writers, as expression of a general unconscious Canadian archetype.

Archetype of the Dying Hero: the Winter Phase

Finally, the story of aging and dying is the inevitable ending of individual life, giving way to a next generation, a next day, a next turn of the wheel. Does the Canadian author, facing the thought of death, linger significantly over one aspect of this part of the universal cycle?

Traditional literature presents classic scenes of tragic heroes gently going into a night of peace and mystery. Tiresias, the old blind prophet, is the legendary epitome of the dimming of experience in age. In Canada, where aging represented a serious drain on the community's work potential on the land, there are many poignant portraits of old men and women. The note of resignation in Duncan Campbell Scott's old woman abandoned on the ice in the poem "Forsaken" recurs even in more modern poems. Dale Zieroth's "Father" and Alden Nowlan's "And He

[24] Raymond Souster, "Roller Skate Man", in *Canadian Anthology*, p. 465.
[25] Eli Mandel, "Minotaur Poems", in *Trio* (Toronto, 1954).

Wept Aloud" are poems that linger over the thought of an old
man stripped of rugged strength.[26]

On the other hand, recent Canadian writing has produced
a surprising number of studies of vigorous, tough old women
battling and resisting, at the point of death. Mrs. Potter in
The Double Hook, Hagar in *The Stone Angel*; Layton's "Keine
Lazarovitch"—in part these portraits are a reaction against the
old tear-jerking pieties of the "death-bed scenes" of sentimental
fiction. In part they are a tribute to the real gusto and persistence
of Canadian women—persistence outlasting gentleness and charm,
and fit to be hymned. In part, they reveal a Canadian version
of the dark spot in consciousness at the thought of death. To
focus that thought in a mother-figure, a life-giver, creates a
paradoxical shock in both writer and reader.

Indeed, the focus on death seems neurotically strong among
the writers of the fifties. Layton, in particular, consistently directed
his thoughts towards cemeteries, funerals, death scenes. He wrote
of deceased public figures such as Vishinsky, Marilyn Monroe; he
wrote epitaphs of nameless people as in "Death of a Construction
Worker".[27] Is this focus a Canadian phenomenon? Leonard Cohen
understands Layton's obsession, and its sources when he describes
him:

> . . . drunk
> to know how close he lived to the breathless
> in the ground . . . [28]

The emphasis on death is part of Layton's rejection of what
he considered the politeness and propriety of his contemporaries.
He attacked his fellow-poets in Canada as "children lost in a
painted forest . . . intent on proving to the world how sensitive they
are, how perceptive, how erudite and archetype-crammed . . . "[29]
Layton, in all his work, but particularly in his poems on death,
explores the dark destructive forces in the universe: "filth,
irrationality, and evil". He analyzes the terrible meanings of
the times, symbolized in death scenes. Curiously, in many of these

[26] Dale Zieroth, "Father",
in *Listen! Songs and Poems
of Canada*, p. 84; Alden
Nowland, "And He Wept
Aloud", in *Fifteen Cana-
dian Poets*, p. 119.
[27] Irving Layton, "Death
of a Construction
Worker", *Collected Poems*
p. 100.
[28] Leonard Cohen, "To My
Old Layton", in *Selected
Poems*, p. 102.
[29] Irving Layton, "Foreword
to *Balls for a One-Armed
Juggler*", in *Canadian
Anthology*, p. 548.

he invokes the archetypal symbol of water usually associated
with life and birth.

Today mythopoeic poetry puts the emphasis on metamorphosis,
the movement from one archetypal phase to another. Eli
Mandel's poem "Houdini", Gwendolyn MacEwen's "Manzini":
Escape Artist", and Douglas Jones' "Summer is a Poem by Ovid"
all focus on the magic moment of emergence and escape from
bondage.[30] Robertson Davies' novel *Fifth Business* presents a
comparable story of magic and of metamorphosis from winter to
spring, from death to rebirth, from despair to creativity.[31]

Theatrical Colours in the Dark

When writers read and accept the archetypal theories, do they
begin to manipulate their own stories to bring out the patterns?
Do metaphors become markers in some game of correspondences?
Perhaps so in minor writers. In a sophisticated poet like James
Reaney, awareness of myth and of archetype becomes one
controlling and structuring convention contributing to a fine
and subtle work of art.

In *Colours in the Dark*, 1969, Reaney presented a dramatic
version of the archetypal life cycle, conceived in intensely Canadian
detail. Reaney, like most mythopoeic writers, was fascinated by the
theatre, as a place of ritual enactment, and he designed *Colours in
the Dark* to exploit all the mysterious power of stage performance.

Reaney's work happily coincided with a resurgence of strength
in the Canadian theatre. Drama has had a strange half-life in
Canada. After early enthusiasm for travelling shows, operas, and
amateur productions, theatre simmered down to an occasional folk
festival and a sporadic flare-up of "little Theatre" groups, fostered
by the Dominion Drama Festival. Then radio performances
gave good experimental dramatists a chance to experiment in the
1940's and 1950's. Lister Sinclair, Robertson Davies, Joseph Schull,
Mavor Moore, and Len Peterson played with some of the deeper
possibilities of theatre. The radio plays of the "Stage" series, such

[30] Eli Mandel, "Houdini",
in *Fifteen Canadian Poets*,
p. 151; Gwendolyn
MacEwen, "Manzini:
Escape Artist", in *Listen!
Songs and Poems of Canada*,
p. 79; Douglas Jones.
"Summer is a Poem by
Ovid", in *Fifteen Canadian
Poets*, p. 105.
[31] Robertson Davies, *Fifth
Business* (Toronto, 1971).

as Lister Sinclair's *Return to Colonus*, included many reworkings
of mythic materials. Such writers relished the power of stirring
audiences at a deep psychic level.

Then the fortunes of patronage and popular whim brought
success to the stage of the Stratford Festival. Here pomp and
pageantry emphasized the ritual qualities of stage performance.
In Centennial year, Stratford prepared to present *Colours in the Dark*.

In the original performance, the audience could see and
hear a mixture of sounds, objects, letters, colours, and flowers
on the stage at all times, coordinated with scenes of child life,
of schooldays, of city experience, or of lonely death. All these
outward visible and audible signs seemed focused in the experience
of the child who sat front-stage, his eyes bandaged so that the
sensual eye could be dimmed. At the beginning of the play
a huge white trillium was projected on a screen centre stage.
"White", says the dramatist's note, "suggests Sunday, Alpha,
white trillium, Harmonium, the Sun, 'Shall We gather at the
River', 'The Big Rock Candy Mountain' ".[32] The stage presented
a melange of all those things, to take the person in the audience
"back to the source of your being when your soul gets born—clear
white Sunday afternoon". By the end of the play, the stage had
toned from white to green to red to orange to yellow, blue,
purple, and black. "Black for Some Day, Omega, Indian Pipes . . . "
The screens showed all these. In front of the screens, the players
had enacted the whole life-to-death cycle.

The play itself was a metaphor of the poet's ideal for art.
Like any deeply moving work, it showed the colours of Canadian
life, caught in the dark of the mind.

[32] James Reaney, *Colours in
the Dark* (Vancouver,
1969), p. 17.

For Further Study

Archetype of the Child: the Spring-time Phase

In Print:

Buckler, Ernest. *The Mountain and the Valley*. Toronto: McClelland and Stewart, 1961.

Cohen, Leonard. *The Favourite Game*. London: Secker and Warburg, 1963.

Cohen, Leonard. "A Kite is a Victim". In *Selected Poems*. Toronto: McClelland and Stewart, 1968.

Cohen, Leonard. "The Story of Isaac". In *Listen! Songs and Poems of Canada*, ed. Homer Hogan. Toronto: Methuen, 1972.

Egoff, Sheila. *The Republic of Childhood*. Toronto: Oxford, 1967.

Jones, Douglas. "Beautiful Creatures Brief as These". In *Canadian Anthology*, eds. C.F. Klinck and R.E. Watters. Toronto: Gage, 1966.

Klein, A.M. "Pastoral of the City Streets". In *Canadian Anthology*, eds. C.F. Klinck and R.E. Watters. Toronto: Gage, 1966.

Livesay, Dorothy. "The Child Looks Out . . . ". In *Canadian Anthology*, eds. C.F. Klinck and R.E. Watters. Toronto: Gage, 1966.

Mitchell, W.O. *The Kite*. Toronto: Macmillan, 1962.

Mitchell, W.O. *Who Has Seen the Wind*. Toronto: Macmillan, 1947.

Reaney, James. "Antichrist as a Child". In *Canadian Anthology*, eds. C.F. Klinck and R.E. Watters. Toronto: Gage, 1966.

Reaney, James. "The Two Kites". In *Canadian Anthology*, eds. C.F. Klinck and R.E. Watters. Toronto: Gage, 1966.

Saunders, Marshall. *Beautiful Joe*. Toronto: McClelland and Stewart, 1934.

Souster, Raymond. "Beautiful Children". In *Canadian Anthology*, eds. C.F. Klinck and R.E. Watters. Toronto: Gage, 1966.

Souster, Raymond. "Kites". In *Canadian Anthology*, eds. C.F. Klinck and R.E. Watters. Toronto: Gage, 1966.

Waddington, Miriam. "Night in October". In *Canadian Anthology*, eds. C.F. Klinck and R.E. Watters. Toronto: Gage, 1966.

On Record:

Fowke, Edith. *Sally Go Round the Sun and Sally Go Round the Moon*. Toronto: McClelland and Stewart. 1969.

Archetype of the Young Hero: the Quest Motif

In Print:

Cohen, Leonard. "As the Mist Leaves no Scar". *Selected Poems*. Toronto: McClelland and Stewart, 1968.

Layton, Irving. "Berry-Picking". In *Canadian Anthology*, eds. C.F. Klinck and R.E. Watters. Toronto: Gage, 1966.

Layton, Irving. "Philosophy 34". In *Collected Poems*. Toronto: McClelland and Stewart, 1965.

Layton, Irving, ed. *Love Where the Nights are Long*. Toronto: McClelland and Stewart, 1959.

LePan. "Net and the Sword". In *Canadian Anthology*, eds. C.F. Klinck and R.E. Watters. Toronto: Gage, 1966.

Livesay, Dorothy. "The Condemned". In *Canadian Anthology*, eds. C.F. Klinck and R.E. Watters. Toronto: Gage, 1966.

Livesay, Dorothy. "The Metal and the Flowers". In *Listen! Songs and Poems of Canada*, ed. Homer Hogan. Toronto: Methuen, 1972.

MacEwen, Gwendolyn. *Julian the Magician*. Toronto: Macmillan, 1963.

MacEwen, Gwendolyn. *King of Egypt, King of Dreams.* Toronto: Macmillan, 1971.
Macpherson, Jay. "Ordinary People in the Last Days". In *Canadian Anthology,* eds. C.F. Klinck and R.E. Watters. Toronto: Gage, 1966. Gage, 1966.
Mandel, Eli. "Marina". In *Fifteen Canadian Poets*, eds. Gary Geddes and Phyllis Bruce. Toronto: Oxford, 1971.
Nowlan, Alden. "I, Icarus". In *Listen! Songs and Poems of Canada*, ed. Homer Hogan. Toronto: Methuen, 1972.
Page, P.K. "The Condemned". In *Canadian Anthology*, eds. C.F. Klinck and R.E. Watters. Toronto: Gage,1966.
Purdy, Al. "Song of the Impermanent Husband". In *Fifteen Canadian Poets*, eds. Gary Geddes and Phyllis Bruce. Toronto: Oxford, 1971.
Radin, Paul. *The Trickster.* London: Routledge and K. Paul, 1956.
Reaney, James. "The Heart and the Sun". In *Canadian Anthology*, eds. C.F. Klinck and R.E. Watters.Toronto: Gage, 1966.
Richler, Mordecai. *The Apprenticeship of Duddy Kravitz.* Toronto: McClelland and Stewart, 1959.
Scott, F.R. "Eden". In *Canadian Anthology*, eds. C.F. Klinck and R.E. Watters. Toronto: Gage, 1966.
Yates, J.M. *Man in the Glass Octopus.* Vancouver: Sono Nis, 1968.

Archetype of Maturity: the City

In Print:

Callaghan, Morley. *The Loved and the Lost.* Paperback edition. Toronto: Macmillan, 1970.
Cohen, Leonard. "I Have Not Lingered". In *Selected Poems.* Toronto: McClelland and Stewart, 1968.
Dudek, Louis. "O Contemporaries". In *Canadian Anthology*, eds. C.F. Klinck and R.E. Watters. Toronto: Gage, 1966.

Layton, Irving. "De Bullion Street". In *Collected Poems.* Toronto: McClelland and Stewart, 1965.
MacLennan, Hugh. *The Return of the Sphinx.* Toronto: Macmillan, 1964.
Mandel, Eli. "The Castle". In *Fifteen Canadian Poets*, eds. Gary Geddes and Phyllis Bruce. Toronto: Oxford, 1971.
Mandel, Eli. "Minotaur Poems". In *Trio.* Toronto: Contact, 1954.
Mitchell, Joni. "Big Yellow Taxi". In *Listen! Songs and Poems of Canada*, ed. Homer Hogan. Toronto: Methuen, 1972.
Simmons, Robert E. and James Simmons. *Urban Canada.* Toronto: Copp Clark, 1969.
Souster, Raymond. "Roller Skate Man". In *Canadian Anthology*, eds. C.F. Klinck and R.E. Watters. Toronto: Gage, 1966.
Waddington, Miriam. "Investigator". In *Canadian Anthology*, eds. C.F. Klinck and R.E. Watters. Toronto: Gage, 1966.

Other Media:

Mandel, Eli. *Poetry Readings.* Toronto: High Barnet Cassettes, 1970.

Archetype of the Dying Hero: the Winter Phase

In Print:

Atwood, Margaret. "Eden is a Zoo". In *Fifteen Canadian Poets*, eds. Gary Geddes and Phyllis Bruce. Toronto: Oxford, 1971.
Cohen, Leonard. "To My Old Layton". *Selected Poems.* Toronto: McClelland and Stewart, 1968.
Laurence, Margaret. *The Stone Angel.* New Canadian Library edition. Toronto: McClelland and Stewart, 1964.
Layton, Irving. "Death of a Construction Worker" In *Collected Poems.* Toronto: McClelland and Stewart, 1965.
Layton, Irving. "Keine Lazarovitch". In *Canadian Anthology*, eds. C.F. Klinck and R.E. Watters. Toronto: Gage, 1966.
Layton, Irving. Preface to "Balls for a One Arm Juggler". In *Canadian Anthology*, eds. C.F. Klinck and R.E. Watters. Toronto: Gage, 1966.

Nelligan, Emile. "Before Two Portraits of My Mother". In *Listen! Songs and Poems of Canada*, ed. Homer Hogan. Toronto: Methuen, 1972.

Nowlan, Alden. "And He Wept Aloud". In *Fifteen Canadian Poets*, eds. Gary Geddes and Phyllis Bruce. Toronto: Oxford, 1941.

Watson, Sheila. *The Double Hook*. New Canadian Library edition. Toronto: McClelland and Stewart, 1959.

Zieroth, Dale. "Father". In *Listen! Songs and Poems of Canada*, ed. Homer Hogan. Toronto: Methuen, 1972.

On Record:

Layton, Irving. Poems. *Six Montreal Poets*. New York: Folkways, 9805. 1958.

Layton, Irving. Poems. *Canadian Poets I*. Toronto: Canadian Broadcasting Corporation. 1966.

On Tape:

Layton, Irving. *Poetry Readings*. Toronto: High Barnet Cassettes. 1970.

Theatrical Colours in the Dark

In Print:

Edwards, M.D. *A Stage in Our Past*. Toronto: University of Toronto Press, 1968.

Frazer, Sir James. *The Golden Bough*. London: Macmillan, 1923.

Frye, Northrop. *Anatomy of Criticism*. Princeton: Princeton University Press, 1957.

Frye, Northrop. *Fearful Symmetry*. Boston: Beacon, 1965.

Hooke, Hilda Mary. *Thunder in the Mountain*. Toronto: Oxford, 1947.

Jung, Carl. *Essays on a Science of Mythology*. Trans. R.F.C. Hull. New York: Harper, 1943.

Jung, Carl. *The Archetypes of the Collective Unconscious*. Trans. R.F.C. Hull. Princeton: Princeton University Press, 1971.

Macpherson, Jay. *Four Ages of Man*. Toronto: Macmillan, 1962.

Reaney, James. *Colours in the Dark*. Toronto: Talon Books with Macmillan, 1969.

Reaney, James. *The Kildeer and Other Plays*. Toronto: Macmillan, 1962.

Watson, Wilfred and Marshall McLuhan. *From Cliché to Archetype*. New York: Viking, 1970.

New Messages:
Understanding Media

11

1970

Marshall McLuhan theorizes that we are entering a significantly new epoch of human life—the electronic age of film, television, phonograph records, telephone. McLuhan says that the appearance of these media marks the waning of the age of print. The "Gutenberg Galaxy"—a whole universe of books and printed media—is dimming. Our eyes and ears, muffled since the Middle Ages because of the dominance of print as a channel to the imagination, are now re-sensitized. We receive the messages flashed by the sounds and images electronically transmitted. The result is a transformation or a mutation of the human consciousness today.

Professor McLuhan's ideas must be considered in their own right in any account of modern literature. In a study of Canadian Literature, he is doubly important, since his own books are a world-renowned part of that literature, and also since he has become a kind of "guru" to younger Canadian artists. He has taught them to consider carefully the media—the channels that purvey messages and the senses they invade. The medium is the message, he says. We must consider the messages propounded by the existence and nature of new media in Canada.

It is natural that in a country so spacious and so sparsely settled as Canada much emphasis should be placed on systems of communication. Before McLuhan, another Canadian scholar, Professor Harold Innis, studied connections between the economy and the communication processes in *The Fur Trade in Canada*, 1956, and *The Bias of Communication*, 1964. Still another social scientist, John Porter, has exposed the role of the mass media in the Canadian class structure. Porter's *Vertical Mosaic*, 1965, presents important analyses of the ways the media are used to maintain a closed system, in which power is held by certain "charter-group" elites.

Whatever may be said of the mass media, in the less-commercial channels of communication there is little sign of any closed system of a rigid hierarchy. In the little presses, the little magazines, the little theatres, and in the recording and film-making outfits that flourish in Canada today, there is great mobility, innovation, and openness. These media as well as the mass media tell part of the Canadian story.

According to Marshall McLuhan, understanding the new media is a way to freedom and energetic change. McLuhan points out three aspects of the impact of the new media on modern communication. The medium is used as a channel for the message; the medium changes the kind of message; the medium, itself, becomes a message which the communicator absorbs and transmits.

Print as Medium

In colonial days, Mrs. Moodie and others were already writing about the literary magazines established in the Canadas, and about their struggle to compete for sales and support against British and American journals.[1] The story of early presses and journals is a very important part of Canadian history. So too is the story of the sequence of editors and publishers who selected the efforts of Canadian writers to be printed. The kind of print used, the kind of binding, the pattern of sales and distribution of books are all aspects of the print medium which bear great significance in the development of Canadian Literature.

The Confederation writers worked to establish national magazines. The look of the late nineteenth century books published by Roberts and Carman expresses the taste and conventions of the times almost as clearly as the poems themselves. The early years of the twentieth century brought big successful publishing houses, ready to encourage Canadian writers, by bringing out little books of poetry, solid-looking easy-to-read novels, and handsome

[1] Susanna Moodie, "Early Canadian Periodicals", in *Canadian Anthology*, eds. C.F. Klinck and R.E. Watters (Toronto, 1966), p. 63.

histories. The old farm papers, *The Family Herald and Weekly Star* and *The Farmer's Advocate*, helped form literary habits, and helped push writers into certain kinds of writing, "for hearth and home".

Avant-garde writers congregated and brought out little magazines, reflecting their own special brand of ideology. From the twenties on, "little mags" proliferated in Canada. First came the university magazines: the *McGill Fortnightly*, the *University of Toronto Quarterly*, *Queen's Quarterly*, *Dalhousie Review*. Then *Contemporary Verse*, established in 1941 in Vancouver, welcomed serious experimental verse. The War ended, a generation of new poets tumbled into print in rival little mags that bickered and bridled and attacked each other, coalesced, separated again and eventually dimmed down. In Montreal, clustering around John Sutherland, their editor-publisher, Louis Dudek, Irving Layton ,and others brought out *First Statements*, 1942-1945. This little magazine was a rival to *Preview*, the magazine of the older established Montrealers like Smith and Scott. Coalescing in *Northern Review*, 1945-1947 the Montreal writers enjoyed a brief peace. [2]

Meanwhile in Toronto a much handsomer journal, *Here and Now*, flowered briefly. Then Raymond Souster emerged as spark for a series of publications, including *Contact*, 1952-1959, and *Combustion*, 1957-60. Those were good years in Toronto publishing: the time of the flourishing of the New Canadian Library Series by McClelland and Stewart, reinforced by strong efforts to support serious Canadian publishing by Macmillan, Clarke Irwin, Gage, Ryerson, and other established commercial publishers, and by the University of Toronto Press. *Tamarack Review* printed good reviews as well as creative writing, the *Canadian Forum* continued strong, and the slicker commercial magazines such as *Macleans* and *Saturday Night* were lively and experimental.

In the Maritimes *Fiddlehead* began publication in 1953. In 1958 *Canadian Literature*, a more solid-looking journal of criticism, marked the growing respectability of Canadian literary studies. But the little magazines continued to pop up,anti-respectable in every way. Out West in the early sixties, there was *Tish*, *Prism*,

[2] Michael Gnarowski, "The Role of the 'Little Magazines' in...Montreal", in *The Making of Modern Poetry in Canada*, eds. Louis Dudek and Michael Gnarowski (Toronto, 1967), p. 212 ff.; see also Wynne Francis, "Montreal Poets of the Forties", in *A Choice of Critics*, ed. George Woodcock (Toronto, 1966), p. 36.

Blew ointment, in varying degrees of raggedness and impropriety.
In the Mid-West *Imago*, in Toronto *Moment*, in Hamilton *Mountain*,
in Montreal *CIV'n*, plus dozens of other brief-lived media appeared. [3]

The names and the very look of many of these journals
carry a message. Many modern writers reflect an interest in
impermanence, both in manner and in matter. They write with
a sense of wispy, ephemeral experience. They settle for unimposing
format—mimeographed sheets, and dittos. They want quick
circulation and don't mind quick oblivion. George Bowering,
who has been involved with many of the little magazines, uses
the phenomenon of impermanent printed stuff as a metaphor of
random, impermanent life-style:

Every day I add an inch
to the pile of old newspapers
in the closet . . . [4]

On the political side, the sense of spontaneity is reflected in
the spurt of underground newspapers. Political activism is voiced
in quickly-produced, cheap and impermanent forms. Underground
presses in particular use the swiftest and cheapest form of
publishing: printing on off-set press, which consists of a process
of photographing and reproducing typed copy. Cheap, quick,
disposable, it is a good medium for mobile confrontation of a
rapidly-changing, randomly-changing world. For radicals, cheap
production is itself a form of prôtest against a consumer-oriented,
materialistic world.

Among the smaller publishing houses, some have experimented
with every kind of cheap and quick method of production. Oberon
Press, House of Anansi, New Press, and Sono Nis Press all show
that a willingness to experiment exists in Canadian publishers. Bigger
publishers have also tried all kinds of experiments in making books
cheap and quickly available. The result is a change in tone and
appearance of many books—a lighter look that enhances the casual
experimental artist.

Other publishers lavish care on the tiniest detail of the

[3] See Frank Davey,
"Anything But Reluctant",
in *The Making of Modern
Poetry in Canada*, p. 222 ff.
[4] George Bowering,
"News", in *Fifteen
Canadian Poets*, p. 224.

presentation of the poem or story. The packaged offerings of *Porcépic*
from Coach House Press are an example. Such works assume
the significance of the printed word—in spite of the death-knell
of literacy sounded by Marshall McLuhan.

Books, little magazines, and mimeographed sheets are the
writers' main channels for publication in print. But the main
channel in this medium as far as public consumption is concerned
is the newspaper. Canadian newspapers have been chronicled by
W.K. Kesterton in *A History of Canadian Journalism*,1967. Their
force in maintaining social cohesion and perpetuating the interests
of the Canadian power elite has been underlined in Porter's *Vertical
Mosaic*. And their physical impact on human consciousness has been
provocatively analyzed in McLuhan's *Understanding Media*, 1964.

It is this last aspect which becomes clear when we study the
form and content of contemporary poetry and fiction. Newspapers,
says McLuhan, present a mosaic configuration. Multiple items
are arranged on one sheet of a newspaper in a mosaic that
bombards the eye with disparate bits of information, exhortation,
pictures, typographic oddities all blocked and spaced in an
apparently random way. Much modern verse seems designed to
have a similar impact.

Typographical poetry plays with letters, and with the placing
of letters on the page. A poet like bp Nichol makes arrangements
of letters that will form words diagonally, or spirally, or in shapes
that reproduce the things described.

<pre>
                          th

        er   god   ew

                       n
                       l
                       y

                      as[5]
</pre>

[5] bp Nichol, "Scraptures",
in *Alphabet*, No. 2., p. 72.

These cruciform words could be rearranged in the mind as "there
was only God" or "Only God was there". But the poem itself
will not specify any lineal order. The visual effect is the message;
the poem cannot be "sounded out". A similar effect in print
is in Doug Fetherling's "There's this old vaudeville skit . . . "[6]

A second response to McLuhanite awareness of the impact
of print is in object poems. The American poet William Carlos
Williams wrote "no ideas but in things": things are sacred and
ought to be celebrated. Poetry should place the names of things
on the page. Let the perception of these things jostle into position,
and create a field of experience for the reader. Facts, rather than
sounds, will create an effect of rhyme. Among the younger poets,
Victor Coleman and George Bowering are most successful in
composing their perceptions into an arrangement of words on the
page, to communicate a maximum sense of the objects perceived,
and of the voice of the perceiver.

Found poetry is a different response to print. Words found
in work not intended to be read as poetry are lifted out of context,
and set as verse to emphasize natural rhythm and intensity. John
Robert Colombo "finds" a poem in a game of Monopoly:

Go to jail.
Move directly to jail
Do not pass "GO"
Do not collect $200.00.[7]

Colombo issued in *John Toronto*, 1969, a volume of early Canadian
poems "found" in the writings and speeches of Archbishop
Strachan.

The New Sound

Professor McLuhan called radio "the tribal drum", and the
phonograph "music hall without walls . . . the toy that shrank the
national chest".[8] Most modern writers show impact of the electronic

[6] Doug Fetherling,
"There's This Old
Vaudeville Skit", in *Listen!
Songs and Poems of Canada*,
ed. Homer Hogan, p. 125.

[7] John Robert Colombo,
"Monopoly" in *Made in
Canada*, eds. Raymond
Souster and Douglas
Lochhead, (Toronto, 1971),
p. 54.

[8] Marshall McLuhan,
Understanding Media (New
York, 1966), chs. 28, 30.

sound media. Communication aimed at the ear—radio broadcasts, phonograph records, poetry readings, and festivals of song— has greatly affected writers, both by increasing their awareness of aural effects and also by emphasizing the sense of impermanence and non-repeatability of some very intense experiences.

Radio was one of the first of the electronic media to re-shape Canadian writing. The Canadian Broadcasting Corporation has always bought Canadian scripts and featured Canadian short story writers and poets.[9] Several major collections of short stories have been edited by Robert Weaver, who has long been in charge of the CBC programme *Anthology*, as well as general director of programming. There is nothing like this phenomenon in the United States; and the situation differs from that of the British Broadcasting Corporation, since English writers have so many more alternative media.

Since the radio became part of daily life, all writers have developed ways of using the effects of commercials, newscasts and weather reports. The strong sense of voice in stories by Rudy Wiebe, for instance, or Alice Munro, or Shirley Faessler,[10] seems striking, particularly when you compare their work with stories written in pre-radio days by C.G.D. Roberts or D.C. Scott.[11] The insistence on the audible has sharpened our sense of sound.

The medium that has had the most direct impact on poetry is the phonograph record. Popular music, especially in the 1960's, has led to the exploration of the hypnotic, incantatory effects of sound. It has also led to experiments with refrain, repetition, and sound-chaining.

Leonard Cohen, Gordon Lightfoot, Neil Young, and Joni Mitchell are among the Canadian writers who have contributed to the popularity of records.[12] The lyrics of their popular songs are poetry—complicated and polished, catering to a mass audience, but giving that audience poetic subtlety and variety. These Canadian lyricists have joined Dylan, the Beatles, and Simon and Garfunkel in the recording media: tapes, casettes, stereo records.

The recording medium induces a feeling of intimacy. It

[9] See Mavor Moore, "Come Away , Come Away", in *Encounter: Canadian Drama in Four Media*, ed. Eugene Benson (Toronto, 1973); Lister Sinclair, "Return To Colonus", in *Canadian Anthology*, pp. 445 ff.

[10] See stories in *The Narrative Voice*, ed. John Metcalfe (Toronto, 1972); *Fourteen Stories High*, eds. David Helwig and Tom Marshall (Ottawa, 1971); *Sixteen by Twelve*, ed. John Metcalfe (Toronto, 1970).

[11] See stories in *Canadian Short Stories*, ed. Robert Weaver (Toronto,1960).

[12] See songs by these poets in *Listen! Songs and Poems of Canada*.

depends on repetition for its effects. It has encouraged a readiness
to listen to lyrics, and let them drift into consciousness by re-play.
Much poetry—including poetry not set to music and not designed
for recording—shows the influence of the recording medium.
Alden Nowlan in "July 15", writes a percussive, repetitive, poem
with refrain:

> Trees sing. The grass walks.
> Nothing is happening.[13]

Outgrowth of recordings, the song festivals of the sixties and
early seventies are themselves a kind of medium for artists. They
emphasize spontaneity and cooperation; they have helped Canadian
poets like Cohen find an instant international audience. Festivals,
such as the Mariposa Festival, encourage a response to a mosaic
overlap of styles and forms. They also emphasize the element
of random or chance excitement.

That random quality, the sense of a spontaneous "happening",
is also reflected in much modern art. Stories and poems about the
sudden flare-up of a sense of total relatedness reflect the "happening"
experience. They also reflect the deeper metaphysical interest in
chance among moderns. Among poems that capitalize on spontaneity
or chance are the poems that introduce allusions to the I-Ching
or the Tarot pack. George Bowering in *Geneve* pulls a card from
the Tarot pack at random; this sets off a lyric. The arrangement
of the lyrics in a printed order is also left to chance. An extension
of this is the box of findings produced by bp Nichol. This is a
box which contains the lines of poetry that one can arrange in any
order. Interest in improvisation is also the note in Gwendolyn
MacEwen's "Poem improvised around a first line"—the first line,
we learn in a foot-note, is now lost.[14] Eli Mandel meditates on
the implications of our interest in fortune-telling in "The I-Ching":
and raises the possibility that the seemingly-random throw of the
I-Ching letters may be fated.[15]

Perhaps the drug culture has been an outgrowth of the
willingness to resign control. Drug-induced poetry has been a

[13]Alden Nowlan, "July 15", in *Fifteen Canadian Poets*, p. 121.
[14] Gwendolyn MacEwen, "Poem Improvised Around a First Line", in *Breakfast for Barbarians* (Toronto: Ryerson, 1966), p. 16.
[15] Eli Mandel, "The Meaning of the I CHING" in *Fifteen Canadian Poets*, p. 149.

strong part of recorded music and of festival singing. Some of Cohen's songs had the surreal random quality of a drug-induced vision. Victor Coleman uses metaphors drawn from drug use. Joe Rosenblatt concocts a book called *L.S.D. Leacock.*

Sound and Image: Television, Film

Traditionally, the medium coordinating experiences of sight and sound is the legitimate theatre. In Canada, playwrights have long struggled to find a stage and an audience for their dramatic writing. Now television and film bring new possibilities for the playwrights. At the same time, these new media effect changes in the way all writers work—dramatists, poets and novelists. One work of grim seriousness by Gratien Gélinas, *Yesterday the Children were Dancing,* produced on stage at Charlottetown in 1967, reached a much wider audience through television. This was a curiously prophetic play about slogans and symbols, and the *Québec libre* movement. When the F.L.Q. acted in 1970, television plugged the nation into that action. Brian Moore, in an interesting documentary report, *The Revolution Script,* emphasizes the role of television in that moment of national crisis. In *Return of the Sphinx*, 1966, the novelist Hugh MacLennan had likewise focused prophetically on the probable role of the electronic media in a separatist crisis.

Less ominously, television is one of the subjects of a very funny modern Canadian book, *Arkwright,* by Leo Simpson. Haliburton, Leacock, Robertson Davies—the line of Canadian satiric humour continues in Leo Simpson. His satire is directed against the levelling of taste, the mediocrity of material purveyed on television—and the connection between that mediocrity and the business interests involved in the medium.

But television has made its impact on modern writers less through its service as medium and as subject for their work, and more through its suggestion of a new method of composition. One feeling always connected with an event in the theatre is a sense of impermanence. The spotlight turns off; the event is gone forever. This feeling is in accord with the tone of a throw-away, fade-out, self-destruct age. Television intensifies this fragmentary effect, by interrupting the dramatic sequence with commercials. This seems to be one major message carried over into poetry from modern experience in television. Writers experiment with the collage of ill-assorted materials. In imitation of the TV effect of discontinuity, Don Bailey ends an anti-war poem:

red cap's
on draft today.[16]

Like writers everywhere, young Canadians have been experimenting with ways of introducing film techniques into writing. If television threw the spotlight on discontinuity, and the ability of the perceiving mind to accept very ill-assorted materials in rapid succession, film focused attention on the opposite element in art: continuity. Students of film are fascinated by the way one frame edges imperceptibly into another, by infinitesimal changes, the way a series of still shots flow into a single continuous action or gesture. Process and kinetics are key words for the people who are involved in experiments with form today.

For many modern poets, this has become an essential part of technique. They repeat words or facts with tiny modifications; they may drop the use of rhyme, which was an old-fashioned version of the same principle of slight modifications, or small phonetic changes within a recurring sound.

Joe Rosenblatt moves in "Bumblebee Dithyramb":

physical animal
taste th' Passion Lily
lick th' Passion Lily
draw th' tongue in
draw th' tongue out
& th' Passion Lily
taste th' bumblebee
draw th' tongues in
draw th' tongues out

[16] Don Bailey, "Saint Paul . . ." in *Soundings*, p. 28.

taste, taste,
'here's th' fertile powder, 'cry the white
                            flower
'here's th' burden
here's th' rent . . .'[17]

The use of after-image, and the zoom technique are common today, a stylistic borrowing from the world of cinema. Like a camera, the writer zooms in on a telling detail. Creative young people, who a generation ago might have been immersed in writing a novel, are now dreaming of movies. They often by-pass the formal script stage and compose directly, camera in hand, on film. Films like *Goin' Down the Road* and *Mon Oncle Antoine* show both the power of film techniques and also the attraction of this medium for innovative artists. Margaret Atwood has worked her novel, *The Edible Woman*, into a screenplay—a serious exploration of the visual qualities of her own work. Reading a film script such as Joan Finnigan's *The Best Damn Fiddler,* we see the way an artist adapts to the technical possibilities of the medium.[18]

As well as being a medium, film has an impact as a subject on work in other media. The world of film-makers is the topic of several stimulating and satiric novels: Mordecai Richler's *Cocksure,* 1968, and *The Apprenticeship of Duddy Kravitz*, 1959, and Hugh Hood's *The Camera Always Lies*, 1967. In *The Apprenticeship*, Richler brilliantly illuminates the world of modern media. Duddy's first major exploit in his tilt with the world is the production of a movie. This part of the novel, beside being outrageously funny, is a documentary report on the reaction of a traditional audience to an experimental medium.[19] Duddy, as modern hero in a McLuhanite age, moves through other adventures dominated by technological devices: telephones, trains, taxis, newspapers, comic books. His world touches the fringes of crime and drug-culture. But in this world, Duddy moves as a genuinely free agent—inventive, restless, ingenious. He understands the media, and proves that they *can* be resisted, and turned to the service of energy and invention.

[17] Joe Rosenblatt, "Bumblebee Dithyramb", in *Impulse,* vol. 1, no. 3, Toronto, Spring 1972, p. 28.
[18] See film and television scripts in *Encounter: Canadian Drama in Four Media*.
[19] Mordecai Richler, *The Apprenticeship of Duddy Kravitz*, (Toronto, 1959).

Understanding the Messages

The enormous complexity of the electronic media may be felt as a menace to the individual creative artist, the solo man, unique and unmechanized. But Marshall McLuhan presents the theory that the ultimate message of the electronic age is one of freedom. The new media are extensions of man. He made them; he can control them. The machine he has created frees man for entry into a new era. McLuhan concludes *Understanding Media*, 1964, with this emphasis:

Persons grouped around a fire or candle for warmth or light are less able to pursue independent thoughts, or even tasks, than people supplied with electric light. In the same way, the social and educational patterns latent in automation are those of self-employment and artistic autonomy.[20]

Among the messages most powerful in the electronic age is a surprising insistence on mystic individual experience. A return to nature in search of enhanced quality of life is a common theme in poems and stories. Experiments with drugs can be seen as another protest against standardized, computerized life. Humour, including absurdity, is a similar reaction. Restlessness and openness are reflected in the themes as well as the forms of contemporary Canadian writing.

[20] Marshall McLuhan, *Understanding Media* (New York, 1964), p. 311.

For Further Study

Print as Medium

In Print:

Bassem, Bertha. *The First Printers and Newspapers in Canada.* Toronto: University of Toronto Press, 1968.

Birney, Earle. *The Creative Writer.* Toronto: Canadian Broadcasting Corporation, 1966.

Bowering, George. "News". In *Fifteen Canadian Poets*, eds. Gary Geddes and Phyllis Bruce. Toronto: Oxford University Press, 1971.

Colombo, John Robert. *John Toronto: New Poems by Dr. Strachan.* Ottawa: Oberon Press, 1969.

Colombo, John Robert. "Monopoly". In *Made in Canada: New Poems of the Seventies*, eds. Douglas Lochead and Raymond Souster. Ottawa: Oberon, 1970.

Colombo, John Robert. *New Directions in Canadian Poetry. A Book of Concrete Poetry.* New York: Holt, 1971.

Davey, Frank. "Anything but Reluctant". *The Making of Modern Poetry in Canada*, eds. Louis Dudek and Michael Gnarowski. Toronto: McGraw-Hill, 1969.

Dudek, Louis. *Literature and the Press.* Toronto: Ryerson, 1960.

Fetherling, Douglas. "There's this old vaudeville skit . . .". In *Listen! Songs and Poems of Canada*, ed. Homer Hogan. Toronto: Methuen, 1972.

Gnarowski, Michael. "The Role of the 'Little Magazines' in . . . Montreal." In *The Making of Modern Poetry in Canada*, eds. Louis Dudek; Michael Gnarowski. Toronto: McGraw-Hill, 1967.

Kesterton, W.H. *A History of Journalism in Canada.* Toronto: McClelland and Stewart, 1967.

McLuhan, Marshall. *The Mechanical Bride.* Boston: Beacon, 1967.

Moodie, Susanna. "Early Literature in the Canadas". In *Canadian Anthology*, eds. C.F. Klinck and R.E. Watters. Toronto: Gage, 1966.

Nichol, bp. *The Cosmic Chef: An Evening of Concrete.* Ottawa: Oberon, 1970.

Nichol, bp. *ABC.* Ottawa: Oberon, 1971.

Ondaatje, Michael. *The Collected Works of Billy the Kid.* Toronto: Anansi, 1970.

Stevenson, Warren. "Poets for Lunch". *Soundings*, eds. Jack Ludwig and Andy Wainwright. Toronto: Anansi, 1970.

Weaver, Robert. *The First Five Years.* Toronto: Oxford, 1962.

Wynne, Francis. "Montreal Poets of the Forties". In *A Choice of Critics*, ed. George Woodcock. Toronto: Oxford, 1966.

The New Sound

In Print:

Bowering, George. *Genève.* Toronto: Coach House, 1971.

Gormely, Sheila. *Drugs and the Canadian Scene.* Toronto: Burns and MacEachern, 1970.

Hughes, Ed. *Tribal Drums.* Toronto: McGraw-Hill, 1970.

MacEwen, Gwendolyn. "Poem Improvised Around a First Line". In *Breakfast for Barbarians.* Toronto: Ryerson, 1972.

Mandel, Eli. "The Meaning of the I-Ching". In *Listen! Songs and Poems of Canada*, ed. Homer Hogan. Toronto: Methuen, 1972.

Metcalfe, John, ed. *The Narrative Voice.* Toronto: McGraw-Hill Ryerson, 1972.

Nowlan, Alden. "July 15". In *Fifteen Canadian Poets*, eds. Gary Geddes and Phyllis Bruce. Toronto: Oxford, 1971.

Ondaatje, Michael. *Leonard Cohen*. Toronto:
McClelland and Stewart, 1970.
Rosenblatt, Joe. *The L.S.D. Leacock*. Toronto:
Coach House, 1966.
Weaver, Robert, ed. *Canadian Short Stories:
Second Series*. Toronto: Oxford, 1968.

On Film:

Cohen, Leonard. Prose Poem from *Beautiful
Losers*, read by Cohen. National Film Board.
1968. Black and white. 4 1/2 minutes.
Cohen, Leonard. *Ladies and Gentlemen, Mr.
Leonard Cohen*. National Film Board. 1965.
Black and white. 41 minutes.

Musical Score:

Cohen, Leonard. *Songs*. New York: Amsco,
1969.
Mitchell, Joni. *The Music of Joni Mitchell*.
Miami Beach: Reprise, 1969.

On Record:

Atwood, Margaret. "The Journals of Susanna
Moodie", *Canadian Poets II*. Toronto: Canadian
Broadcasting Corporation. 1970.
Cohen, Leonard. *Songs of Leonard Cohen*. New
York: Columbia. 1968. CL2733.
Cohen, Leonard. *Songs from a Room*. New
York: Columbia. 1969. C79767.
Cohen, Leonard. Poems in *Canadian Poets I*.
Toronto: Canadian Broadcasting Coporation.
1966.
Mitchell, Joni. "Big Yellow Taxi". *Ladies of
the Canyon*. 1970. Reprise R56376.

Sound and Image: Television, Film

In Print:

Atwood, Margaret. *The Edible Woman*.
Toronto: McClelland and Stewart, 1969.
Bailey, Paul. "Saint Paul/as another sex/
slipping into/something more comfortable".
In *Soundings*, eds. Jack Ludwig and Andy
Wainwright. Toronto: Anansi, 1970.
Gélinas, Gratien. *Yesterday the Children Were
Dancing*. Toronto: Clarke, Irwin, 1967.

Goldberg, Gerry. *I Am A Sensation*. Toronto:
McClelland and Stewart, 1971.
Hood, Hugh. *The Camera Always Lies*. New
York: Harcourt, Brace and World, 1967.
MacLennan, Hugh. *Return of the Sphinx*.
Toronto: Macmillan, 1967.
Richler, Mordecai. *The Apprenticeship of Duddy
Kravitz*. New Canadian Library edition.
Toronto: McClelland and Stewart, 1959.
Richler, Mordecai. *Cocksure*. Toronto:
McClelland and Stewart, 1968.
Rosenblatt, Joe. "Bumblebee Dithyramb". In
Impulse, vol. I, no. 3. Toronto: Spring, 1972.
Simpson, Leo. *Arkwright*. Toronto:
Macmillan, 1971.

Film Script:

"The Best Damn Fiddler". In *Encounter:
Canadian Drama in Four Media*, ed. Eugene
Benson. Toronto: Methuen, 1973.

On Film:

Angel. Music by Leonard Cohen. National Film
Board. 1966. Colour. 7 minutes.

Understanding the Messages

In Print:

Grant, George. *Technology and Empire*.
Toronto: Anansi, 1969.
Innis, Harold A. *The Bias of Communication*.
Toronto: University of Toronto Press, 1964.
Innis, Harold A. *The Fur Trade in Canada*.
Toronto: University of Toronto Press,1956.
McDayter, W.E. ed. *A Media Mosaic*. New
York: Holt, 1971.
McLuhan, Marshall. *Understanding Media*.
Toronto: The New American Library of Canada,
1968.
Porter, John. *The Vertical Mosaic*. Toronto:
University of Toronto Press, 1965.

On Film:

This is Marshall McLuhan. McGraw-Hill. 1967.
Colour. 53 minutes.

Epilogue:
Butterfly on Rock

Canadian pioneers used to talk about "making land". By this, they meant working the soil into a form useful for human life.

Canada was also made by generations of men and women who moved from "making land" into "making a social environment": constructing roads, buildings, schools, stores, churches, mills. The land was "made" also by people working out ways of electing governors; ways of coping with sickness, crime, and aggression; ways of celebrating; ways of introducing innovation and of eliminating the obsolete.

Then there is a third way of making a nation. This is the creation of a reflection, an inspiration, a goad and a goal—in art. The artists tell us what they think we are. They help us to hear our own voice, recognize our own shape, laugh at our own follies, rejoice in our own powers. Accepting or rejecting the artists' views, we become more thoroughly ourselves. Now Canadians have never agreed whether they really want a national literature or not—but that very indecision is itself a national characteristic. "Patterns I deny," says the poet George Bowering, "and that/ is part/of a pattern."[1]

The artist in Canada has always been erratic. Who could have guessed from reading C.G.D. Roberts' gentle "Tantramar Revisited" that he would become a teller of harsh and tragic animal stories? Who could have predicted that E.J. Pratt would move from the terse little lyrics of *Newfoundland Verse* into the epic sweep of *Toward the Last Spike?* What in Hugh MacLennan's socio-political *Two Solitudes* foreshadowed the psychological *Each Man's Son?* Read the poetry of Dorothy Livesay and you swing from filigree to prettiness to social wrath and on to personal confession. The country changes, the times change, and the writers change.

[1] George Bowering, "Circus Maximus", in *Fifteen Canadian Poets*, eds. Gary Geddes and Phyllis Bruce (Toronto, 1970), p. 226.

The archetypal image of the artist is the butterfly. Its metamorphosis from pupa to cocoon to winged form typifies the amazing changes that artists undergo. It is brief-lived, bright, and subject to smashing storms. The phrase "Butterfly on Rock" is used as a title of a fine book of literary criticism by Douglas Jones. Jones' book isolates certain themes and images in Canadian Literature and theorizes that through these images Canada's cultural identity is clarified. The artist gives voice to the country. "The cultural vision grows out of the rock, whether the rock is the Laurentian shield or the globe itself."[2] The butterfly—the artist's vision—is the rock's grace.

Metamorphosis in Roles

Canada has not always regarded her artists as her "grace". Sometimes they have seemed her nuisance, sometimes her goad, sometimes her publicists and salesmen, and sometimes her freaky idiot children. The artists' images of themselves and their role has also changed—another surprising metamorphosis.

Mrs. Brooke, in 1769, felt that the artist would be hard put to play any role in Canada. "The rigour of the climate," she says, "suspends the very powers of the understanding; what then must become of those of the imagination?"[3] Too cold for art: a judgment that hasn't altogether disappeared.

For a garrison lady like Mrs. Moodie, the function of the artist was to disregard the climate and the wilderness. Mrs. Moodie wrote to prove to herself and to her neighbours that the human imagination is not subservient to the environment.

A few years later, the notion of the artist was reversed. The theory in early years of the Dominion was that the artist should express the environment. The writer should describe the landscape to the world. "There is something in the autumn that is native to my blood," Bliss Carman wrote.[4] In his poetry, the blood sings a song of scarlet maples, purple asters, golden birches.

[2] Douglas Jones, *Butterfly on Rock* (Toronto, 1970), p. 11.
[3] Frances Brooke, from *The History of Emily Montague*, in *Canadian Anthology*, eds. C.F. Klinck and R.E. Watters (Toronto, 1966), p. 4.
[4] Bliss Carman, "A Vagabond Song", in *Canadian Anthology*, p. 113.

"Painting the native maple" came to seem a foolish job to the artists of a later generation. For Scott and Smith and company the artist's role was to import modern ideas. The artist, they said, is "not in the exporting business, for maple sugar is a sickly and cloying commodity".[5]

"I serve", says the artist of the next generation. "As a mouth I serve".[6] The phrase is Irving Layton's; the idea of the artist's role as that of giving voice to the inarticulate creation is the one emphasized by many of the writers studied in Jones' *Butterfly on Rock.*

Other images of the poet's function follow. Poet as Noah, drawing into the ark of his consciousness all the universe—that is an emergent image of the fifties, explored by Jay Macpherson.[7] Poet as anvil, on whom the new politics of activism are hammered out—that image appears in the sixties. Poet as reader of the world—Gwendolyn MacEwen says:

I should read all things like braille in this season
with my fingers and I should read them
lest I go blind in both eyes reading with
that other eye the final hieroglyph . . .[8]

Then there is the image of the poet as swimmer—Layton's image.[9] ("At the bottom of the sea", Klein once added sardonically.[10])

The shifting images of the artist reflect the shifting nature of his role and of the demands society makes of him. Recently Canadian society and the Canadian artist have reached a new basis of rapport. Three things have happened: new presses have proliferated; the positions of "artist-in-residence", "poet-in-residence", "novelist-in-residence" have opened the university environment to the working artist, without onerous teaching duties attached; and the Canada Council has established generous policies of support. The effect of Canada Council support is psychological as well as financial. Its enormous effect on the work

[5] A.J.M. Smith, "Foreword", in *The Book of Canadian Poetry*, 3rd ed. (Toronto, 1957), p. 32.
[6] Irving Layton, "The Birth of Tragedy", in *Canadian Anthology*, p. 387.
[7] Jay MacPherson, "The Boatman", in *Canadian Anthology*, p. 482.
[8] Gwendolyn MacEwen, "Poems in Braille", in *Fifteen Canadian Poets*, p. 183.
[9] Irving Layton, "The Cold Green Element", in *Canadian Anthology*, p. 388
[10] A.M. Klein, "Portrait of the Poet as Landscape", in *Canadian Anthology*, p. 344.

of the artists is expressed by bill bissett in a note to *nobody owns th earth:*

Receivd three Canada council grants without which all that ive bin abul to help do cud no way have happend.[11]

The role of the artist changes when he is given official sanction—and the images of the artist change again. Why watch the images? Because this is the way artists' work, obliquely, by indirection, by correlatives and metaphors. Looking at the images, we clarify the object:

Undersense the kept webs widen of spidery light and sudden centres of comprehension.[12]

These are Gwendolyn MacEwen's words about the way the poetic mind works. MacEwen takes us back to the image of the butterfly:

butterflies of monarch myriad with orange alphabets on their wings are flying dictionaries.[13]

Alphabet of Authors

The artists who spell out Canada's cultural life at this moment are indeed myriad. An alphabet of established authors could be compiled, from "Acorn" to "Zieroth", listing all the writers appearing steadily now with poetry, fiction, film-scripts, non-fiction. Compiling such a list is easy today because of the sudden fluttering of new collections of poetry, collections of short stories, collections of speculative essays. *Read Canadian* is the title of a book directing us to all sorts of reading possiblities.[14] *Survival* is the grimmer title of a similar publication.[15] Even without such bibliographic aids it is easy to see evidence of the booksellers' efforts to sell Canadian writing in bright forms.

[11] bill bissett, *nobody owns th earth*, (Toronto, 1971).
[12] Gwendolyn MacEwen, "Poem for G. W.", in *Canadian Anthology*, p. 491.
[13] Gwendolyn MacEwen, "Poem for G. W.".
[14] Robert Fulford, David Godfrey, and Abraham Rotstein, eds., *Read Canadian* (Toronto, 1972).
[15] Margaret Atwood, *Survival*, (Toronto, 1972).

As we complete the dictionary of authors, the list changes. As we complete the analysis of themes and topics in Canadian Literature, they change too. New media, new messages, and new names pressing in, making a brand-new alphabet of Canadian writers. Call the new roll quickly before it changes! It may run like this: Amabile, Blaise, Cooperman, Davey, Everson, Faessler, Gibson, Helwig, Inkster, Jonas, Kearnes, Ludwig, Marshall, Newman, Ondaatje, Persky, Q?, Rosenthal, Schroeder, Thompson, Ulrich, Valgardson, Wayman, X?, Yates, Zend.

Compiling the list, we would still have trouble naming a "Q" or an "X". That's as it should be, leaving room for query and for mystery.

Who is missing from such a list? Perhaps the best writer in Canada today. Perhaps, like Pratt, he won't publish till he's forty. Perhaps like Purdy, he won't find a big audience till he's fifty. Perhaps, like Birney, he'll begin innovating, stretching into a new dimension when he's sixty. Many of our best Canadian poets next year—same as last year—will be "late apples". The same can be predicted for prose writers, if we remember Stephen Leacock, Frederick Philip Grove, and Ethel Wilson. Don't be surprised if some of the little old ladies or the quiet middle-aged fellows suddenly start a literature of the seventies percolating. But then again—we have some early shiners too: James Reaney, Rosanna Leprohon, Morley Callaghan, all under twenty when producing some of their best work. So it's hard to say whether our alphabetical net has caught any of the real new writers; indeed it doesn't catch all those already showing promise. We should keep the list open. Keep an eye on the young Canadians, the people still in school. They are ready to respond with incredible alacrity to any appeal to their writing ability.

Whoever they are, our new writers will be in part determined by their life in the Canadian environment. Of all the colours in the spectrum, their eyes will be adjusted to those tints that show up in Canadian light. Of all the sounds in the air, they will hear those that fit in with the Canadian accent. But it is

unlikely that a modern writer will pin himself down to a narrowly
Canadian scene or theme.

As we come to the end of a study of Canadian writing
we know the review is not complete. We have merely marked
a few butterfles. The phrase is Irving Layton's:

We'll mark the butterflies . . .
with tiny wristwatches on their wings.[16]

The phrase is both an accurate description of the appearance
of design on the butterfly's wing, and also a metaphor implying
the impermanence of butterflies—and of the watching artist.

Like the butterfly, like art itself, Canada is in a state of
metamorphosis. Canada is a mystery; and Canada is a miracle.
And we have the literature to prove it.

The rock has borne this:
The butterfly is the rock's grace.[17]

[16] Irving Layton, "The
Fertile Muck", in *Fifteen
Canadian Poets*, p. 49.
[17] Irving Layton,
"Butterfly on Rock", in
Collected Poems (Toronto,
1965), p. 282.

For Further Study

Metamorphosis in Roles

In Print:

Birney, Earle. *The Writing and Reading of Poetry*. New York: Holt, 1971.
Cameron, Donald. *Conversations with Canadian Novelists*. Toronto: Macmillan, 1972.
Clarkson, Stephen, ed. *Visions 2020*. Edmonton: Hurtig, 1970.
Colombo, J.R. *How Do I Love Thee?* Edmonton: Hurtig, 1970.
Geddes, Gary. *Canadian Poetry and Poetics*. Toronto: Oxford, 1969.
Jones, Douglas. *Butterfly on Rock*. Toronto: University of Toronto Press, 1970.
Macpherson, Jay. *The Boatman*. Toronto: Oxford, 1968.

On Record:

Bowering, George. Poems. *Canadian Poets I*. Toronto: Canadian Broadcasting Corporation. 1966.
MacEwen, Gwendolyn. Poems. *Canadian Poets I*. Toronto: Canadian Broadcasting Corporation. 1966.
Webb, Phyllis. Poems. *Canadian Poets I*. Toronto: Canadian Broadcasting Corporation. 1966.

On Tape:

Atwood, Margaret. *The Twist of Feeling*. Toronto: Canadian Broadcasting Corporation Learning Systems. 1972. 30 minutes.
Frye, Northrop. *The Canadian Imagination*. Toronto: Canadian Broadcasting Corporation Learning Systems. 1971. 30 minutes.

MacLennan, Hugh; Al Purdy; Miriam Waddington. *My Country Tis of Thee*. Toronto: Canadian Broadcasting Corporation Learning Systems. 1971. 1 hour.
Layton, Irving. *Power and Poetry*. Toronto: Canadian Broadcasting Corporation Learning Systems. 1972.

Alphabet of Authors

In Print:

Atwood, Margaret. *The Circle Game*. Toronto: Anansi, 1967.
Bacque, James. *Big Lonely*. Toronto: New Press, 1970.
Bowering, George. *The Gangs of Kosmos*. Toronto: Anasi, 1969.
Coleman, Victor. *One/Eye/Love*. Toronto: Coach House, 1967.
Davies, Robertson. *Manticore*. Toronto: Macmillan, 1972.
Dudek, Louis. *Collected Poetry*. Montreal: Delta, 1971.
Everson, R.G. *The Dark is not so Dark*. Montreal: Delta, 1969.
Fetherling, Douglas, ed. *Thumbprints*. Toronto: Peter Martin, 1969.
Gotlieb, Phyllis. *Ordinary, Moving*. Toronto: Oxford, 1969.
Grier, Eldon. *Selected Poems*. Montreal: Delta, 1971.
Helwig, David. *The Sign of the Gunman*. Ottawa: Oberon, 1969.
Hood, Hugh. *A Game of Touch*. Toronto: Longmans, 1970.
Johnston, George. *The Cruising Auk*. Toronto: Oxford, 1959.

Kilgallin, Tony, ed. *The Canadian Short Story.*
New York: Holt, 1971.
Kroetsch, Robert; J. Baque; Paul Gravel.
Creation. Toronto: New Press, 1972.
Lee, Ronald. *Goddam Gypsy.* Montreal:
Tundra, 1971.
Marshall, Tom. *Magic Water.* Kingston:
Quarry, 1971.
Mayne, Seymour. *Mouth.* Kingston: Quarry,
1970.
Nowlan, Alden. *Bread, Wine and Salt.*
Toronto: Clarke, Irwin, 1967.
Newlove, John. *Black Night Window.*
Toronto: McClelland and Stewart, 1968.
Ondaatje, Michael. *The Collected Works of Billy
the Kid.* Toronto: Anansi, 1970.
Peate, Mary. *The Girl in a Red River Coat.*
Toronto: Clarke, Irwin, 1970.

Purdy, Alfred. *Wild Grape Wine.* Toronto:
McClelland and Stewart, 1968.
Scott, Chris. *Bartleby.* Toronto: Anansi, 1971.
Souster, Raymond. *Colour of the Times.*
Toronto: Ryerson, 1964.
Vanier, Jean. *Tears of Silence.* Toronto: Griffin,
1971.
Waddington, Miriam. *Say Yes.* Toronto:
Oxford, 1969.
Wainwright, Andy. *Moving Outward.*
Toronto: New Press, 1970.
Wright, Richard. *The Weekend Man.* Toronto:
Macmillan, 1970.
Wall, Ann, ed. *Mindscapes.* Toronto: Anansi,
1971. Poems by Zieroth, Jiles, Musgrave and
Wayman.
Yates, J. Michael. *Great Bear Lake Meditations.*
Ottawa: Oberon, 1970.

Survey Chart

Historical Chronology	Canadian Literary Events	Literary Events Elsewhere
1497—John Cabot discovers Newfoundland		
1534—Jacques Cartier travels up the St. Lawrence as far as Montreal		1516—Thomas More, *Utopia*
	1576—Earliest extant Canadian Literature —Accounts of voyageurs and explorers	
1578—Francis Drake's *Golden Hind* skirts the West Coast		
1583—Newfoundland claimed for Britain		
		1589—Edmund Spenser, *The Faerie Queene*
	1598-1600—Richard Hakluyt's *Principal Navigations* covers voyages to Canada	
1603—Champlain founds Port Royal		
1608—Founding of Quebec City	1608—Cultural development of English Canada lags far behind that of the French-Canadian territories —No literary work of the 17th century with Canada as its main subject	
1610—Hudson explores Hudson and James Bays		
		1611—William Shakespeare, *The Tempest* —King James Version of the Bible
		1624—John Smith, *The General History of Virginia**
1632—Jesuits arrive in the Great Lakes region to set up missions	1632—*The Jesuit Relations,* important documents recording the progress of the missions	

Note: * marks American publication

Historical Chronology	Canadian Literary Events	Literary Events Elsewhere
	1641—Fr. Brébeuf, "Jesous Ahatonhia" (Huron Christmas Carol)	
1648-49—Fort Ste. Marie destroyed		
		1650—Anne Bradstreet, *The Tenth Muse Lately Sprung up in America**
1654—Radisson and Groseillers begin exploration west of the Great Lakes		
		1662—Michael Wigglesworth, *Day of Doom**
	1668-1669—Pierre Radisson, *Voyages*	1667—John Milton, *Paradise Lost*
1670—Charter of the Hudson's Bay Co.		
		1678—John Bunyan, *Pilgrim's Progress*
1697—England's maritime settlements ceded to France		
	circa 1700—Henry Kelsey, *Diary of Hudson's Bay*	
		1702—Cotton Mather, *Magralia Christi Americana**
		1711-14—Joseph Addison and Richard Steele, *The Spectator*
1713—Treaty of Utrecht, France yields possession of Hudson Bay, Acadia and Newfoundland to Britain		
		1719—Daniel Defoe, *Robinson Crusoe*
		1726—Jonathan Swift, *Gulliver's Travels*
		1730—James Thomson, *The Seasons*
1731—Pierre de la Verendrye initiates the establishment of fur-trading posts on the prairies		
		1733-1734—Alexander Pope, *An Essay on Criticism, An Essay on Man*
	1736—John Gyles, *Memoirs of Old Adventures*	

Historical Chronology	Canadian Literary Events	Literary Events Elsewhere
		1740—Samuel Richardson, *Pamela*
		1741—Jonathan Edward, *Sinners in the Hands of an Angry God**
1749—First permanent English settlement at Halifax		1749—Henry Fielding, *Tom Jones*
	1751—Bartholomew Green establishes the first printing press at Halifax	1751—Thomas Gray, *Elegy Written in a Country Churchyard*
	1752—*Halifax Gazette* established	
	—Joseph Robson, *An Account of Six Years Residence on Hudson's Bay*	
1755—Expulsion of Acadians from Nova Scotia		
1756—Seven Years' War begins		
		1758—Benjamin Franklin, *The Way to Wealth**
1759—Battle of the Plains of Abraham, British rule established		1759—Samuel Johnson, *Rasselas*
1760-1776—Travels of Alexander Henry		1760—James Macpherson, *Ossian*
1763—Treaty of Paris, Britain gains control of most French possessions in the northern New World		
1763-1764—Pontiac's conspiracy, massacre at Michilimackinac	1764—*Quebec Gazette/La Gazette de Québec* established	
	1766—Nova Scotia *Gazette* published	1765—Bishop Percy, *Reliques*
		1766—Oliver Goldsmith, *The Vicar of Wakefield*
	1769—*Nova Scotia Chronicle and Weekly Advertiser,* the third Nova Scotian newspaper	
	—Frances Brooke, *The History of Emily Montague*, first Canadian novel and first novel emanating from any part of North America	
		1770—Oliver Goldsmith, *The Deserted Village*

Historical Chronology	Canadian Literary Events	Literary Events Elsewhere
1774—Quebec Act guarantees French-Canadian liberties		
1776—American War of Independence, first United Empire Loyalists come to Maritimes and "Ontario"		
		1777—Richard B. Sheridan, *School for Scandal*
1778—James Cook arrives at Nootka		
	1780—John Howe founds the *Halifax Journal*	
		1782—St. Jean de Crèvecouer, *Letters From an American Farmer**
1783—North West Company formed —Treaty of Versailles gives U.S.A. possession of the Ohio, the Mississippi, and much of the Great Lakes regions —Loyalists settle in Maritimes	1783—*Royal St. John's Gazette* established in New Brunswick which later becomes the *St. John's Gazette*	
1784—New Brunswick erected as Province	1784—James Cook, *A Voyage to the Pacific Ocean . . .*	1784—Thomas Jefferson, *The Declaration of Independence**
	1785—Fleury Masplet founds the *Montreal Gazette,* a bilingual publication	
		1786—Robert Burns, *Poems,* Kilmarnock edition
	1787—*Royal American Gazette* established on Prince Edward Island	
		1788—Philip Freneau, "The Indian Burying Ground"*
1789-1793—Alexander Mackenzie's voyages		1789—Benjamin Franklin, *Autobiography** —William Blake, *Songs of Innocence and Experience*
1791—The Constitutional Act, separation of Upper and Lower Canada		1791—James Boswell, *Life of Samuel Johnson* —Thomas Paine, *The Rights of Man**

Historical Chronology	Canadian Literary Events	Literary Events Elsewhere
	1793—Lady Simcoe's *Journal* —Louis Roy publishes the *Upper Canada Gazette* at Niagara-on-the-Lake	
1794—The Napoleonic Wars encourage the Canadian lumber trade		
	1795—Samuel Hearne, *Journey . . . to the Northern Ocean*	
1796—Road-building begins in the Maritimes and Canada	1796—William Cobbett, *Peter Porcupine*	
	1799—Isaac Weld, *Travels . . .*	
		1800—William Wordsworth, *Lyrical Ballads*
	1801—Alexander Mackenzie, *Voyages from Montreal . . .* —Charles Vancouver, *A Voyage of Discovery . . .*	
	1806—Henry Alline, *Life and Journal*	1806—Thomas Moore, "Canadian Boat Song"
	1807—George Heriot, *Travels through the Canadas*	
1808—Simon Fraser explores the Fraser Canyon		
1809—Steamship service opens on the St. Lawrence, Montreal-to-Quebec City	1809—Alexander Henry, *Travels and Adventures . . .*	
	1810—Stephen Miles publishes the *Kingston Gazette* —John Lambert, *Travels through Canada . . .*	1810—Sir Walter Scott, *Lady of the Lake*
1812—War with the U.S. —Red River Settlement established	1812—War produces many anonymous ballads —John Richardson, *War of 1812*	
1813—Death of Tecumseh at Moraviatown		1813—Jane Austen, *Pride and Prejudice*
		1814—Sir Walter Scott, *Waverley*
1815—Wave of European emigration to Canada following the Napoleonic Wars		
1815-1840—Enforced emigration to the New World from Scottish Highlands		
1816—Skirmish at Seven Oaks		1816—Mary Wollstonecraft Shelley, *Frankenstein*

Historical Chronology	Canadian Literary Events	Literary Events Elsewhere
1817—Rush-Bagot treaty cuts naval armament off the Great Lakes		
		1818—George Gordon, Lord Byron, *Childe Harold's grimage*
		1819—John Keats, *Odes*
		1820—Percy Bysshe Shelley, *Prometheus Unbound*
		—Washington Irving, *Ske Book**
	1821—Thomas McCulloch, *Letters of Mephibosheth Stepsure* appear in *Acadian Recorder*	
	1823—John Franklin, *Journey to the Polar Sea*	
	1824—Julia Beckwith, *St. Ursula's Convent*	
	1825—Oliver Goldsmith, *The Risng Village*	
		1826—James Fenimore Coop *The Last of the Mohica*
	1828—John Richardson, *Tecumseh*	
1829—Completion of the Welland Canal		
1831—James Ross discovers the North Magnetic Pole	1831—John Galt, *Bogle Corbet*	1831—Edgar Allan Poe, *Poem*
1832—Rideau Canal opened	1832—John Richardson, *Wacousta*	1832—William Cullen Bryant, Forest Hymn''*
	—Tiger Dunlop, *Statistical Sketches of Upper Canada*	
		1833—Thomas Carlyle, *Sarto Resartus*
		1834—Edward Bulwer-Lytton, *Last Days of Pompeii*
1836—First Canadian Railway, LaPrairie-St. John's, P.Q.	1836—Catherine Parr Traill, *The Backwoods of Canada*	1836—Charles Dickens, *Pickv Papers*
	—Thomas Haliburton, *Sayings and Doings of Sam Slick, The Clockmaker* (first series)	—Ralph Waldo Emerson *Nature**

Historical Chronology	Canadian Literary Events	Literary Events Elsewhere
1837—Rebellions in Upper and Lower Canadas —Militant reform groups headed by Louis Joseph Papineau and William Lyon Mackenzie	1837—A. Gerin-Lajoie, "Un Canadien Errant"	1837—Nathaniel Hawthorne, *Twice-Told Tales**
	1838-1851—*The Literary Garland,* society gossip, poems, dramatic sketches —Anna Jameson, *Winter Studies and Summer Rambles*	
1839—Lord Durham's *Report* —Aroostook War on New Brunswick-Maine border		
		1840—Edgar Allan Poe, *Tales**
1841—Union of the Canadas	1841—James Evans publishes the *Cree Syllabic Hymn Book*	1841—James Fenimore Cooper, *Deerslayer** —Ralph Waldo Emerson, "Self-Reliance"*
	1842—R.H. Bonnycastle, *Newfoundland in 1842* —Standish Haliburton, *The Attaché* —Standish O'Grady, *The Emigrant, A Poem*	1842—Alfred, Lord Tennyson, *Collected Poems*
	1843—Thomas Haliburton, *The Attaché*	
1844—U.S. election slogan: "54'40 or Fight"	1844—Joseph Doutre, *Les Fiancés de 1812*	
	1845—F.-X. Garneau, *Histoire du Canada*	
1846—Britain gives up claim to Oregon, loss of Pacific outlet for fur trade	1846—George Warburton, *Hochelaga*	
	1847—John Richardson, *Eight Years in Canada*	1847—Charlotte Brontë, *Jane Eyre* —William Makepeace Thackeray, *Vanity Fair* —Emily Brontë, *Wuthering Heights* —Henry W. Longfellow, *Evangeline*
	1848—Royal Lyceum Theatre opens in Toronto —P. Lacombe, *La Terre Paternelle* —Alexander Ross, *Adventures of the first settlers on the Oregon or Columbia River*	

Historical Chronology **Canadian Literary Events** **Literary Events Elsewhere**

Historical Chronology	Canadian Literary Events	Literary Events Elsewhere
1849—Vancouver Island Colony established		1849—Charles Dickens, *David Copperfield*
1849-1864—Political deadlock in Canada East and West		—Thomas Macaulay, *History*
1850—Poverty and successive potato famines cause mass Irish immigration into British North America		1850—Nathaniel Hawthorne, *The Scarlet Letter**
		1851—Herman Melville, *Moby Dick**
		—John Ruskin, *Stones of Venice*
	1852—Susanna Moodie, *Roughing It in the Bush*	1852—Harriet Beecher Stowe, *Uncle Tom's Cabin**
	1853—P.J.O. Chauveau, *Charles Guérin*	
	—Toronto *Globe* becomes a daily newspaper	
	—Jacob Bailey, *The Frontier Missionary*	
1854—Reciprocity Treaty with U.S.A.		1854—Henry David Thoreau, *Walden**
	1855—Samuel Strickland, *Twenty-Seven Years in Canada*	1855—Robert Browning, *Men and Women*
		—H.W. Longfellow, "Hiawatha"*
		—Walt Whitman, *Leaves of Grass**
	1856—Mrs. Traill, *Little Mary and her Nurse*	
	—Charles Sangster, *The St. Lawrence and the Saguenay*	
	—R.M. Ballantyne, *The Young Fur Traders*	
1857—Ottawa chosen as national capital by Queen Victoria	1857—Charles Heavysege, *Saul*	1857—Anthony Trollope, *Barchester Towers*
1857-1860—John Palliser leads Prairie explorations		—Oliver Wendell Holmes, *The Autocrat of the Breakfast Table**
1858—Fraser River Gold Rush in British Columbia	1858—Four newspapers published in Victoria including the *Victoria Gazette* and the *British Gazette* by Amor de Cosmos	
	—D'Arcy McGee, *Canadian Ballads*	

Historical Chronology	Canadian Literary Events	Literary Events Elsewhere
1859—Charles Darwin, *The Origin of Species*	1859—Wm. Buckingham and Wm. Coldwell found the *Norwester* newspaper —Paul Kane, *Wandering of an Artist*	1859—Edward Fitzgerald, *Omar Khayyam*
		1860—George Eliot, *Mill on the Floss*
	1861—Alexander MacLachlan, *The Emigrant* —John Robson founds the *British Columbian* —Mrs. Leprohon, *Le Manoir de Villerai*	
1862-1865—Building of Cariboo Road		
	1863—P.A. de Gaspé, *Les Anciens Canadiens* 1863-1906—J.M. LeMoine, *Maple Leaves* (6 vols.)	
1864—Charlottetown Conference —Quebec Conference —Karl Marx, *Communist Manifesto*	1864—Mrs. Leprohon, *Antoinette de Mirecourt* —E.H. Dewart (ed.), *Selections from Canadian Poets*	
	1865—Viscount Milton and W.B. Cheadle, *The North-West Passage by Land*	1865—Lewis Carroll, *Alice in Wonderland* 1865-1892—Francis Parkman, *France and England in North America**
1866—Fenian Raids		1866—J.G. Whittier, ''Snow-Bound''*
1867—Confederation, John A. MacDonald Canada's first Prime Minister —U.S. purchases Alaska from Russia	1867—J.H. Morgan, *Bibliotheca Canadensis*	
	1868—Charles Mair, *Dreamland and Other Poems*	
1869-1871—Red River Rebellion		1869—Mark Twain, *Innocents Abroad**
1870—''Canada First'' Movement —Manitoba created as province —Northwest Territories transferred to Canada by Hudson's Bay Company		1870—D.G. Rossetti, *Poems* —Bret Harte, *The Luck of Roaring Camp and Other Sketches**

Historical Chronology	Canadian Literary Events	Literary Events Elsewhere
1871—Treaty of Washington —British Columbia enters Confederation	1871—Alexander Begg, *Dot-it-Down* 1872—Wm. F. Butler, *The Great Lone Land* —James Marmette, *L'Intendant Bigot* 1872-78—*Canadian Monthly and National Review* published	1871—Edward Eggleston, *Hoosier Schoolmaster**
1873—Royal Canadian Mounted Police formed	1873—George M. Grant, *Ocean to Ocean* 1874—Joseph Howe, *Poems and Essays* —Agnes Machar, *For King and Country* 1875—Earl of Southesk, *Saskatchewan and the Rocky Mountains*	
1876—Intercolonial Railway completed to Halifax		1876—Mark Twain, *The Adventures of Tom Sawyer**
	1877—William Kirby, *The Golden Dog* —J.T. Lesperance, *Les Bastonnais* 1878-1882—*Rose-Belford's Magazine* in Toronto	1877—Henry James, *The American** 1878—Thomas Hardy, *Return of the Native*
1880—"O Canada" composed by Calixa Lavallée 1881—Royal Canadian Academy of Art established 1882—Royal Society of Canada founded	1880—Charles G.D. Roberts, *Orion* 1881—J.C. Dent, *The Last Forty Years* 1882—James Marmotte, *Les Machabees de la Nouvelle France* —A. Tonas, *Un Heros Canadien* 1883-1896—*The Week* published in Toronto 1884—I.V. Crawford, *Old Spookses Pass and Other Poems*	1880—Lew Wallace, *Ben Hur** 1882—Robert Louis Stevenson, *Treasure Island* 1884—Mark Twain, *Huckleberry Finn**
1885—The second Riel Rebellion —Louis Riel hanged 1886—Canadian Pacific Railway completed	1886—C.G.D. Roberts, *In Divers Tones* 1887-1898—William Kingsford, *History of Canada*	1885—Wm. Dean Howells, *Rise of Silas Lapham** 1886—Robert Louis Stevenson, *Dr. Jekyll and Mr. Hyde*

Historical Chronology	Canadian Literary Events	Literary Events Elsewhere
	1888—Archibald Lampman, *Among the Millet* —James de Mille, *Strange Manuscript* 1889—W.D. Lighthall (ed.), *Songs of the Great Dominion* 1890—Sara Jeannette Duncan, *A Social Departure*	1888—J.M. Barrie, *Auld Licht Idylls* 1889—A.C. Swinburne, *Poems and Ballads* 1890—Emily Dickinson, *Poems** —James Frazer, *The Golden Bough* 1891—Oscar Wilde, *Portrait of Dorian Gray* —Arthur Conan Doyle, *Sherlock Holmes*
1892—Stanley Cup for Hockey donated by Governor-General	1892—Gilbert Parker, *Pierre and his People* 1893—Bliss Carmen, *Low Tide on Grand Pré* —*Queen's Quarterly* established —Archibald Lampman, *Lyrics from the Earth* 1894—Marshall Saunders, *Beautiful Joe* —Robert Barr, *In the Midst of Alarms* —K. Phillips-Wolley, *Gold, Gold in Cariboo!*	 1893—Ian Maclaren, *Beside the Bonnie Briar Bush* 1894—George Du Maurier, *Trilby*
		1895—W.B. Yeats, *Poems* —Stephen Crane, *Red Badge of Courage** —Rudyard Kipling, *Barrack Room Ballads*
1896—Wilfrid Laurier elected Prime Minister	1896—D.C. Scott, *In the Village of Viger* —Gilbert Parker, *The Seats of the Mighty*	1896—A.E. Houseman, *A Shropshire Lad* —Sarah Orne Jewett, *Country of the Pointed Firs**
1897—Manitoba School compromise by Laurier —Klondike Gold Rush —First Women's Institute founded by Adelaide Hoodless	1897—W.H. Drummond, *The Habitant* 1897-1900—J.C. Hopkins (ed.), *Canada: An Encyclopaedia*	1897—C.M. Sheldon, *In His Steps**

Historical Chronology	Canadian Literary Events	Literary Events Elsewhere
1898—Yukon created as a separate territory	1898—E.T. Seton, *Wild Animals I Have Known* —Ralph Connor, *Black Rock*	1898—George Bernard Shaw, *Plays Pleasant and Unpleasant*
1899—Boer War	1899—Ralph Connor, *The Sky Pilot*	
1900—Sigmund Freud, *Interpretation of Dreams*	1900—Archibald Lampman, *Collected Poems*	1900—Joseph Conrad, *Lord Jim* —Theodore Dreiser, *Sister Carrie**
1901—Marconi receives trans-Atlantic wireless message at St John's, Newfoundland	1901—W.H. Drummond, *Johnny Courteau* —Ralph Connor, *The Man from Glengarry*	1901—Frank Norris, *The Octopus**
	1902—C.G.D. Roberts, *Kindred of the Wild*	1902—Owen Wister, *The Virginian** —E.A. Robinson, "Richard Cory"*
1903—Wright Brothers' flight	1903-1908—*Makers of Canada*	1903—Frank Norris, *The Pit** —Henry James, *The Ambassadors** —Jack London, *Call of the Wild**
1904—Charles Saunders develops Marquis wheat	1904—S.J. Duncan, *The Imperialist* —Norman Duncan, *Dr. Luke of the Labrador*	1904—J. M. Barrie, *Peter Pan*
1905—Albert Einstein, Theory of Relativity	1905—W.H. Drummond, *The Voyageur*	
	1906—Marion Keith, *The Silver Maple* —Agnes Machar, *Roland Graeme, Knight*	1906—John Galsworthy, *Man of Property* —Upton Sinclair, *The Jungle**
1907—First air flight in Canada by Alexander Graham Bell's Cygnet	1907—Robert Service, *Songs of a Sourdough* —W.A. Fraser, *The Lone Furrow*	
	1908—L.M. Montgomery, *Anne of Green Gables* —Nellie McClung, *Sowing Seeds in Danny*	
1909—Boundary Waters Treaty, formation of International Joint Commisssion with the U.S. —Perry reaches the North Pole —Ford's Model T		
		1910—W.B. Yeats, *The Green Helmet*

Historical Chronology	Canadian Literary Events	Literary Events Elsewhere
1911—Robert Borden elected Prime Minister	1911—Stephen Leacock, *Nonsense Novels* —Pauline Johnson, *Legends of Vancouver*	
1912—Titanic sinks	1912—Stephen Leacock, *Sunshine Sketches of a Little Town* —Basil King, *The Street Called Straight* —Pauline Johnson, *Flint and Feather*	1912—*Poetry Magazine* founded in Chicago —Ezra Pound, *Ripostes**
	1913—Marjorie Pickthall, *The Drift of Pinions* —Louis Hemon, *Maria Chapdelaine*	1913—D.H. Lawrence, *Sons and Lovers* —Willa Cather, *O! Pioneers**
1914—World War I begins		1914—Robert Frost, *North of Boston** —Vachel Lindsay, *The Congo*
	1915—A.J. Stringer, *The Prairie Wife* —Peter McArthur, *In Pastures Green*	1915—Somerset Maugham, *Of Human Bondage* —Edgar Lee Masters, *Spoon River Anthology**
1916—Karl Jung, *Psychology of the Unconscious*		1916—James Joyce, *A Portrait of the Artist as a Young Man* —E.A. Robinson, *Man Against the Sky** —Carl Sandburg, *Chicago Poems* —T.S. Eliot, *Prufrock and other Poems*
1917—Conscription Crisis —*"Deux Nations"* —Bolshevik Revolution —Franchise extended to women in Canadian soldiers' families	1917—Frank Packard, *Jimmy Dale, Detective*	
1918—Easter Riots in Quebec		1918—G.M. Hopkins, *Poems*
1919—Winnipeg General Strike —U.S. Prohibition begins —Canada seated at Peace Conference —Group of Seven formed	1919—John McCrae, "In Flanders Fields" —*Canadian Bookman* established	1919—Sherwood Anderson, *Winesburg Ohio** —Somerset Maugham, *The Moon and Sixpence* —W.B. Yeats, *Wild Swans at Coole*
1920—Arthur Meighen elected Prime Minister	1920—*Canadian Forum* begins publication	

Historical Chronology	Canadian Literary Events	Literary Events Elsewhere
1921—William Lyon Mackenzie King elected Prime Minister —Civil War in Ireland —Imperial Conference —Banting and Best discover insulin	1921—Canadian Author's Association established —*Dalhousie Review* established	1921—William Carlos Williams, *Sour Grapes** —Sinclair Lewis, *Main Street**
1922—Mussolini comes to power	1922—F.P. Grove, *Over Prairie Trails* —M. Pickthall, *The Woodcarver's Wife*	1922—Edith Sitwell, *Façade* —James Joyce, *Ulysses* —T.S. Eliot, *The Wasteland** —John Galsworthy, *The Forsythe Saga* —Eugene O'Neill, *Hairy Ape* —Sinclair Lewis, *Babbitt**
1923—Hitler's Munich Putsch —U.S.S.R. established —Canada signs Halibut Treaty as independent power	1923—Laura Salverson, *The Viking Heart* —Mazo de la Roche, *Possession*	1923—e.e. cummings, *Tulips and Chimneys** —Wallace Stevens, *Harmonium** —George Bernard Shaw, *Saint Joan* —Franz Kafka, *The Trial*
	1924—F.O.Grove, *Settlers of the Marsh* —J.D. Logan, D.G. French (eds.), *Highways of Canadian Literature*	1924—E.M. Forster, *Passage to India* —Thomas Mann, *Magic Mountain*
1925—Lucarno Treaties	1925—M. Ostenso, *Wild Geese*	1925—Virginia Woolf, *Mrs. Dalloway* —F. Scott Fitzgerald, *The Great Gatsby** —Theodore Dreiser, *American Tragedy**
	1926—L.M. Montgomery, *The Blue Castle* —R.J.C. Stead, *Grain*	1926—Ezra Pound, *Personae** —Ernest Hemingway, *The Sun Also Rises** —Sean O'Casey, *Plough and the Stars*
1927—Lindbergh's flight —Canada's first representative in Washington	1927—Mazo de la Roche, *Jalna* —Lorne Pierce, *Outline of Canadian Literature* —*McGill Fortnightly Review*	
	1928—Morley Callaghan, *Strange Fugitive*	1928—Aldous Huxley, *Point Counter Point* —D. H. Lawrence, *Lady Chatterley's Lover*

Historical Chronology	Canadian Literary Events	Literary Events Elsewhere
1929—Beginning of the Great Depression	1929—Raymond Knister, *Short Stories; White Narcissus*	1929—William Faulkner, *The Sound and the Fury** —Ernest Hemingway, *Farewell to Arms** —Thomas Wolfe, *Look Homeward Angel**
1930—R.B. Bennett elected Prime Minister —Beaverbrook leads an "Empire Crusade" in Britain	1930—H.A. Innis, *The Fur Trade in Canada* —W.W.E. Ross, *Laconics*	1930—Hart Crane, *The Bridge** —John Dos Passos, *42nd Parallel**
1931—Statute of Westminster, self-government within the Empire attained		1931—Eugene O'Neill, *Mourning Becomes Electra**
1932—Founding of the CCF—J.S. Woodsworth first leader —establishment of the Canadian Radio Broadcasting Commission which later becomes the CBC —Farmers' delegations to Ottawa	1932—E.J. Pratt, *Many Moods*	1932—W.H. Auden, *The Orators* —Aldous Huxley, *Brave New World* —Erskine Caldwell, *Tobacco Road**
1933—"New Deal" in the U.S.	1933—F.P. Grove, *Fruits of the Earth*	1933—Stephen Spender, *Poems* —Gertrude Stein, *Autobiography of Alice B. Toklas**
	1934—Morley Callaghan, *Such is my Beloved* —Jean-Charles Harvey, *Les Demi-Civilises*	1934—Nathanael West, *A Cool Million* —Henry Miller, *Tropic of Cancer**
1935—Wheat Board re-established —Social Credit Party formed under William Aberhart in Alberta —L'Union Nationale formed under Maurice Duplessis —At Regina, RCMP break up "March to Ottawa" of unemployed	1935—Leo Kennedy, *The Shrouding* —Frederick Niven, *The Flying Years* —Initiation of annual *Letters in Canada* in the *University of Toronto Quarterly* —E.J. Pratt, *Titanic* —Grey Owl, *Pilgrim's of the Wild*	1935—Thomas Wolfe, *Of Time and the River**
1936—Spanish Civil War begins —Padlock Law in Quebec —Abdication crisis in England	1936—Phillip Child, *God's Sparrows* —F.R. Scott (ed.), *New Provinces* —*New Frontier* founded	1936—Roy Campbell, *Gum Trees*

Historical Chronology	Canadian Literary Events	Literary Events Elsewhere
1937—Governor General's Awards established	1937—Morley Callaghan, *More Joy in Heaven* —Donald Creighton, *The Commercial Empire of the St. Lawrence*	1937—John Steinbeck, *Of Mice and Men** —Archibald MacLeish, *Fall of the City**
	1938—Ringuet, *Trente Arpents* —Kenneth Leslie, *By Stubborn Stars*	1938—John Buchan, *39 Steps* —e.e. cummings, *Collected Poems**
1939—Canada enters World War II —National Film Board established —Visit to Canada of King George VI and Queen Elizabeth	1939—Anne Marriott, *The Wind our Enemy* —Irene Baird, *Waste Heritage* —Laura Salverson, *Confessions of an Immigrant's Daughter*	1939—Dylan Thomas, *Selected Writings* —John Steinbeck, *Grapes of Wrath** —James Joyce, *Finnegan's Wake* —W.H. Auden, *Journey to War*
1940—Rowell-Sirois Report on federal-provincial powers —Battle of Britain involves Canadian airmen	1940—A.M. Klein, *Hath Not a Jew* —E.J. Pratt, *Brébeuf and his Brethren*	1940—Ernest Hemingway, *For Whom the Bell Tolls** —Graham Greene, *The Power and the Glory* —Carson McCullers, *The Heart is a Lonely Hunter** —Richard Wright, *Native Son**
1941—Hitler invades Russia —Pearl Harbour —Atlantic Charter signed by U.S. and U.K.	1941—Hugh MacLennan, *Barometer Rising* —Sinclair Ross, *As for Me and My House* —Emily Carr, *Klee Wyck*	1941—Noel Coward, *Blithe Spirit* —Budd Schulberg, *What Makes Sammy Run?*
1942—Conscription plebiscite —Dieppe Raid —Food rationing in effect	1942—Thomas Raddall, *His Majesty's Yankees* —Earle Birney, *David and other Poems* —*First Statement* founded by John Sutherland —*Preview* founded by Patrick Anderson	
1943—Quebec Conference of Allied leaders	1943—A.J.M. Smith, *News of the Phoenix*	1943—William Saroyan, *The Human Comedy** —T.S. Eliot, *Four Quartets** —Delmore Schwartz, *Genesis**
1944—D-Day invasion of France	1944—Roger Lemelin, *Au Bout de la Pente Douce* —Gwethalyn Graham, *Earth and High Heaven* —Hugh Garner, *The Storm Below*	

Historical Chronology	Canadian Literary Events	Literary Events Elsewhere
	1944—Dorothy Livesay, *Day and Night* —Donald Creighton, *Dominion of the North*	
1945—Atomic bomb —End of World War II —Canada joins the United Nations —Russian espionage in Canada exposed by Gouzenko	1945—F.R. Scott, *Overture* —Irving Layton, *Here and Now* —M. Fairley (ed.), *Spirit of Canadian Democracy* —Hugh MacLennan, *Two Solitudes* —Merger of *First Statement* and *Preview* into *Northern Review* —*Fiddlehead* founded by Fred Cogswell	1945—Thomas B. Costain, *The Black Rose** —George Orwell, *Animal Farm* —Tennessee Williams, *The Glass Menagerie** —Richard Wright, *Black Boy** —Karl Shapiro, *Essay on Rime**
1946—Kinsey Report on Sexual Behaviour	1946—P.K. Page, *As Ten As Twenty* —Raymond Souster, *When We Are Young* —Louis Dudek, *East of the City* —Selwyn Dewdney, *Wind Without Rain* —Ralph Allen, *Home Made Banners* —Patrick Anderson, *The White Centre* —Edward Meade, *Remember Me* —A.R.M. Lower, *Colony to Nation*	1946—Evelyn Waugh, *Brideshead Revisited* —R. Penn Warren, *All the King's Men**
	1947—Northrop Frye, *Fearful Symmetry* —Gabrielle Roy, *The Tin Flute* (tr.) —W.O. Mitchell, *Who Has Seen the Wind* —Lionel Shapiro, *Sealed Verdict* —Malcolm Lowry, *Under the Volcano* —Paul Hiebert, *Sarah Binks* —Edgar McInnis, *Canada: A Social and Political History* —Edward McCourt, *Music at the Close* —Dorothy Livesay, *Poems for My People*	1947—Tennessee Williams, *A Streetcar Named Desire**

Historical Chronology	**Canadian Literary Events**	**Literary Events Elsewhere**
1948—Louis St. Laurent elected Prime Minister	1948—A.M. Klein, *The Rocking Chair* —A.J. Elliott, *The Aging Nymph* —Roger Lemelin, *Les Plouffe* —Henry Kreisel, *Rich Man* —Roy Daniells, *Deeper into the Forest*	1948—Norman Mailer, *The Naked and the Dead** —Alan Paton, *Cry the Beloved Country* —B.F. Skinner, *Walden Two*
1949—Newfoundland enters Confederation —Massey Commission to investigate Canadian arts —Canadian Citizenship Act —NATO formed	1949—James Reaney, *The Red Heart* —Hugh Garner, *Storm Below* —Earle Birney, *Turvey* —Kathleen Coburn, *The Grandmothers* —Len Peterson, *Chipmunk* —Robertson Davies, *Fortune my Foe*	1949—George Orwell, *Nineteen Eighty-Four* —Elizabeth Bowen, *Heat of the Day* —Henry Miller, *Death of a Salesman**
1950—War in Korea —Establishment of joint Canada-U.S. weather stations on Ellesmere Island	1950—Thomas Raddall, *The Nymph and the Lamp* —Edward McCourt, *Home is the Stranger* —H.A. Innis, *Empire and Communications*	
1951—Report on Arts, Letters, Science by the Massey Commission —"Cold War" with Russia begins —*Théâtre du Nouveau Monde* founded in Montreal	1951—Marshall McLuhan, *The Mechanical Bride* —André Langevin, *Evadé de la Nuit* —R. de Roquebrune, *Testament de mon Enfance* —Morley Callaghan, *The Loved and the Lost* —Roderick Haig-Brown, *Fisherman's Spring* —Kay Smith, *Footnote to the Lord's Prayer* —A.M. Klein, *The Second Scroll* —Hugh Garner, *Cabbage Town* —Hugh MacLennan, *Each Man's Son*	1951—J.D. Sallinger, *The Catcher in the Rye** —Jas. Jones, *From Here to Eternity** —William Styron, *Lie Down in Darkness** —C.P. Snow, *The Masters* —Wm. Carlos Williams, *Paterson** —Isaac Asimov, *Foundation*
1952—Television introduced in Canada	1952—Ernest Buckler, *The Mountain and the Valley* —E.J. Pratt, *Towards the Last Spike*	1952—Ernest Hemingway, *The Old Man and the Sea** —Ralph W. Ellison, *Invisible Man**

Historical Chronology	Canadian Literary Events	Literary Event Elsewhere
	1952-1954—*Contact* magazine edited by Raymond Souster	1952—George Lamming, *In the Castle of My Skin*
1953—Lester Pearson, President of United Nations General Assembly —National Library established in Ottawa —Stratford Festival begins —Korean War ends —McCarthyism in U.S.	1953—Bruce Hutchison, *The Incredible Canadian* —Douglas Le Pan, *The Net and the Sword*	1953—Saul Bellow, *Adventures of Augie March**
	1954—Ethel Wilson, *Swamp Angel* —Eli Mandel, *Trio* —Yves Theriault, *Aaron* —Jay Macpherson, *O Earth Return* —Edith Fowke and Richard Johnston (eds.), *Folk Songs of Canada* —Robertson Davies, *Leaven of Malice* —Malcolm Ross (ed.), *Our Sense of Identity*	1954—Randall Jarrell, *Pictures from an Institution** —Kingsley Amis, *Lucky Jim* —Samuel Beckett, *Waiting for Godot* —Wm. Golding, *Lord of the Flies* —Iris Murdoch, *Under the Net*
	1955—Mordecai Richler, *Son of a Smaller Hero* —Miriam Waddington, *The Second Silence* —Anne Wilkinson, *The Hangman Ties the Holly*	1955—Allen Ginsberg, *Howl and Other Poems** —Jean Genet, *The Balcony*
1956—Debates on Pipeline, crisis in Canadian Parliament —Suez crisis	1956—Adele Wiseman, *Sacrifice* —Mavis Gallant, *The Other Paris* —Leonard Cohen, *Let Us Compare Mythologies* —William Kilbourn, *The Firebrand* —*Tamarack Review* established —Farley Mowat, *Lost in the Barrens*	1956—Nelson Algren, *A Walk on the Wild Side** —Graham Greene, *The Quiet American* —John Osborne, *Look Back in Anger*
1957—John Diefenbaker elected Prime Minister —Sputnik launched by U.S.S.R. —Canada Council established	1957—Frank Scott (ed.), *The Blasted Pine* —Jay Macpherson, *The Boatman* —Northrop Frye, *The Anatomy of Criticism*	1957—John Braine, *Room at the Top* —J.G. Cozzens, *By Love Possessed** —Bernard Malamud, *The Assistant**

Historical Chronology	Canadian Literary Events	Literary Events Elsewhere
1957—DEW (Distant Early Warning) line opened for U.S.-Canada defence		1957—Boris Pasternak, *Dr. Zhivago* —Jack Kerouac, *On the Road**
1958—NORAD agreement —Disaster in Spring Hill, Nova Scotia coal mine	1958—Douglas Jones, *Frost on the Sun* —Yves Theriault, *Agaguk* —*Alphabet* founded by James Reaney —Robertson Davies, *Mixture of Frailties* —Pierre Berton, *Klondike* —Colin MacDougall, *Execution*	1958—T.H. White, *The Once and Future King* —Iris Murdoch, *The Bell* —Alan Sillitoe, *Saturday Night and Sunday Morning* —Theodore Roethke, *Words for the Wind** —John Updike, *Poorhouse Fair** —William Burroughs, *Naked Lunch** —Archibald MacLeish, *J.B.** —Harold Pinter, *The Caretaker*
1959—St. Lawrence Seaway opened —Canada condemns South African apartheid at Imperial Conference	1959—George Johnston, *The Cruising Auk* —Ronald Bates, *The Wandering World* —Mordecai Richler, *The Apprenticeship of Duddy Kravitz* —Fred Cogswell, *Descent from Eden* —Hugh MacLennan, *The Watch That Ends the Night* —Sheila Watson, *Double Hook* —*Prism*, *Tish*, and *Canadian Literature* established	1959—Philip Roth, *Goodbye Columbus** —Ian Fleming, *Goldfinger** —Norman Brown, *Life Against Death*
1960—Jet air travel, Vancouver to Toronto. —Wheat contracts with China	1960—Marie-Claire Blais, *Mad Shadows* (tr.) —Margaret Avison, *Winter Sun* —Eli Mandel, *Fuseli Poems* —Claire Martin, *Doux-Amer* —David Walker, *Where the High Winds Blow* —Brian Moore, *Luck of Ginger Coffey* —Ralph Gustafson, *Rivers among Rocks* —Kenneth McRobbie, *Eyes without a Face*	1960—Edward Albee, *The American Dream** —Flannery O'Connor, *The Violent Bear It Away** —Charles Olson, *The Maximus Poems** —John Barth, *The Sotweed Factor** —Laurence Durrell, *Alexandria Quartet* —Muriel Spark, *Ballad of Peckham Rye*

Historical Chronology	Canadian Literary Events	Literary Events Elsewhere
1961—First Mariposa Festival	1961—Malcolm Lowry, *Hear Us, O Lord, From Heaven Thy Dwelling Place* —Douglas Jones, *The Sun is Axeman* —Sheila Brunford, *The Incredible Journey* —William Morton, *The Canadian Identity* —Robert Finch, *Dover Beach Revisited; Acis in Oxford*	1961—Joseph Heller, *Catch 22** —John Updike, *Rabbit Run**
1962—Missile crisis in Cuba, involving U.S.A., U.S.S.R.	1962—Jacques Godbout, *L'Aquarium* —James Reaney, *Kildeer; Twelve Letters to a Small Town* —Marshall McLuhan, *The Gutenberg Galaxy* —John Coulter, *Riel* —St. Denys Garneau and Anne Hébert, *Poems,* tr. F.R. Scott	1962—Robert Creeley, *For Love** —Anthony Burgess, *A Clockwork Orange* —Doris Lessing, *Golden Notebook* —Vladimir Nabokov, *Pale Fire*
1963—Lester Pearson elected Prime Minister —Canada supports U.S. involvement in Viet Nam —FLQ bombings in Quebec —President Kennedy assassinated in Texas —Winter Works Programme established	1963—Mordecai Richler, *The Incomparable Atuk* —Leonard Cohen, *The Favourite Game* —Margaret Laurence, *The Tomorrow Tamer* —bill bissett founds *Blewointment* —Irving Layton, *Balls for a One-Armed Juggler*	1963—Mary McCarthy, *The Group** —James Baldwin, *Go Tell It on the Mountain; The Fire Next Time**
1964—Columbia River treaties re hydro-electric power —Royal Commission on Bilingualism and Biculturalism	1964—Claude Jasmin, *Ethel et el Terroriste* —Marie-Claire Blais, *Une Saison dans la Vie d'Emmanuel* —Marshall McLuhan, *Understanding Media* —Earle Birney, *Near False Creek Mouth* —Leonard Cohen, *Flowers for Hitler* —*Quarry* founded at Kingston —Raymond Souster, *The Colour of the Times*	1964—Saul Bellow, *Herzog** —William Golding, *The Spire* —Le Roi Jones, *The Dead Lecturer** —Philip Larkin, *Whitsun Wedding* —Robert Lowell, *For the Union Dead**

Historical Chronology	Canadian Literary Events	Literary Events Elsewhere
	1964—Margaret Laurence, *Stone Angel* —Douglas Le Pan, *The Deserter* —Douglas Lochhead, *Poet Talking*	
1965—Civil Rights march in Alabama joined by Canadian sympathizers	1965—Alfred Purdy, *Cariboo Horses* —John Newlove, *Moving in Alone* —Jacques Godbout, *Le Couteau sur la Table* —Hubert Aquin, *Prochaine Episode* —John Porter, *Vertical Mosaic* —Gabrielle Roy, *Where Nests the Water Hen* (tr.) —Phyllis Web, *Naked Poems* —Daryl Hine, *The Wooden Horse*	1965—James Baldwin, *Going to Meet the Man** —Robert Lowell, *The Old Glory** —John Osborne, *Inadmissible Evidence* —Muriel Spark, *Mandelbaum Gate* —Norman Mailer, *The American Dream**
1966—War in Vietnam intensifies	1966—Margaret Avison, *The Dumbfounding* —Leonard Cohen, *Beautiful Losers* —Réjean Ducharm, *L'Avalée des Avalées* —Margaret Laurence, *A Jest of God* —Mordecai Richler, *St. Urbain's Horseman* —Ralph Gustafson, *Sift in an Hour Glass* —Robert Kroetsch, *Words of my Roaring* —Joe Rosenblatt, *The L.S.D. Leacock*	1966—John Barth, *Giles Goat Boy** —Denise Levertov, *The Sorrow-Dance**
1967—Canada's Centennial —"Expo" in Montreal focuses national sentiment —de Gaulle's "Vive Québec Libre!" speech in Québec	1967—Eli Mandel, *An Idiot Joy* —P.K. Page, *Cry Ararat* —Alden Nowlan, *Bread, Wine and Salt* —Dorothy Livesay, *The Unquiet Bed* —Raymond Souster, *As Is* —Gratien Gélinas, *Yesterday the Children Were Dancing (tr.)*	1967—Flannery O'Connor, *Three by Flannery O'Connor** —Robert Creeley, *Words** —Ted Hughes, *Woodwo* —Norman Podhoretz, *Making It** —Angus Wilson, *No Laughing Matter* —Harold Pinter, *The Tea-Party and other Plays*

1967—Hugh MacLennan, *Return of the Sphinx*
—Louis Dudek, *Atlantis*
—David Stein, *Scratch One Dreamer*
—John Robert Colombo, *Abracadabra*
—Michael Ondaatje, *The Dainty Monsters*
—bp Nichol, *Journeyings and the Return*

1967—Norman Mailer, *Why Are We in Vietnam**

1968—Pierre Trudeau elected Prime Minister
—"Trudeaumania" in Canada
—Martin Luther King assassinated; student unrest in U.S.
—Biafran dispute in Nigeria
—Company of Young Canadians founded

1968—John Newlove, *Black Night Window*
—Al Purdy, *Wild Grape Wine*
—Margaret Atwood, *The Animals in that Country*
—Sinclair Ross, *Lamp at Noon and other Stories*
—Victor Coleman, *One-Eye-Love*
—bill bissett, *of the land divine service*
—Alice Munro, *Dance of the Happy Shades*
—Jacques Godbout, *Knife on the Table* (tr.)
—Dorothy Livesay, *Documentaries*
—Jack Ludwig, *Above Ground*
—Mordecai Richler, *Cocksure*
—Dennis Lee, *Civil Elegies*
—W.W.E. Ross, *Shapes and Sounds*
—Marshal McLuhan, *Understanding Media*
—George Bowering, *Rocky Mountain Foot*

1968—Iris Murdoch, *The Nice and The Good*
—John Updike, *Couples**
—Beatles, *Yellow Submarine*
—Norman Mailer, *Armies of the Night**

1969—First men on the moon
—Student unrest flares at Sir George Williams University
—National Arts Centre opened in Ottawa
—Canada discusses exchange of ambassadors with Peking

1969—Gwendolyn MacEwen, *The Shadow-Maker*
—Margaret Atwood, *The Edible Woman*
—Graeme Gibson, *Five Legs*
—R.G. Everson, *The Dark is Not so Dark*
—Margaret Laurence, *Fire-Dwellers*

1969—James Dickey, *Buck-dancer's Choice*
—Iris Murdoch, *Bruno's Dream*

	1969—Lawrence Garber, *Garber's Tales From the Quarter*	
	—George Bowering, *The Gangs of Kosmos*	
	—Francis Sparshott, *A Cardboard Garage*	
	—John Robert Colombo, *New Poems by Dr. Strachan*	
	—James Bacque, *The Lonely Ones*	
	—Lionel Kearnes, *By the Light of the Silvery McLune*	
	—Robert Kroetsch, *The Studhorse Man*	
	—Phyllis Gotlieb, *Ordinary, Moving*	
	—David Helwig, *Sign of the Gunman*	
	—Milton Acorn, *I've Tasted My Blood*	
	—Miriam Waddington, *Say Yes*	
	—Alden Nowland, *The Mysterious Naked Man*	
1970—Committee for an Independent Canada formed	1970—Alice Munro, *Lives of Girls and Women*	1970—Saul Bellow, *Mr. Sammler's Planet**
—Youth Projects for summer employment	—George Ryga, *The Ecstasy of Rita Joe*	—John Fowles, *French Lieutenant's Woman*
—Front de la Libération de Québec (FLQ) crisis	—Henry Beissel, *Face in the Dark*	—Charles Reich, *The Greening of America**
—Sale of Ryerson Press	—Seymour Mayne, *Mouth*	—Richard Brautigan, *Revenge of the Lawn**
—Canadian Federation of Native Peoples exerts political pressure	—Sarrain Stump, *There is my People Sleeping*	—Lawrence Ferlinghetti, *Back Roads to Far Palaces**
	—Norman Levine, *From a Seaside Town*	
	—Markoosie, *Harpoon of the Hunter*	
	—Robertson Davies, *Fifth Business*	
	—James Bacque, *Big Lonely*	
	—Roch Carrier, *La Guerre, Yes Sir!* (tr.)	
	—Marian Engel, *The Honeyman Festival*	

Canadian Literary Events

1970—Michael Ondaatje, *The Collected Works of Billy the Kid*
—Dave Godfrey, *New Ancestors*
—Alan Fry, *How a People Die*
—Pierre Berton, *The National Dream*
—Adrienne Clarkson, *Hunger Trace*
—J. Michael Yates, *The Great Bear Lake Meditations*
—Douglas Jones, *Butterfly on Rock*
—John Newlove, *The Cave*
—George Jonas, *The Happy Hungry Man*
—George Woodcock, *Canada and the Canadians*

Historical Chronology

1971—Provincial elections and long regimes in British Columbia, Alberta, Newfoundland, Manitoba
—Alaska via Mackenzie Valley Pipeline construction debate
—Department of Environment established
—Dow Chemical and other companies prosecuted for industrial pollution
—U.S.-Canada agreement to clean up the Great Lakes
—Bomarc Missile squadrons discontinued
—Trudeau visits Moscow
1972—Massacre at Olympic games in Munich
—Team Canada in world hockey matches against U.S.S.R.
—U.K. moves to join European Common Market
—James Bay Development halted

Canadian Literary Events

1971—Victor Coleman, *America*
—Pierre Vallières, *White Niggers of America* (tr.)
—Tom Marshall, *Magic Water*
—Eldon Grier, *Selected Poems*
—Stuart MacKinnon, *Skydeck*
—Ronald Lee, *Goddam Gypsy*
—David Helwig, *The Day Before Tomorrow*
—bill bissett, *nobody owns th earth*
—Margaret Laurence, *A Bird in the House*
1972—Gwendolyn MacEwen, *Armies of the Moon; King of Egypt, King of Dreams*
—Margaret Atwood, *Survival; Surfacing*
—bp Nichol, *Martyrology*
—Robertson Davies, *The Manticore*
—Joe Rosenblatt, *Bumblebee Dithyramb*

Literary Events Elsewhere

1971—Anthony Powell, *Books That Furnish a Room*
—Bernard Malamud, *Tenants**
—Alain Robbe-Grillet, *The Immortal One*
—William Golding, *The Spire*
—L.P. Hartley, *The Harness Room*
—Terry Southern, *Red-Dirt Marijuana*
—Alexei Solzhenitsyn, *The Cancer Ward*
—William Maxwell, *The Ancestors**
—Claude Levi-Strauss, *Mythologiques IV*

1972—Doris Lessing, *Story of a Non-Marrying Man*
—H.E. Bates, *The Song of the Wier*
—Herman Wouk, *The Winds of War**
—Dee Brown, *Bury My Heart at Wounded Knee**
—Peter Schrag, *Decline of the Wasp**

Historical Chronology	**Canadian Literary Events**	**Literary Events Elsewhere**
1972—Peace talks on Vietnam —Liberal Government of Trudeau returned with narrow majority	1972—Tim Inkster, *Topolobampo Poems* —Hugh Hood, *You Can't Get There from Here* —Frank Davey, *4 Myths for Sam Perry* —John Metcalf, *Going Down Slow* —Leonard Cohen, *The Energy of Slaves*	1972—James Baldwin, *No Name in the Street** —Barry Commoner, *The Closing Circle* —Auberon Waugh, *A Bed of Flowers* —Chimua Achebe, *Girls at War* —Richard Bach, *Jonathon Livingston Seagull*

Index